THE BATTLES OF GERMANTOWN

In the series *History and the Public,*

edited by STEVEN CONN

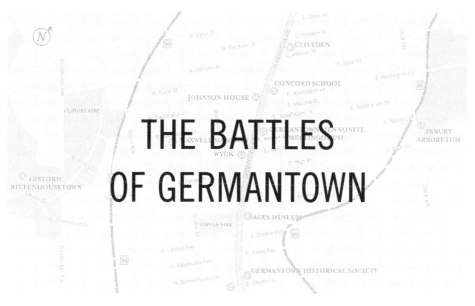

THE BATTLES
OF GERMANTOWN

↠ Effective Public History in America ↞

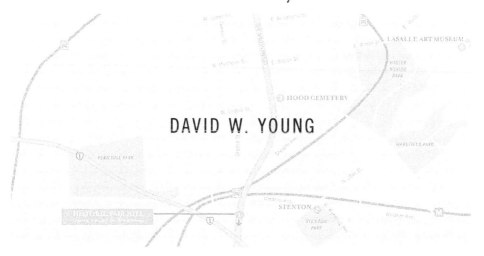

DAVID W. YOUNG

TEMPLE UNIVERSITY PRESS
Philadelphia · *Rome* · *Tokyo*

TEMPLE UNIVERSITY PRESS
Philadelphia, Pennsylvania 19122
tupress.temple.edu

Library of Congress Cataloging-in-Publication Data

Names: Young, David W., 1964– author.
Title: The battles of Germantown : effective public history in America /
    David W. Young.
Description: Philadelphia : Temple University Press, [2019] | Series: History
    and the public | Includes bibliographical references and index. |
    Description based on print version record and CIP data provided by
    publisher; resource not viewed.
Identifiers: LCCN 2018054717 (print) | LCCN 2019000791 (ebook) |
    ISBN 9781439915561 (E-book) | ISBN 9781439915547 (cloth : alk. paper) |
    ISBN 9781439915554 (pbk. : alk. paper)
Subjects: LCSH: Germantown (Philadelphia, Pa.)—Historiography. | Public
    history—Pennsylvania—Philadelphia. | Historic preservation—Pennsylvania—
    Philadelphia. | Collective memory—Pennsylvania—Philadelphia. | Community
    life—Pennsylvania—Philadelphia. | Philadelphia (Pa.)—Historiography. | Public
    history—United States—Methodology—Case studies.
Classification: LCC F159.G3 (ebook) | LCC F159.G3 Y68 2019 (print) |
    DDC 974.8/11—dc23
LC record available at https://lccn.loc.gov/2018054717

Printed in the United States of America

9 8 7 6 5 4 3 2

To Sloan,

whose choice of neighborhoods

made such a difference

Contents

List of Illustrations

THE BATTLES OF GERMANTOWN

Prologue

Historians, like the histories they write, are products of the circumstances that produce them, and so it's worth reflecting on how I came to write this book.

When I moved to the Germantown section of Philadelphia in late 1994, I was an unemployed graduate student with some experience teaching history at the high school and college levels. I am not a public historian by training. Nor am I native to Germantown, the neighborhood so rich in history where I made my home, raised my son, and fell into the public history business.

Shortly after moving to Philadelphia, I lost interest in finishing my dissertation about local politics in postwar Germany. I also found that academic history was not for me. But I wondered whether I might apply my interest in history in a way that was more engaging than the ivory tower approach, which seemed to me to be insular, about arcane research for a limited audience and irrelevant to people who are not experts. All my adult life I had prepared to be a university professor. Now, removed from graduate school and a new father, I needed a job. Little did I know that the streets of Philadelphia had much to teach me about how history happens, gets crafted, and can make a difference to a broad public.

While teaching history as an adjunct at a local college, I answered an ad for a weekend coordinator at Historic RittenhouseTown, a colonial-era site down the street from my home. My introduction to public history came when a large coach bus carrying a group of Rittenhouse descendants pulled up at the site. The tour was running late, and my boss, the director, handed me a bullhorn, saying: "Here, I have to go. You give the tour." I had not yet been trained to give a tour, but fortunately my outgoing personality and experience as a waiter gave me the confidence I needed to sell the visitors on the fascinating history of America's first paper mill. My experience at RittenhouseTown was good, but the job paid only $8.50 an hour.

I started a second part-time public history job interviewing Holocaust survivors. The Survivors of the Shoah Visual History Foundation (now the University of Southern California's Shoah Foundation) was collecting the testimonies of Jewish survivors on digital video; the foundation paid fifty dollars per interview to cover the time and travel expenses of the mainly volunteer corps of retirees who conducted the interviews. I was one of the youngest trainees. It was a tremendous experience because it allowed me to use my German language skills and my knowledge of European history and because the whole project was an example of effective public history. The Shoah Project was created by the filmmaker Steven Spielberg, following the success of his award-winning film *Schindler's List,* to record the testimonies of as many living Holocaust victims as possible before they disappeared. Information in the interviews could be accessed through a giant database. The results are available at the Holocaust Museum in Washington, DC, the Yad Vashem memorial in Israel, and several other repositories. I did not realize until later how helpful the project would be to my own growth as a historian.

The project provided outstanding training for collecting oral histories. I learned how crucial the planning and pre-interview process is: getting important bits of data before the actual conversation is recorded under lights and in front of the camera. Sometimes this phase entailed a phone call or a one-on-one visit to gather information. But as critical as it was to get details such as names, dates, and locations of camps, the pre-interview also started the vital process of building trust. Training in active listening was crucial, and so was empathy. Simply put, the process involved going to the homes of elderly people and encouraging them to share their worst memories and deepest emotions on camera. Ensuring that such an intense encounter would be a positive experience was one of the important goals of the Shoah Project.

Conducting the interviews made clear how much it means to people to be able to share their own history. Most people do not have their sto-

ries in the historical record; without projects like this one, much information would be lost. In this case, the people interviewed felt honored to be
heard—though not at first. At times it took nudging. Most survivors would
say something like, "Oh, my story is not that important" or "I was not at
any of the well-known camps like Auschwitz, but only at smaller work
camps." Interviewers had a sense of racing against the clock to compile a
record of voices that would soon be lost—and any voice lost would be a
missed opportunity. Witnesses' stories are complicated, especially for the
period of displacement and relocation camps after 1945, and every piece
of information entered into the database allows dots to be connected and
the Holocaust as a whole to be better understood. The true wisdom of that
project, however, went beyond the mere act of collecting data; it derived
from the personal connection needed to insure its success.

The project's planners gave the volunteer corps of interviewers the
historical background and trained them in how to conduct conversations.
We were citizens interviewing citizens, listening to their stories simply
because people agreed that this exercise was important. When both interviewers and subjects were well prepared, the discussion went well, and
the process often revealed a deeper truth because people felt empowered
by being heard. Actively listening and maintaining a respectful dialogue
makes it easier for a stranger to bring difficult memories into the open.
The information we collected, whether tragic or exciting, mundane or
associated with an important event, mattered less than how people felt
having their stories heard. I am not Jewish, but by working to maintain a
mutually respectful relationship, I made connections with people who are.
Many of those connections proved unforgettable.

My first interview did not go well, but it gave me perspective. I arrived
late, harried, with notes disheveled and fearful that an awful first impression would ruin the interview. My car battery had died and I had had to
use the honorarium to take a cab to Northeast Philadelphia to interview
a ninety-year-old tailor, the only sibling from a family of fifteen children
to survive the Nazi regime. Just before we began filming, I confessed my
anxiety and apologized. The interviewee said, "Let's not hurry bad news."
Here was a man who had lost so much in his life, yet he was the one smil-
ing and reassuring me.

Another time I was tapped to interview a woman in the morning and
her husband in the afternoon. They had come to Philadelphia from Israel for their granddaughter's wedding. The pre-interviews took place in a
hotel near the airport, and the man was taciturn to the point of being un-

friendly. The next day we interviewed them on camera. The morning session with the wife went well. At the afternoon interview, though, I could not get the husband to reveal details. Every question received a one-word response.

Then everything changed. He told me that his parents had hosted parties in 1930s Vienna, fashionable events featuring music played on a phonograph, and I asked him to describe the music. Had any of the songs been in the Klezmer style popular at the time? His eyes grew wide, he straightened up in his chair, and suddenly he began to describe in colorful detail the music and the parties from his childhood. He recounted stories that painted a picture of his parents, their friends, and the life of his family. Wondrous and specific memories poured out, as if he had not shared them in years, or ever. After the interview, while the video crew was dismantling the equipment, he waited outside the room, repeatedly checking his watch. When the crew wrapped up, he asked whether he could approach me, stepping so close that I was afraid I had done something wrong. He reached out and grabbed me by the shoulders, and then he leaned in and kissed me. He said he could not leave without thanking me. I was stunned but relished the thought that he had engaged those memories of his family in time to bring positive spirits to his granddaughter's wedding. I never did another interview for the project, but I learned that encountering history together can produce a powerful bond, even among strangers. My introduction to public history illustrates its unique blend of public and personal importance and its foundation in a social compact. Building knowledge about the past is a shared endeavor.

My experience with the Survivors of the Shoah deepened my commitment to public history and informed my work as a public historian. Interviewing Holocaust survivors instilled in me the awareness and respect necessary to hear those who were not always considered significant or who were not allowed in the room when decisions about what is considered historic got made. Soon after my Shoah work ended, I started an oral history project to get people to share stories about the evolution of my neighborhood in the early twentieth century. I considered myself less a historian than a community member walking around the neighborhood, an urban enclave of Philadelphia at the edge of the forested Wissahickon Valley, with my son in a stroller, talking with people to learn about my new home. Methods from the Shoah Project—pre-interview surveys to get details about parents, schools, and addresses and establish a rapport—allowed me to gather facts while also triggering memories that could build knowledge, get verified, and somehow be used later in programs, publications, or exhibitions. The project turned into a website in 1997, and people interested in the neighborhood's past and present logged on to add their own stories and photographs or whatever they had uncovered researching their own houses. It was public history as a kind of picnic blanket, where people could set out and share their own discoveries about the history and beauty of Germantown.

I observed some interesting dynamics on that project, for which long-time middle- and working-class residents joined newcomers like me to learn the history of our neighborhood. Both groups clearly appreciated local connections to American history that transcended race and class differences—connections that in this neighborhood included finding ancient arrowheads in the woods or playing around colonial-era buildings and imagining the historical events that might have happened in their own backyards. People liked remembering the old days. And everyone agreed that Germantown's history and beauty should be stewarded. That sentiment united people whose ancestors had settled the neighborhood with people who were more recent arrivals. Yet people also had strong opinions about the negative aspects of the neighborhood. I was under no illusions myself.

One afternoon I was mugged on my way to give tours at Rittenhouse-Town. Not long after that, my house was robbed. When I interviewed my neighbors, the conversations invariably turned to politics and the state of the community. Long-time residents wanted to tell newcomers about their experiences with crime, neglect, and poverty. Nostalgic for the "good old days," they were ready to lay blame for the present on politicians, this or that ethnic group, or one political party or another—the list was endless. Everyone had a reason why Germantown's best days were in the past. When I pointed out the opportunities we had to learn more together, they put me on the defensive, demanding to know why there should be hope for a neighborhood that had seen better days. I was frustrated and annoyed by these simplistic explanations for why, despite its rich history and beautiful blend of nature and architecture, Germantown had such a bad rap.

The neighborhood project landed me a full-time job as an educator at the city's history museum, designing programs that drew on community input and audience participation to create a fuller picture of history than the museum's collections could illuminate by themselves. All too often at conferences or public lectures, the most interesting discussions happen after the presenter stops talking. I have noticed how, as the audience departs, people come up to the podium to pose questions, often very personal questions, that they don't want the whole room to hear. Only when the microphone is off do people reveal their real selves to the speaker, and frequently with great questions that everyone might have benefited from hearing. I began to plan programs in which the audience could take an active role.

One such program at the Philadelphia History Museum involved people who had worked at the Curtis Publishing Company, where the *Saturday Evening Post* and other magazines were produced in the mid-twentieth century. Participants shared their memories of Norman Rockwell. Someone who knew the cartoonist Ted Key brought original *Hazel* comic strips. Once again, the program became a picnic blanket, gathering memories and stories, yet audience members would never have seen themselves as part of history. For another program we brought in women who had worked in factories during World War II to talk about their experiences. When we first pitched the idea to the one-time Rosie the Riveters, they resisted; but with a little encouragement, one by one they agreed to take part—once they were assured that they would not be alone or have to do all the talking. It was not colonial history or military history, just their everyday lives, which they didn't see as historic, but when talking in a group, they recognized their connection to the larger historical narrative. And this truly public participation in a history event pleased them very much. Frankly, it was hard to get them to stop talking.

Involving the audience as active participants revealed new perspectives on the twentieth century. By hearing and empathizing with another person's point of view, everyone gained something from the program. The work made me a better historian, while participating in a safe, respectful, welcoming group setting, learning from one another and putting their own experiences into context reminded everyone involved that we are part of something larger than ourselves.

Not everyone, however, agreed with my assessment—including people within the institutions where I worked. The boss at RittenhouseTown told me that Germantown's industrial history and its evolution in the nineteenth and twentieth centuries might be interesting to the surrounding community, but colonial history brings visitors to the site. He made it clear that only one history matters—the site's colonial and Revolutionary War connections. That is why it is a National Historic Landmark. And yet the oral history project was popular, and people were donating artifacts and memories because the project connected them to the place. The boss insisted that if people were really committed, they would have been participating financially and becoming members. Donations or ticket sales counted more than relationship building.

Nor did everyone at the history museum want a two-way street when it came to information gathering. The curators decided who got to see the collections; as gatekeepers of the historical artifacts, they saw the museum's role as keeping the collections safe. Changing the museum's relationship to the public would take leadership and commitment from the entire organization, and not just from a few educational programmers. I knew that to make the change I hoped to see in historic sites and museums, I needed to direct one myself.

I started at a traditional county historical society in southern New Jersey. Historical societies reflect all the challenges and opportunities of public history. This one, like many others, was a centuries-old institution with a large assortment of old buildings, collections, and artifacts, accompanied by intense scrutiny from the descendants of the people who made or donated them, all eager to protect their family's heritage. Frequently reminded that I was not from the county, I had to earn my stripes and learn the local history. I was not always entirely welcome, but I was not alone.

I learned from talking with local residents that many had no idea that the historical society was open, much less open to them. Yet the society employed all the building blocks of public history: archives, artifacts, museum displays, historic buildings, a newsletter to stimulate advocacy and showcase ongoing research, and collections of newspapers, yearbooks, and family Bibles. It was a repository for the component parts of public memory. As director, my job was to use these parts as connectors and teaching devices to engage people of all backgrounds and build their support for the historical society. The first step was to overcome the perception that the society was closed to outsiders—to involve more people, shine light on the volunteers who were writing books about their discoveries, and encourage people to share their own memories, according to the picnic blanket model of participatory programming. It was hard, rewarding work.

My first full-time job in Germantown began in 2004, when I was hired as the first director of the Johnson House, named a National Historic Landmark on the Underground Railroad in 1997. I was hired by an African American board of directors. The 1768 building was new as a historic site, with long-deferred maintenance needs, a small staff, and few resources. Though the passionate board members and I had little preservation experience or background in fundraising, we shared a resolve to get the house's story told. A significant portion of the black experience in America, and especially in Germantown, was not being presented. And the Johnson House's board was resolved with me to remedy that lack by expanding what was considered "historic" in Germantown beyond the traditional focus on colonial and Revolutionary War history.

At Johnson House, the context is everything. People feel the power and spirit of an intact Underground Railroad station and the stories and emotions connected with it—the danger, the impulse to seek freedom, the willingness to risk everything. Merely standing in a room of the house or walking up the back stairs or crouching in the attic hiding places moves people of all ages and backgrounds. People encounter the Johnson House in wonder, using their imaginations to fill spaces and consider what they might have done.

As director of the Johnson House, I worked with the directors of three other Germantown house museums on the History Hunters Youth Reporter Program, an interactive program to bring elementary school students to the neighborhood's historic sites. Those three—Wyck, Cliveden, and Stenton—were among Philadelphia's grandest historic houses. Stenton led the initiative to address a national problem: how to make history relevant to the community. The directors of the house museums, all middle-class, educated white people, were under no illusions about the need to matter more to the surrounding African American neighborhood. Not all of the directors were Germantown residents, but they all understood that house museums were in trouble. Since the late 1990s, trade journals, conference panels, policy papers, and even daily newspapers had bemoaned their declining visitation, lack of foundation support, and increasing separation from their surrounding communities.

Yet the Germantown organizations were still wary about working together. Their boards of directors included people whose ancestors had lived in the house or had founded the house museum, and the resistance to change was sometimes fierce. Some sites had no interest in opening their doors to school groups on a common schedule. Or one site might prefer to devote its fundraising energy to fixing a roof or installing a better security system, rather than starting a collective education program that might benefit other institutions at the expense of its own.

The repeated use of the words "survival" and "dire" in discussions of house museums, however, made it clear that collaboration was desperately needed. The four directors understood the urgency and committed to a joint project. Time was running out for traditional house museums: Loudoun and Upsala, both in Germantown, had closed. Maintaining the status quo had become the riskiest option, prompting the professional site directors to push their organizations to make changes and look beyond their own narrow needs.

In 2006 I left the Johnson House and moved a block and a half up Germantown Avenue to become director of Cliveden. I was leaving the Underground Railroad freedom station for the slave owner's mansion on the hill. Moving between two houses connected as opposing elements of the same story made me realize that the power of the larger narrative transcends either site by itself. It sharpened my understanding of public history as a point of connection for people. I set out to bring this understanding to Cliveden, with its Revolutionary War battlefield, cannon ball marks, and historic decorative arts and furniture, as well as its plantations.

Cliveden, once home to the elite Chew family, stands behind a locked gate and dark stone walls, visibly set apart from the community. I was frustrated by how off-putting and sterile such a beautiful and compelling place could seem. Tours of the house tended to highlight the 1770 Affleck Chippendale sofa that had been made for the William Penn family. I was reminded of how my mother used to say, "Get off the sofa and make yourself useful!" Cliveden holds deep connections to the past, some of which have been hidden. It should not be all about the sofa. The board of directors also wanted to make Cliveden's history useful, and so they hired not a historian of the Revolutionary era or a historic preservationist but a former history teacher.

In 2009 I finally completed my doctoral dissertation—a history of how twentieth-century Germantown was preserved and remembered. Germantown still has a way to go, but so far the neighborhood's twenty-first-century history embraces a broad public working to make the neighborhood better, safer, and more economically viable, building on the efforts of the past one hundred years and overcoming the defects that remain. This book offers examples that people may find useful in their own communities.

I wrote this book to demonstrate what public history and historic preservation must do to thrive—not merely survive. Its chapters describe controversies and battles, but my intent is not to "hurry bad news." Time is of the essence, but this account also highlights the good news that people are eager to learn more about the past, even a difficult and painful past, because through history we learn what makes us human. Public history can offer many ways to encounter the past, discuss it openly, connect it to what matters to people, and make it useful. When it does this, any encounter with a historic place can be a powerful, effective experience.

Introduction

This book is about Germantown, a Philadelphia neighborhood established in 1683. It is also about public history, history that takes place outside a classroom and actively involves people from varied backgrounds and with varied points of view.[1] Germantown is a perfect place to explore public history in America—its strengths and possibilities, its limits and the ways in which it can be truly effective.

Germantown is rife with contradictions. Old enough for many to find themselves in its compelling history, whose physical evidence is apparent in well-preserved artifacts and buildings, Germantown is also riddled with abandoned structures, racial politics, and crime, despite more than a century of efforts to use its connections to important events in American history for the benefit of the community.

From 1683 to 1854 Germantown stood on its own, legally separate from the city of Philadelphia. As the name implies, it was founded by people from what is now Germany. Anabaptists, mainly Mennonites and Quakers, came from the German and Dutch areas of the Rhine seeking religious toleration and freedom from persecution in William Penn's Pennsylvania. Five years after the first settlers arrived, four members of the town's Quaker meeting drafted the "Germantown Protest against Slavery." At the beginning of the twentieth century, "Germantown" referred to the entire pre-1854 German Township, which comprised Germantown,

Mount Airy, and Chestnut Hill. Economic efforts to promote the township centered on the Germantown and Chestnut Hill Improvement Association, which spanned all three neighborhoods but focused on the commercial district that is the main artery of the community, Germantown Avenue. Shortly after World War II, as the population of the region changed from white upper and middle class to predominantly black and working class, first Chestnut Hill (today an upper-middle-class neighborhood) and then Mount Airy (today largely middle class) separated their economic fates from that of Germantown and its increasingly African American population. In this book "Germantown" refers to the neighborhood rather than the township designation that became obsolete after 1854. Bounded by Windrim Avenue in the Logan section of North Philadelphia north to and including Upsal Street in Mount Airy and bounded on the east roughly from Stenton Avenue west to the Wissahickon Creek, Germantown, for this book, refers to an area that encompasses the historic sites of Northwest Philadelphia that have been or are now open to the public.[2]

Germantown developed as a rustic strip village of small-shop manufacturers, farms, and mills where raw materials from outlying counties were turned into products that could be sold in Philadelphia. It had lost its "Germanness" by the early 1800s and was incorporated into Philadelphia under the Consolidation Act of 1854. After the Civil War, Germantown's population grew rapidly, from seventeen thousand people in 1860 to sixty-five thousand in 1900, largely because of influxes of Irish and Italian immigrants and African American migrants from the South. Since consolidation, Germantown and other Philadelphia neighborhoods have cultivated community identities separate from the city, with distinct founding narratives and histories and their own historical societies to celebrate them. Losing political independence prompted Germantown to use history to establish its own sense of place. Well into the middle of the twentieth century, for instance, people identified themselves as coming from "Germantown, Pennsylvania" rather than Philadelphia.[3]

For well over a hundred years, markers, monuments, and house museums identified attempts to document and preserve Germantown's history. Germantown Avenue, the spine of the neighborhood, was once known as the "Great Road." Today, a two-mile stretch of Germantown Avenue starting in North Philadelphia and ending near Cliveden is the longest National Colonial Historic Landmark District in the country. Along with Annapolis, Maryland, it was also one of the first districts so designated. The pathbreaking Historic American Buildings Survey began in Germantown in 1935, and the neighborhood's many house museums are owned or operated by prominent local and national preservation stewards, such as the Philadelphia Society for the Preservation of Landmarks, the National Society of Colonial Dames, the National Park Service, and the National Trust for Historic Preservation. History has been crucial to the neighborhood's identity, as seen in its many (and often competing) history festivals, and vital to its economic well-being, as demonstrated by successive heritage tourism and urban planning initiatives. Yet Germantown's preservation goals have fallen short of making its place in American history lastingly useful for the neighborhood's overall benefit. In many ways, Germantown's public history offers a parable for what happens when insular practices of public history and preservation fail to overcome entrenched interests or are unable to involve broad sections of the population, such as immigrants and people of color.

The most recent generation of people working to preserve and make known Germantown's history, motivated by an urgent sense that the way history has been practiced is not financially or socially sustainable, recognizes that change needs to be made. With dedicated leadership, ongoing research, and the willingness to use new methods to reckon with the results of selective historical memory, Germantown's citizen historians, amateur and professional, have pushed boundaries and changed inert patterns. They recognized and took responsibility for the limitations of previous generations of stewards, which had almost doomed its public history to irrelevance. A narrow public history leaves a legacy of division. These new public historians began to overcome tendencies to insular, self-serving narratives with openness to innovative ways of looking at the colonial period that have encompassed the difficult histories of slavery, racism, and class distinctions. Recent efforts to reckon with Germantown's history-making have embraced the history of the twentieth century to show how politics, economic forces, and population shifts shaped how the neighborhood looks today, adding new chapters to well-chronicled colonial and Victorian narratives. The resulting collaborations among historic sites and with community institutions have not been easy, nor have they solved all the problems, but they have generated powerful responses from a wider public that finds itself involved in honest, inventive, and good faith efforts to preserve and remember all the stories that Germantown's history contains.

Public history played a big role in this shift over the past one hundred years, providing a source of community pride and a context that allows people to address present-day issues by considering the history of the community, good and bad. Because Germantown has always been a cauldron for understanding preservation and public history in America, the resulting signs have implications for the wider field, especially at a time when people in the preservation movement are considering its future.

Publications abound about public history and preservation, the demise of house museums, and the need to change how we think about preserving the past. Few, however, are written by someone leading the work, building coalitions of stakeholders, overcoming institutional resistance, or raising money and allocating resources to make the necessary changes. Those that are tend to be alarmist rather than instructive. Yet in my case a practitioner's perspective clarifies how hard, political, socially engaged, and ultimately satisfying it is to forge a common experience of making history meaningful to the public. Writing about making history public as a participant observer seems especially appropriate in Germantown, with its tradition of citizen historians who made a difference. John Fanning Watson, J. Gordon Baugh Jr., Edwin Jellet, David Richardson, Edward Robinson, Margaret Tinkcom, Shirley Parham, and many others whose work is described here, wrote, collected, or advocated for a sense of place based on the belief that putting the past and present into a broader context might improve current and future conditions.

I believe my practitioner's perspective offers needed context and real world examples showing a record of community engagement that stretches back a century and helps explain current circumstances. And Germantown offers lessons that can be applied in other communities.

As a neighbor, a historian, and a leader of a historic site, I have based my analysis on my own research, observations, and experiences, which need to be taken as informed yet personal and limited. The book is not a complete chronology of Germantown but an exploration of its struggles and contested discussions about how to apply its history in publicly accessible ways. This account of making Germantown history truly public is more than a collection of impressions, though. It shows how heritage practitioners like me are finding their place in the United States and in the community life of places like Germantown.

My experience suggests that when public history is used to address equity, fairness, and agreed-on community needs, it can help a place like Germantown not only survive but also thrive. Examples appear throughout this book. At certain points in the past century, public history came to Germantown's aid through documentation, preservation, and creative forms of stewardship—but with the limitations inherent in the practices of the times and the interests of people with the political or economic influence to dictate what was preserved and remembered. As the field has evolved to embrace new ways of knowing history and involve more perspectives, public history has also helped Germantown evolve. The examples in this book show that it would be wrong to cast Germantown in either/or terms; instead, we must embrace a both/and approach in order to make local history beneficial in sustainable ways. Germantown stands as a parable about the limits of public history and a laboratory for understanding what makes it effective.

Effective public history is an active group endeavor that transcends any one view of the past. "Effective," like many words associated with public history, carries multiple meanings. "Effective public history" means history done accurately and with scholarly rigor in ways that make it come alive for a variety of people; it also actually builds on a German concept (*Wirkungsgeschichte*) of ways of knowing history that address personal perspectives that affect one's view of the past.[4] In this book I argue that Germantown has begun to practice effective public history by addressing the limitations and biases it has inherited from earlier stewards in ways that transform individuals and their understanding of the past, so that public history can help address the social ills plaguing the neighborhood today. Public history will not solve income inequality or racism or housing problems or the shortcomings of the education system. But all of these things intersect in public history, and that is where Germantown's public history practitioners have begun to do more to reveal context and stimulate discussion. Public history can democratize which stories matter, contextualize new information openly and with critical awareness, and boldly embrace the personal passions that make encounters with history meaningful, even if the subjects are less than celebratory, even if they are tragic.

Interpretation of historic sites can raise people's consciousness, inspire them, and lift them to an unanticipated level of understanding. But, like weightlessness, it can be scary in practice. Effective public history provides a kind of "antigravity." Encounters with artifacts and places often evoke visceral responses, powerful emotions, even cognitive changes in the brain.[5] The result is an opportunity to change people. But such fraught encounters have to be managed and led carefully. Effective public history, therefore, requires time and resources to overcome resistance, as well as intentional communication, facilitation of difficult conversations, and leadership of organizational change. In the end, these encounters are rewarding because they can take people beyond one story to understand that there are many more ways to see the past and ourselves in it.

We lay the foundations for effective public history by broadening the level of input, lowering barriers to participation for expert and nonexpert historians, and deepening our sense of the past by plumbing the sources more expansively and examining all stories accurately and fairly. The result is an active, adaptable process that can elevate public discourse by providing context, expanding our point of view to consider new ways of understanding, and transcending parochial limitations to raise our shared sense of the past. By uncovering history, working toward partnerships, and openly striving for dialogue, effective public history in Germantown builds a platform for preserving stories in as full a context as possible in ways that usefully inform the neighborhood's often competing needs.

Revivals Colonial and Economic

Visitors to the neighborhood are often struck by what the novelist Mat Johnson calls the "urban depression that is Germantown," a place "frozen in an architectural class war."[6] In 1983 German journalists visiting Philadelphia to celebrate the three hundredth anniversary of the first permanent German settlement in America were aghast at the neighborhood's dilapidated condition. I have heard university students call it "ghetto Williamsburg." Whites simplistically blame the last generation of black politicians, while blacks assign the problems to white flight and discriminatory business practices. In the 1990s, Germantown's white state representative, Robert O'Donnell, the speaker of the state legislature, was often heard saying, "Places like Germantown will never die, but they will always be dying."[7] What makes "places like Germantown"?

You might say that public history—in particular, the way people apply history to make sense of change in the present—has made Germantown and places like it. Germantown is a very old neighborhood where many of the ills that beset U.S. cities in the twentieth century are easy to spot. Other old neighborhoods with unique architecture or significant historical resources have used them for economic revival. But not Germantown. Why not? Many remarkably creative approaches to contemporary problems in Germantown have had historic preservation at their core. Several times a year, news headlines proclaim some new project or initiative that will provide the spark and allow it to reach its elusive potential.[8] A look at what has been tried, what has succeeded, and what has failed in Germantown helps to illustrate how urban planning, heritage tourism, architectural preservation, and museum studies have evolved in the country overall. Each decade has offered examples of attempted solutions and success stories, frequently setting standards for historic preservation nationally. Why did history fail to provide the development spark that people expected?

Part of the answer lies in how public history has been practiced: occasionally, by people with insular, self-interested motives who are trying to justify their own power or place by establishing connections to the past. Germantown lost its status as an independent town when it was incorporated by the city of Philadelphia in 1854. At that point its leaders pushed for a distinctive identity for the neighborhood by rekindling ancestral associations with the colonial and Revolutionary War generations. Our record of this contested process begins with John Fanning Watson (1779–1860), who started the evolution of Germantown's public memory by establishing markers, collecting objects from the Revolutionary War, commissioning photographs of colonial buildings, and interviewing people who were alive when President George Washington lived in the neighborhood. Though Watson's work was error-prone, inaccurate, and highly bigoted, his influence lasted well into the twentieth century. Guidebooks used his *Annals of Philadelphia* as a source, and it shaped the papers read before meetings of descendant groups. In 1900 the Germantown Site and Relic Society was founded to maintain Watson's approach to local history by preserving "souvenirs and mementos of Washington."[9] Watson's model of progressive historic preservation, combined with his conservative politics, informed a century's worth of efforts in what amounted to one prolonged, localized Colonial Revival.[10]

Though generations of antiquarians followed Watson's model, many groups claim Germantown, with pride, as a vessel for their own heritage. Because of William Penn's bold idea of toleration for all Christian sects in his colony, many people sought a religious home in Germantown. The influx of settlers resulted in the establishment of scores of congregations but also a tendency to fragment and exclude. Thus, the Germantown Friends meeting and school (built in 1845) stands across from the reform Quaker meeting and school, Greene Street Friends, founded ten years later. Rittenhouse Street, on what was once called "Poor House Lane," has more than a dozen churches, mostly storefront congregations established by successive waves of African American migrants after the Civil War. They and other immigrants and migrants saw opportunity in Germantown's natural beauty and architecture. Even as its German identity gave way to

Irish, Italian, and African American, the neighborhood's history helped to Americanize new groups. So strong was the impulse to connect to Germantown's icons of colonial America that in February 1928 the black YWCA hosted a ladies' tea where African American women celebrated Washington's birthday by dressing as George and Martha.

A Day in Germantown

On a bright August day not long ago, the historic site where I worked, Cliveden, gathered a team of historians, architects, designers, museum conservators, and professional tour guides to study its two kitchens. The construction of Cliveden was completed in 1767. Today the property consists of a large stone mansion, two separate outbuildings, and a stone and wood carriage house, reconstructed after a 1970 fire, that today contains staff offices, interpretive exhibition space, and rooms for community use. Though built by local craftsmen out of locally quarried stone, the sixteen-room mansion stands apart from the German-style architecture on the avenue. Significantly, it reveals certain differences between spaces where the workers lived and worked, such as a hidden staircase that slaves, servants, and children used, and the 1767 kitchen, one of two "dependencies"—outbuildings on which the household depended for laundry, food, and other products of the service quarters. Workers lived in the service spaces but also on upper floors of the mansion. Thus, the spaces where the family lived and the ones where the workers lived and worked sometimes intersect. Enslaved and indentured workers served the large household, which included twelve children in the first generation that occupied Cliveden. The seven generations of Chew descendants who owned the house until 1972 modified and modernized the stone structure several times, particularly the service spaces (see Chapter 5), but, because of the house's role in the Battle of Germantown during the Revolutionary War, they never altered the façade.

On October 4, 1777, General George Washington attacked British forces at Germantown in a battle that extended over the entire neighborhood. Planned as an attack on the British army to liberate occupied Philadelphia, the Battle of Germantown engaged twenty-one thousand troops and could be heard sixty miles away. The most intense skirmishes took place at Cliveden as the Continental Army tried unsuccessfully to remove approximately a hundred British soldiers who were using its thick stone walls as a fortress. Though an American defeat, the Battle of German-

Figure I.1 Cliveden, 2018. The mansion was built between 1763 and 1767 on a site that became the scene of intense fighting during the 1777 Revolutionary War Battle of Germantown. Except for a brief period after the Revolution, the Chew family owned the property until it was transferred to the National Trust for Historic Preservation in 1972. (Photo by the author.)

town was a key event in the Philadelphia campaign, for it persuaded European allies to support the Continental cause. Cliveden was permanently linked to the 1777 battle, just as the neighborhood as a whole cherished its connections to America's colonial and revolutionary history as a source of pride and identity.

Cliveden had received a major grant to involve consulting scholars and neighborhood residents in a project to uncover the history of its kitchens in order to preserve them appropriately and program the spaces for regular exhibitions and tours. Even simple spaces can yield historical insights that are accessible, relevant, and even provocative to visitors and neighbors. One kitchen is located in an original 1767 structure—a two-story outbuilding or dependency—former slave quarters that were remodeled into a twentieth-century apartment and later damaged by water and neglect. The second, located inside the Cliveden mansion itself, is a 1959 kitchen filled with bright green cabinets and what were modern appliances for the time. As surprised as visitors are to enter a "modern" kitchen in a colonial house museum, they are consistently shocked to learn that the family that owned Cliveden until 1972, the Chews, were once among the largest slave owners in Pennsylvania. This history was a shock, too, to the experts visiting on that August day. Some members of the team were unaware that slavery existed in Philadelphia, the City of Brotherly Love in the Quaker State. Learning this history disorients visitors to this revolutionary shrine, challenging them to reconsider their understanding of the site's past.

The kitchens project is the latest initiative to excavate this facet of the history of mid-Atlantic chattel slavery: the enslaved people associated with the Chews of Cliveden. If visitors are taken aback by the presence of slave quarters, then all of Germantown's well-remembered history is worth reconsidering. Only within the past generation have its established museums, monuments, and historic markers—its "memory infrastructure"— acknowledged anything but a celebratory past. How the memory infrastructure of the neighborhood changed and expanded in response to residents' experience and understanding is a central component of this book.[11]

As the team probed Cliveden's kitchens, children from a neighborhood summer camp played on the six acres of grounds, careful to avoid the caution tape that marked off where heavy rains had felled a two-hundred-year-old tree the week before. One of Cliveden's challenges is connecting local children with the sense of wonder the experts felt in their own encounter with the site. The children ran around and played on the grounds, while the experts coaxed a few of them down from the trees.

Leaving Cliveden, at the upper end of Germantown Avenue, the team took to the road to examine historic kitchens at several nearby sites built in the eighteenth century. Most of the twenty experts were seeing the neighborhood's historic resources for the first time. Among these are sixteen historic sites, seven of which are National Historic Landmarks, the highest designation of historic significance conferred by the Secretary of the Interior. The 1777 Battle of Germantown sprawled over the neighborhood, and damage can still be seen on many houses from that period. Three schoolhouses from the time when Washington lived in Germantown remain standing; one of them was adapted for use as a coffee shop, which provided lunch for the team. More than ten thousand residential buildings here are at least a century old. Among the scores of churches in the neighborhood are the founding congregations in North America for Lutherans, Mennonites, and Moravians, who settled in Germantown because of the promise of religious freedom offered in Pennsylvania. The buildings, however, do not reveal all the stories. Burial grounds dating from the seventeenth century include group graves of Revolutionary War dead, buried by neighborhood boys on October 4, 1777, and a "potter's field" with the remains of paupers and nameless African Americans.

The presence of so much history in plain sight makes it practically invisible to most residents. The purpose of our trip was to get to the previously untold stories embedded in the architecture and social history of kitchens and service spaces where workers toiled to provide food and clothing for the wealthy owners of the properties. Even team members familiar with Germantown's history saw it with new eyes. Going in and out of old kitchens, exploring physical evidence of the interplay of labor, wealth, and privilege, prompted us to make connections to today's dynamics of class and power.

The first stop was the Johnson House, constructed in 1768 by the same man who built Cliveden, a Mennonite master carpenter named Jacob Knorr. The team looked through the kitchen, examined the well pump, and peered into the icehouse outbuilding. The site's central air conditioning units had recently been stolen for scrap copper, and the board of directors was trying to raise funds to replace them. A private home until 1908, the Johnson House for most of the rest of the twentieth century was the meeting place for the Germantown Women's Club. Research in the 1980s verified that the Johnson family included abolitionists who offered their house as a station on the Underground Railroad in the early 1850s. The house's history was rewritten, and in 1997 the house was designated a National Historic Landmark. Today it is open as a public house museum whose mission is to tell the story of the slaves' struggle for freedom. The same man who built Cliveden, the slave owner's mansion just one block away, built this house that became a station on the Underground Railroad. Germantown history contains many such juxtapositions, showing how the revelation of events and connections from the past changes the public's sense of a building's importance.

A small bus (a remade trolley car, recalling the Number 23 trolley that operated on the nine miles of Germantown Avenue until the 1990s) brought the group to Historic RittenhouseTown (built in 1688), site of America's first paper mill. Its executive director showed us through two of its kitchens: the 1740 bakehouse and the cooking hearth in the recently renovated 1707 homestead, birthplace of the colonial-era astronomer David Rittenhouse. The restored bakehouse is larger than it appears from

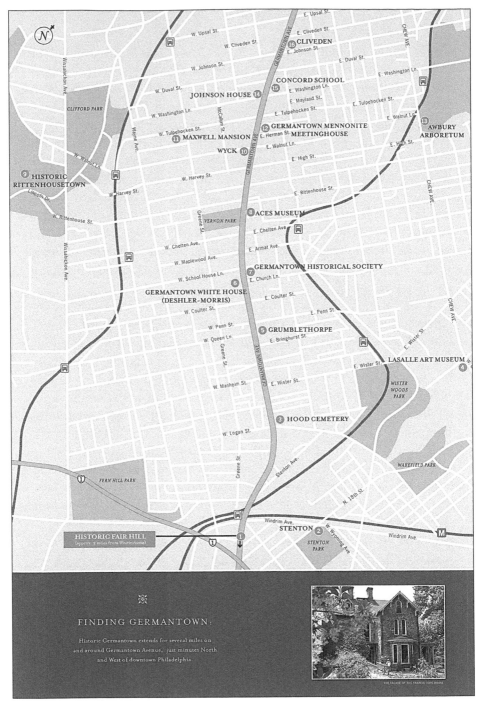

Figure I.2 Publicly accessible sites of Historic Germantown, 2016. This map shows all sixteen members of the Historic Germantown consortium, most of them on or near Germantown Avenue; Cliveden is near the top. (Courtesy of Historic Germantown; design by Caspari-McCormick.)

outside; episodes of a cable television show, *Cooking with History,* have been filmed there, with cooks from Philadelphia's City Tavern preparing meals over multiple fires in its hearth. The 1707 homestead building is now used as the visitor center. The director seemed upbeat about the challenges of maintaining seven historic buildings with a volunteer board of directors consisting of Rittenhouse descendants, local craftspeople, and professionals with varied skill sets and financial capacity, all of whom share a love for the site.

The next stop was the "Germantown White House," as the Deshler-Morris House (built in 1752) is now known, operated by Independence National Historic Park (part of the National Park Service). Washington lived and held cabinet meetings during two summers of his presidency, in 1793 and 1794. The curator showed the team through the kitchen ten at a time because of the delicate state of its recent restoration. Owned by the federal government since 1948, the site has benefited over the past ten years from millions of dollars in investment for meticulous repairs and new exhibitions; the interior spaces and the exterior are exceptionally handsome. Budget cuts resulting from the 2012 federal sequester, however, keep the Deshler-Morris House closed to the public most days of the year.

The bus passed Vernon Park, which includes the 1803 Vernon-Wister House and serves as Germantown's de facto public square. Monuments to the neighborhood's colonial and revolutionary past are spread throughout Vernon Park's spacious lawn. This central Germantown park was the scene of numerous public history festivals during the past century, and in 2008 presidential candidate Barack Obama spoke to twenty thousand people there. The kitchens team saw construction under way to improve the park's landscaping and playground, with funding recently secured through the efforts of Germantown's city councilwoman. The initiative to shift the perception of the park from a hangout for homeless drug addicts to a community gathering place was nearing completion. Banners promoted the project's progress and announced upcoming movie nights and concerts featuring local musicians and poets.

Three prominent buildings not far from Vernon Park stand empty and abandoned: the Young Women's Christian Association, the Germantown Town Hall, and, across the street from them, the old Germantown High School, which closed in 2013. The Y had been the scene of progressive interracial programming in the 1920s. Only a few months before our tour, plans for adapting and reactivating the Y building were scuttled by the councilwoman at a public meeting, and with it hopes for the redevelopment of at least one of Germantown Avenue's vacant, graffiti-tagged institutional ruins. It stands as a reminder that the public does not always get to decide the fate of historic buildings. The other buildings hold some promise. A private developer has purchased the 1914 high school building. As for the 1923 Town Hall, abandoned since 1996, a complicated ownership arrangement with the city of Philadelphia challenges efforts to make the massive marble structure viable. In 2013 public art projects drew attention to the building, currently the greatest test of the neighborhood's ongoing efforts to use its historic architecture for the benefit of the public. Germantown regularly sees creative efforts to reuse existing structures to meet present community needs. (The coffee shop in the 1750 schoolhouse is one such example.) No museum has ever been built in Germantown: All its historic sites are adaptations, mostly former homes preserved and interpreted for the public.

The trolley drove past dollar stores housed in what had been Germantown's grand department stores during the mid-twentieth century. I left the group for a moment to rush into a lawyer's office located in the Clarkson-Watson House (built in 1750–1760), where Thomas Jefferson lived during the summer of 1793. Once a bank, later home to the nineteenth-century historian John Fanning Watson, the building's historic features, including exposed wood panels and door hardware, had been expertly restored in 2010. I was delivering a letter needed to legally dissolve the Upsala Foundation—the nonprofit that had run the 1798 Upsala mansion as a house museum. Rarely visited and overburdened by maintenance costs, Upsala closed in 2003 and was (at the time of the tour) operated by Cliveden, located across the street. As I left to catch up to the trolley, I invited the attorneys to offer promotional fliers to their clients or even purchase a program ad for the history festival held each October to commemorate the 1777 Battle of Germantown on the grounds of Cliveden and Upsala.

The kitchens team moved on to Grumblethorpe to see the kitchen and service cellar at this 1744 site. Located on 2.5 acres, Grumblethorpe remains Germantown's best example of German architecture from the colonial era. Volunteers run an award-winning education program for local students, who tend an urban farm; Grumblethorpe is not open to the public except by appointment. Like many historic sites in Germantown and elsewhere, its financial sustainability is in jeopardy because of declining resources and dwindling visitation. Economics may well force more of Germantown's sixteen historic sites to go the way of Upsala and either close or become something other than a house museum. (These sixteen sites belong to the Historic Germantown consortium, described in Chapter 1.)

The team ate lunch at the 1730 Stenton mansion at the lower end of Germantown. Stenton's prominence in the Historic Germantown consortium of sites stems, in part, from its status as the first house museum in Philadelphia (opened in 1899). More recently, Stenton has managed an exemplary program aimed at promoting history education and literacy through collaboration among five sites in Germantown, no small feat in a community with ninety churches and thirty-nine neighborhood associations, as well as those sixteen historic sites.[12] Stenton's grounds are open to the public, and thousands from the surrounding community take part in an annual Easter egg hunt and other seasonal events. The city of Philadelphia owns Stenton, but the National Society of the Colonial Dames of America in the Commonwealth of Pennsylvania operates the property. Though a traditional and descendant-based organization, the Dames have implemented a strategic vision that transcends mere preservation of the building.

Reviewing our day in Germantown, the scholars, architects, and consultants of the kitchens team saw potential beyond the study of kitchen spaces and the social history of the people who worked in them. Though we were charged with examining and comparing elements of kitchen design and architecture, the give and take of the day allowed us to see the whole neighborhood as a sort of test kitchen for public engagement with history. Many remarked that despite all the issues Germantown faced, they had never experienced such a well-preserved place. They saw the neighborhood as curators would, examining the kitchens for evidence, interpreting archaeological and architectural details, but they also saw Germantown in its larger urban context and wondered how preserving the kitchens could help identify the needs of the surrounding neighborhood. Could the research be made relevant to more than just a small group of experts? What was the symbolic importance of recovering known slave quarters? Can colonial cooking demonstrations show the evolution of traditional foodways, and perhaps connect that knowledge with local restaurants and businesses on the commercial corridor? Finally, the kitchens team noted the strong reactions to the contrast between a modern kitchen and one from colonial times. A relatively simple space architecturally, a kitchen can be the setting for complex social dynamics. Exploring how those played out over time offers opportunities to connect with individual visitors. Making the kitchens more prominent on the tour could lead to more sensory experiences: tastes, sounds, and aromas, triggering reactions to the historic kitchens or sparking memories of their own homes. A kitchen can raise issues of, race, class, status, servitude, and gender roles in a realm that is identifiable for most people. Showing the kitchens as private and public spaces raises key questions of public history. Who owns the history of such spaces? The people who worked in them? The employers and owners? The current stewards? An encounter with the past through a common space like a kitchen can create a powerful historical experience.

The team saw a great opportunity but also the current state of Germantown. Gated shops and abandoned buildings stand alongside beautiful historic architecture. Even the many well-preserved historic sites interconnected through the Historic Germantown consortium stand apart from people walking by on the street, literally fenced off from the everyday life of the neighborhood. The history practitioners who work at the sites, largely white and well educated, are separated from the neighbors they are trying to reach. If Germantown is indeed a test kitchen for public history, and if Germantown's historic places are to provide a common space for all kinds of audiences, its practitioners need to emerge from behind the gates to engage with the community so that the sites can offer inclusive experiences that make the neighborhood's compelling history matter to its residents.

Citizens and Historians

Public history depends on citizens' trying to see themselves in larger cultural narratives. The passions that motivate campaigns to save a place typically stem from a drive to preserve something that illustrates a story of "our people." Whether those impulses are curatorial (saving the buildings and artifacts), urbanist and contextual (saving the place or location), or experiential (saving the feeling and association the place inspires), they derive from groups pushing a specific version of history. National Park Service historians informally call this energy "Criterion P"—referring to the passion and political influence that frequently determine which historic places are designated as nationally significant.[13] Both elements of Criterion P are vital to Germantown. Tension is generated when people delve deep into their ethnic or local roots to make a case for national importance. With personal passions motivating the striving for more general affiliation, people often make their claim to national importance by highlighting culturally specific roots in a larger narrative. Germantown's historical memory comes from its many citizen historians, passionately raising the profile of their own special interest.

Public history and historic preservation have always been political. The national embrace of historic preservation began in the nineteenth century as a reaction to industrialization and the Civil War. Colonial customs and revolutionary heroes recalled the nation's origins: Mount Vernon was saved and New England kitchens were reconstructed for local fairs and national exhibitions to suggest that the sacrifices and sentiments that had built the nation could still be drawn upon. In Germantown, Watson preserved strands of George Washington's hair in a box fashioned from a fragment of the William Penn Treaty Oak. Moments became mementos used to inspire as well as preserve the past against change in the present.

Twentieth-century public history and preservation saw a venerated past vulnerable to urbanization and threatened by more alien newcomers. John D. Rockefeller Jr.'s Colonial Williamsburg, like Henry Ford's Greenfield Village collections and Henry du Pont's Winterthur period rooms, saved and honored structures that were reminders of earlier eras, when, it could be believed, ingenuity, shared values, political virtue, sacrifices for common goals, and even high style distinguished a traditional America. The preservation movement of the 1920s went hand in hand with race-based immigration restriction: The same sources created and funded a vision of a presumably superior homogeneous America and promoted parallel legislative strategies to protect that vision.

Germantown's preservation-based responses to change were built on the Watson model. As immigrants and migrants made their way into Germantown after the Civil War, citizens trumpeted their connections to the colonial generations, using curatorial research or symbols from the historical records. In the 1890s Governor Samuel Pennypacker celebrated the Germanness of early Germantown as it faded from view.[14] The Germantown Site and Relic Society drew attention to buildings, artifacts, and documents that showed how different white Protestant groups each had their roots in the township's colonial heritage.[15]

As its population changed, Germantown's citizens responded by crafting their own sense of place. We have already noted the tradition of antiquarians like John Fanning Watson, carried on by the preservationist Frances Anne Wister (1874–1956) and the founders of the Site and Relic Society (renamed the Germantown Historical Society in 1925). The society operated on Watson's model, treating anything colonial as a sacred relic and pairing a nostalgia narrative that emphasized the authority of the past with the melancholic realization that, amid so much change, Germantown's best days were behind it.

The work of preservation gave rise to a professionalizing preservation community, which shifted the movement beyond its culturally specific origins. The 1906 Antiquities Act and 1935 legislation authorizing the Historic American Buildings Survey prompted architects and historians to draw on disciplinary expertise; since the 1960s, the Secretary of the Interior's Standards for the Treatment of Historic Properties and the National Historic Register nominations process have reinforced the importance of expert knowledge. Professional preservationists extended the movement's purview from battlefields and landscapes into cities; they also came to valorize buildings and specific details of the built environment. These curatorial and urbanist impulses passed from a traditional antiquarian elite to a class of professional experts with similar biases and no less exclusive.[16] At its best, the process upheld rigorous standards for a designation conferring elite status on a site or structure. At its worst, it produced an expert-led "tyranny of best practices," a term frequently cited by critics who feel that house museums have become so boring as to be unsustainable.[17] The result is that only 5 percent of the buildings listed on the National Register have anything to do with women, African Americans, Asian Americans, Latinos, or LGBTQ people,[18] suggesting that, if a building did not tell the story of a famous white person, it did not deserve designation. In 2012 Cliveden applied to update its National Historic Landmark nomination to include the new findings on its history of slavery, based on the Chew plantation records. The effort ran up against the limits of the current rules and guidelines. Cliveden's team had to make the case in terms of the buildings' architecture rather than the experiences of the people who toiled in them.

There was, however, another way to look at Germantown. J. Gordon Baugh Jr. (d. 1946) documented the growing African American population in a remarkable 1913 photograph album that commemorates what blacks in Germantown did in the fifty years after emancipation. Rather than depicting a neighborhood in decline, he captured images of how African Americans had established their own sense of place, contributing jobs, taxes, and associations for what he labeled "our people." Baugh placed the growing African American population in Germantown's history, with a chronology beginning in 1863 rather than 1683. Rather than glorifying what used to be, Baugh depicted the experience of African Americans with a sense of progress and hope. He showed people active in the present, trumpeting their contributions and proclaiming their existence in the community as citizens. Baugh's goals would be extended in 1928, when leaders of the Harlem Renaissance brought an exceptional collaboration to Germantown for one of the first-ever Negro Achievement Week celebrations.

Tension between national connections and ethnic identification played out in many ways. Until the early 1940s, there were separate Young Women's Christian Associations and Young Men's Christian Associations for whites and blacks. The Ys and Germantown Settlement, rooted in organizations founded in 1884 by Quakers to Americanize immigrants, promoted ethnic clubs and associations to advance patriotic American ideals. Such groups found their own ways to connect to the past, invoking the example of Penn's religious toleration or establishing a sense of place in a specific section of the neighborhood. Ethnic heritage festivals were frequent and competing. The ethnically English and the descendants of revolutionary patriots celebrated October 4 with parades and gatherings in Vernon Park to recall the Battle of Germantown. Two days later German groups celebrated German-American Day. It was easier to start a new variation on a theme than to work together. In the early 1970s, when Germantown's emergent African American political leaders gained control over Germantown Settlement, they used that organization to control public investments for the benefit of black political causes, empowering a single group rather than joining with others to address larger neighborhood issues. Efforts to embrace a broader view of American history tended to break down because of entrenched agendas serving narrowly defined interest groups. This endemic parochialism remains enshrined in the neighborhood's constellation of house museums, each celebrating a discrete connection to the past while struggling to establish a niche in a crowded field.

Even as Germantown became more heterogeneous, passions and politics worked together to simplify complex historical narratives, resulting in a public history that was divided and not entirely public. The influence of Colonial Williamsburg proved long lasting. Between 1946 and 1976, Germantown business leaders tried to create their own version of a reconstructed colonial village, and despite that project's failure, one still hears today the myth that the Rockefellers considered reconstructing Germantown before settling on the former Virginia capital.

For decades, the Germantown section of Philadelphia has been a poor, high-crime neighborhood with a declining population. In 1950, there were more than 68,000 residents, of whom fewer than 10,000 were black. By 1980, there were fewer than 49,000 residents, slightly more than 10,000 of whom were white.[19] The 2010 census saw 29 percent of the 46,690 residents living below the poverty line (compared with 14 percent state-wide).[20] The large minority population (73 percent as of 2010) has until recently been disconnected from the neighborhood's established public history. No marker related to Germantown's African American history existed until 1987, when a plaque marking the site of the Joseph Hill Elementary School was placed in the parking lot where it had once stood. The absence of museums and monuments reflecting the history of the neighborhood's black residents was not an indication that these residents were uninterested in history—quite the contrary. Though black residents were not allowed to be members of the Germantown Historical Society (founded in 1900) until the early 1970s, they found ways to put themselves into the history of Germantown.

Applying "Criterion P," black residents took matters into their own hands. In 1967 the recent high school graduate David Richardson Jr. led a walkout of two hundred students from Germantown High School to protest the absence of African American history in the curriculum. Recently, Vashti Dubois opened the Colored Girls Museum in her own home in southern Germantown, and Supreme D. Dow started the Black Writers Museum, which now occupies the 1803 Wister House in Vernon Park. The founders adopted the name "museum" for these institutions that were designed to fill a perceived gap in the public memory: a built environment and memory infrastructure that did not represent the black experience. Some museums have had to close because there are not enough visitors; several more have opened to share the history of "our people" when the memory infrastructure does not reflect them.

This book shows that the issues that divide Germantown go well beyond simplistic oppositions such as white and black, rich and poor, and descendant and newcomer. There have always been many Germantowns. The interplay of class, education, ethnic background, and one's sense of the past helped determine which Germantown one belonged to and which clubs, heritage groups, and neighborhood associations one joined. Separatism was encouraged, rather than mitigated, by religious groups. If public history were solely about white history, there would be one colonial museum rather than a dozen. And if ethnic groups were perfectly cohesive, there probably would not be so many churches, often of the same denomination, in such close proximity. In Germantown, the "sense of place" and identification with "our people" has proved as much a source of division as of unity. It has even been a source of embarrassment at key moments.

In 1983 the German Sunday newsweekly *Zeit Magazin* published a ten-page cover story about Germantown, marking the three hundredth anniversary of its founding. The magazine profiled descendants of the thirteen families who came from the Crefeld area of Germany in the 1680s. One of the highlights of the story was a history parade. Here was the epitome of the wave of Colonial Revivalism that shaped public history after World War II and continued into the 1976 Bicentennial celebrations. Planning for the tercentenary, historic sites formed a loose collaboration, Historic Germantown Preserved, to facilitate the efforts of volunteers and a small group of museum professionals to draw tourists to Germantown. Combined tours, exhibitions of founding documents, and a variety of programs and events celebrated the connection to Germany. The group even succeeded in bringing West German Bundespräsident Karl Carstens to the Germantown Historical Society.

The magazine coverage, however, could not have been more alarming. The front page featured an honor guard of five men dressed in Prussian military uniforms (helmeted in the traditional *Pickelhäube,* two of them carrying rifles), marching past gray buildings with boarded windows splattered with graffiti, on the broken cobblestones of Germantown Avenue, its sidewalks curiously devoid of onlookers. Intended to update colonial connections, the article ignored the fact that Germantown had lost its "Germanness" by the late 1800s.[21] Nor did the northwestern German and Dutch founders who settled that Pennsylvania village have any link with Prussia. Those out-of-context re-enactors, in nostalgic costumes completely at odds with their surroundings, showed the limitations of the Watson approach to public history. *Zeit* used the word "decline" a dozen times to describe the neighborhood, giving special attention to race, crime (crack had arrived in Germantown earlier that year), and the diminishing interest in preservation. "The German Township is a black ghetto. I pass through decaying streets, the spray-paint-soiled façades, and whole city blocks vacant, doors and windows strewn with trash and debris. Is this Philadelphia's future Bronx? The neglected historic dregs of the City of Brotherly Love?"[22]

History Scholarly and Public

As the kitchens team saw, Germantown can use history to connect stakeholders to larger issues of social and economic justice. By 2012, Germantown had reckoned enough with its history to take a step forward in the evolution of the field and its professionalizing efforts. Nearly two decades worth of articles decrying the fate of house museums and labeling public history "irrelevant" stimulated thinking and produced changes that have made Germantown's public history more public.[23] But can a history as compelling as Germantown's—Revolutionary War battles, Underground Railroad, Harlem Renaissance events, to say nothing of deep musical and literary connections—be sustainable? Or are recent efforts too little, too late?

Since the 1980s, Germantown's heritage practitioners have operated with a new sense of urgency. Having inherited the stewardship of buildings, collections, and research from waves of descendant-based colonialists and the professional curatorial and architectural experts who succeeded them, they have taken stock of the realities of dwindling resources, declining visitation, and a local population left out of the standard colonial memory of the neighborhood and the memories constructed by antiquarians like Watson. Rather than promoting national identity in an age of immigration or trying to forestall urbanization by sealing off beautiful architecture, they are struggling for relevance. The survival of public history in the neighborhood depends on a continuing ability to adapt.

Germantown is not Concord or Gettysburg, whose pasts offered pivotal moments that transformed the nation. The 1777 Battle of Germantown was a defeat and did not alter the course of the Revolutionary War. The 1688 Germantown Protest against Slavery—which Katharine Gerbner has argued begat abolitionism in the North—was written for a local meeting and was little known for decades.[24] Even when the protest reached the Philadelphia Friends' Yearly Meeting, it was considered "too weighty a matter" to consider. (And Germantown Quakers, proud as they were of the 1688 Protest, did not allow black people into their meeting until 1947.)[25] Such contradictions occur frequently in Germantown's collective memory, and they point to its true place in history, for they show how people think about history in America.

These contradictions make up what I call the "Germantown problem."[26] We have already encountered its three components: an idealized, nostalgic narrative that tends toward bitterness about the present; too many competing, uncoordinated groups; and neighborhoods with outsized senses of identity that resist change. The problem defies simple explanations, so entangled is Germantown's history with issues of race, class, and politics.[27] Consider housing segregation. Recent events make clear that predatory lending and redlining, while significant, cannot be the only factors in Germantown's housing patterns because there are many integrated enclaves interspersed among African American neighborhoods.[28] Scholars have challenged myths that Germantown was truly integrated while also avoiding the trap of the nostalgic "decline narrative."[29] Germantown's twentieth-century challenges and complications may not all have been overtly racist in intent; the neighborhood's divisions and parochialism stem from many origins and have generated many competing narratives. And Germantown's house museums, until recently, have been ill-equipped to tell nuanced, messy histories because they emphasized celebratory narratives involving members of the elite. As the Cliveden kitchens team saw, there are inconsistencies and pockets of amnesia even in the institutions that embody Germantown's well-remembered past. How do we make recent findings such as the extent of the Chews' slaveholding or events such as Negro Achievement Week and the 1967 high school walkout truly public in a place where commemorating colonial heritage has been primary?

This book, in examining the twenty-first century, shows ways of grappling with this complicated history. It addresses the "Germantown problem" by offering some elements of a "Germantown solution." Recognizing the complexities of history and accepting that we cannot always find certainty about the past, rather than tacitly accepting comfort-preserving explanations and easy categorization, reveals opportunities for public history to make a difference. By recognizing that no two people see the past in the same way and bringing people together to discuss new findings and consider different ways to apply the research, effective public history can provide a point of connection for people in the community and a forum that is broader and more open-ended than books or lectures.

Crafting ways of making history public may be Germantown's most important contribution to American history. The ongoing efforts have involved many conflicts. Traditional ways of applying the neighborhood's connections to American history may have encouraged divisions along lines of race and class. But newer approaches may show alternatives to these divisions and at the same time address the oversaturation of underperforming historic sites. Germantown's contradictions and messiness are part of its history and worth examining. Even the occasions when Germantowners tried and failed to apply the past in order to address current issues are worth examining, for the failures reveal the challenging dynamics of making history public. The chapters in this book ask the following: Why, in such a well-chronicled neighborhood, was a week-long Harlem Renaissance event unremembered? Why have continual attempts to use colonial- and revolutionary-era connections for economic gain only contributed to economic decline? Why did black activists choose the absence of African American history in the school curriculum to spark protests during the civil rights movement? The record shows that solutions depend on coordination, collaboration, broad community input, and uncovering history in ways that look at all stories, not just the simple or celebratory ones.

What Germantown has remembered is rooted less in racism or classicism than in a robust and prideful self-interest—a wish to preserve stories of "our people." Germantown's solution lies in new processes that help to recall stories of "all our people." As Facebook and other social media contribute to interest groups' narrowing insularity, making it ever harder to see differing points of view, some examples of local leadership show how to examine differences usefully.

Two participant observers, Elijah Anderson and Katie Day, have offered local audiences ways to cope with the kinds of differences, disagreements, and divisions that have limited Germantown in the past. Though they are sociologists, not academic historians, they have described elements of effective public history. Anderson is the author of a landmark ethnography of Germantown Avenue, *Code of the Street*. His study of urban spaces, *The Cosmopolitan Canopy*, presents urban islands of civility that can be brought into existence even where segregation is the norm.[30] Public settings such as parks, malls, town squares, and—one can extrapolate—public history sites can be places that maintain civil and comfortable interactions between diverse populations. Where the canopy breaks down, in the workplace, on public transportation, and by extension, through public history done wrong, Anderson shows how people have to address the social dynamics of racial inequality directly and be conscious and intentional about recognizing that each space has multiple points of entry that must be respected, in all their variations. Clothing, conduct, and color all inform and provoke reactions, and it is easy to tear or collapse the civil canopy. Without awareness, attention, and intent, disrespect can occur in many forms. Differences of opinion have to be faced directly if civility is to be maintained. This is a scary step for many. But cosmopolitan civility can be restored by recognizing one's barriers to communication and by stretching to see another person's point of view.

When Anderson spoke at Cliveden in October 2013, he presented examples of ghettos and uncivil conduct to a packed audience of blacks and whites of mixed incomes and backgrounds. His talk was part of the Cliveden Conversations program, which gathers neighbors together to address recent research and hear people's reactions in an open forum (see Chapter 1). Audience members are required to introduce themselves to a stranger and discuss with him or her the topic of the presentation. This open process, which forces neighbors to confront their biases and ways of communicating with strangers, helps people learn in ways that elevate their understanding. "I never thought that coming to Cliveden could change my outlook on life," one participant wrote on an evaluation form. "I didn't think that introducing myself to a person of another color would be so hard, and then it turned out we had so much to discuss." People enter the room as strangers, but they end up discussing the presentation in small groups with people to whom they just introduced themselves, asking, for instance, What surprised you? How should Cliveden tell this story? What are you willing to do to help? Their responses are recorded on notepads in the front of the room (and eventually make their way to the walls of Cliveden's offices, guiding the staff on adjustments to exhibitions or tours and new program ideas).

Anderson's presentation sparked lively discussions, which were in turn shared with the rest of the crowd and the speaker. Anderson ended the evening by saying, "I had no idea it would be like this. Such a forum gives us a vocabulary of hope." There have now been forty-one community conversations about race, class, history, and memory at Cliveden.

Building on Anderson's work, Day studied Germantown's many churches and mosques to explain three insights vital for improving public history. First, people get their history from a variety of sources, and they do so no matter what, collecting data and learning in their own ways. In other words, it is wrong to conclude that because people do not visit house museums, they are not interested in history. In fact, several Germantown churches note their proximity to historic places as a point of pride. Second, faith communities often move and change, especially older ones. "Hermit crab" churches, for instance, move into other places of worship when economics, aging congregations, or diminished resources force them to adapt. Public history institutions that find new ways of operating, beyond house museums or established membership organizations, may prove more sustainable than those that adhere to a single outdated model. Third, even competing faith communities have found ways to share space and mediate differences. Day describes Germantown churches where people who do not share the same faith have negotiated a "détente" in order to maximize resources like shared meeting rooms or green space.[31] Identifying shared values allows them to overcome their differences and meet larger, agreed-on needs.

Day and Anderson both showed that the ability to see past one's own narrow interest depends on establishing mutual trust and respect. Day's study concludes that respect for sacred spaces enables a larger respect for another person's different faith or point of view. Germantown's churches give lessons that historic sites like Cliveden have applied, using history and shared heritage to serve a larger understanding of what is sacred or deserving of the effort to forge a détente with those who see things differently.

Day helped me train students to interview elders about twentieth-century history for a 2009 program called "Germantown Speaks" (see Chapter 1). Several churches helped recruit older parishioners for the project. Participants of varied ages and backgrounds interacted in an open forum, with results that surprised many, pointing to ways in which people learn from one another about history and in the process create community. By carefully forging a trustworthy process among all participants, we learned more than we could have learned alone.

Initiatives that include nonexperts, craft trustworthy experiences, and adapt to new ways of knowing have pulled Germantown's public history closer to the ideal of a "community of memory." This concept was first described in a book about Colonial Williamsburg's use of social history. A community of memory occurs when people agree that they share some kind of cultural heritage and discuss it in ways that celebrate what is good and criticize what is not.[32] Programs such as Cliveden Conservations and Germantown Speaks place Germantown firmly in the conversation about the future of preservation and show that preservation will not be doomed to irrelevance if it becomes more engaged with social justice, equity, and fairness. In the twenty-first century, Germantown's consortium of sites use history as a platform to explore issues of race and class, fully in keeping with calls to use preservation for social aims beyond preserving pretty buildings.[33] By broadening community involvement, we come to a greater sense of the history we share. Openly curating the past, together, and sharing authority over what is considered historic have become regular features of Germantown's approach to preservation and public history.[34] The results can be powerful.

Consider that the Battle of Germantown reenactment at Cliveden annually draws well over five thousand people to the site on the first Saturday of October. Attendance is not, of course, the only measure of success, but this one-day local history festival draws more people than the annual meetings of the National Preservation Conference, the American Historical Association, and the National Council on Public History. Bringing history to people in lively ways can reach a large audience. Even casual contact with the built environment and the stories the buildings represent can reveal meaning, beauty, and craft, which is why finding ways to apply the expert's rigor and the nonexpert's enthusiasm helps point to a more effective public history. But involving more people means more than simply adding more perspectives.

It means seeing public history as a series of relationships, not merely a summary of facts or collection of buildings. It means, in the words of the preservation historian Gail Dubrow, "bringing [people's] experience, insights and perspectives to bear on redefining the scope, policies, participants and priorities of the preservation movement."[35] Germantown's experience shows how the involvement of the broader public can reshape values that generate other narratives, and perhaps a new kind of momentum.

Battles

It takes hard work to build effective, truly public history. Ira Berlin's statement, "History is not about the past; it is about arguments we have about the past" applies to Germantown, past and present.[36] To overcome tendencies to exclusion and embrace the potential for shared history, it was necessary to transform some of the traditional ways of knowing its history.

Germantown's most notable battle took place on the foggy morning of October 4, 1777. Both a tactical defeat for the Americans and a strategic victory because it impressed potential foreign allies, the battle was one of the largest engagements of the Revolutionary War. And though it lasted only a few hours, it had a tremendous impact on Germantown, exerting a strong gravitational pull on future decisions about historic preservation. The public use of the past has been a frequent source of tension in Germantown ever since. Now that living off the glory of one brief colonial battle is no longer viable, a meaningful public history depends on embracing the neighborhood's many episodes of conflict.

Each of the following chapters illustrates a different way in which people have struggled to make history meaningful and lasting. These struggles take the form of contesting sources of evidence or institutional inertia or pushing against intransigent self-interest. In each case, barriers to change have forced people to uncover new methods, find different allies, and engage the past in novel ways so that it matters in the present. Despite the contradictions and the politics and drama of Germantown history, the struggles have generated constructive energy. The fight is not for the squeamish, however.

Chapter 1 examines how Cliveden and the Historic Germantown consortium reckoned with the perceived stagnation of Germantown's public history and created new ways of interpreting some of its sites. Recognizing that its many house museums could have a larger impact on neighborhood affairs, five historic sites employed new approaches in history education, research, and public engagement that brought wider audiences to find meaning in a difficult history. Historic Germantown's embrace of new approaches amid decreasing visitation and dwindling financial resources has helped it counter the decline and nostalgia narratives at work in the neighborhood for so long. The chapter explores in detail the leadership needed to manage Cliveden's embrace of African American history, involving the public in efforts to reveal long-taboo subjects such as slavery and discrimination. Cliveden had been a shrine to the colonial era; the challenge was to make it a forum for discussing the extensive slave-holding history of the Chew family—and to tell one story without obliterating the other. The success of this ongoing project reveals effective public history in action.

Chapter 2 examines an exceptional event: a weeklong celebration of Negro Achievement Week (a forerunner of Black History Month), hosted by Germantown's leading institutions, in 1928. How was this episode forgotten so quickly, even as the number of African Americans in the neighborhood continued to grow? Answering this question, and recalling some other unremembered episodes, turns up some interesting facets of Germantown's style of involving the public in history. Negro Achievement Week was the first modern public history program in America. It involved a broad collaboration of the East Coast's growing population of African Americans at a time when Ku Klux Klan activity was also prominent. The diversity of the content, the national leadership, and the attempt to address broad neighborhood concerns make this a significant and effective example of public history in action, and a powerful contrast to the antiquarian responses to change that were more common in that period.

Chapter 3 explores issues of authority, asking who gets to decide which versions of the past get remembered and which can be used to uncover and rewrite history in persuasive and enlightening ways. Germantown's efforts to remake itself during the period of urban renewal in the 1950s and 1960s showed that heritage tourism was not the solution. The limitations of the traditional, elite-based historical community became highly visible when economic decline, suburbanization, and population change prompted centuries-old anchor institutions to leave the neighborhood for the suburbs. Their departure motivated business leaders to commission architects and urban planners to develop plans to revitalize Germantown. As new plans were proposed, minority groups and the burgeoning corps of professional preservation advocates challenged traditional leadership methods, culminating in a struggle that *Philadelphia Magazine* dubbed "the Second Battle of Germantown" in 1967. Both communities' efforts expanded the memory infrastructure to include African American historic markers and museums.

Chapter 4 describes how social history research proved that Johnson House was a station on the Underground Railroad. In the 1980s, black and white citizen historians, working independently, established the site as a freedom station. Their efforts, growing out of the social activism of Germantown's Mennonites and the power of Germantown's black community in the 1970s, preserved the Dutch-style house on the corner of Germantown Avenue and Washington Lane as something other than a colonial site. Like many Underground Railroad stations, Johnson House has a story based on a blend of fact and legend. Verifying its status as an Underground Railroad landmark likewise involved a blend of evidence and idealization, reflecting some of the contradictions that have propelled Germantown history throughout the twentieth century. This example of effective public history illustrates how a site's meaning for a community goes well beyond its architectural features, heirloom furniture, and association with famous names.

Chapter 5 analyzes several empty buildings in Germantown and the process of finding meaning in them. From its construction in 1854 through its symbolic reconstruction in 1923 and eventual abandonment in 1996, Germantown's now-derelict Town Hall has evolved in the public's memory. Local artists projected their own history of the building in 2013, showing how a place that once stood for a nostalgic past, becoming historic for the wrong reasons, can still become meaningful when empty.

When the Upsala Foundation went out of business as a house museum in 2005, Cliveden devoted several years to a public process to find another use for the 1798 building. Upsala eventually returned to its original use as a private residence in 2017. Not every old building needs to be a museum. Finding alternative uses based on agreed-on community needs is difficult and demanding but not impossible. A mid-twentieth-century housing project was demolished in 2014 and neighbors advocated to have the city commemorate the burials at the colonial-era potter's field on which the building had stood. Finally, Cliveden's interpretation of its 1767 kitchen reveals how empty buildings need not have a single narrative imposed on them. Instead, they must find relevance by allowing several meanings to emerge through the implementation of processes that involve many points of view.

Mere preservation is no longer sufficient. Buildings, places, and spaces need to adapt in order to last. Their practical use as sites of connection for many publics will be the measure of future success. Each battle discussed in these pages was born of an urgent need. Passionate advocates met with pushback but focused their efforts on overcoming entrenched agendas, whether personal, institutional, or political, and found success. These struggles are well documented by preservationists, public historians, and academics. But will doing history well be enough?

Effective Public History

A recent program at Cliveden, *Liberty to Go to See*, used dramatic arts to bring to life stories from the Chew family's plantation records. An evaluation of the performance describes the writer's intimate encounter with Cliveden's history: "Never before have I felt such, I don't know what the word is, but I never felt such a sense of a 'beingness' of a place before."

This comment shows the power of public history as practiced in Germantown. When people actively bring their sense of who they are into an encounter with the past and then share their understanding in a way that informs the encounter, the result is a new understanding. The German term *Wirkungsgeschichte* has come to be translated as "effective history," since it refers to the effect of an observer's subjective experience on the supposed objectivity of a historical fact. I would like to expand it beyond the personal to the public, to include the need not only to reckon with the limits of one's personal perspective but also, using my practitioner's perspective, to consider the limits of institutional and group identifications that effect it. Taking one's personal perspective into its broader social context to consider a fuller and new experience, moves it from the past events to its current situation into a possible application for the future. To involve the observer's experience—including with the effects of institutions that comprise a shared heritage like a neighborhood's history—in order to share authority in an open-ended consideration of the past makes history both effective and public. "Beingness" suggests how "effective history" can become "effective public history."

I am not the first to argue that public history must acknowledge more than one way to view the past. Germantown's concrete examples, however, show how personal experience with the past generates narratives that are to be valued. And when public history welcomes other entry points and sources of evidence, it can be truly effective in the sense of making an impact. Even when embroiled in difficult discussions pitting traditionally opposed views against one another—such as Colonial Revival versus economic revival, citizen historian versus preservation professional, public history versus academic history—effective public history extends the meaning of the past beyond "building-ism" to get to the human feelings embedded in a place.[37] Rather than seeing buildings or landscapes as objectively defined spaces where events happened, effective public history embraces the "storyscape" of how a person encounters a place in order to incorporate how that person is changed through the encounter. Using storyscapes, public history identifies and preserves "landscapes of engagement where individuals actively encounter stories of past lives."[38] Allowing the personal perspective to inform the facts of the past, but with empathy rather than hierarchy, encourages personal encounters that will in turn inform context. And such wider storyscapes extend understanding beyond any one simplistic imposition of meaning by a curator or other authority. Storyscapes allow places to adapt by acquiring new meaning as our understanding changes in relation to them. With open and trustworthy processes as a regular feature of public history, multiple viewpoints can be engaged to challenge how we use history, how we determine who is a citizen, and whether the whole public is being served or only one segment of society. Effective public history makes it possible to preserve more than one intimate encounter with a place and get to a deeper understanding of the past.

By lowering barriers to participation, expanding input to include non-experts, and widening the base of knowledge by considering many sources for each story, we lay the foundations for a public history that moves beyond established ways of knowing. Effective public history promotes open dialogue, transcends parochial self-interests, and contributes to a shared sense of the fuller story, so that the story itself may change. And change brings conflict, so the antigravity of effective public history is challenging as well as transformative. Germantown has been in many ways an exemplar of the limitations of traditional public history practice. But because it has also, increasingly, involved a shared, engaging experience that brings life to history for many people and not just one specific interest or group, Germantown has now become a test kitchen for ways of knowing that build a sense of place greater than any single view of it. Effective public history elevates all those involved, instilling a fuller and more universal sense of stewardship.

Germantown has pushed what is considered "historic" beyond previously accepted narratives. Just as many of the buildings that were once homes or schools have found new uses as historic sites or coffee shops, the history community has adapted too. And it has done so with scholarly rigor, while also allowing new audiences to contribute to the process. Germantown reveals that a historic site, and public history itself, can offer a safe, welcoming, and respectful environment in which to consider difficult issues from the past and discuss how they might inform contemporary challenges. It shows that it is possible to offer new ways to connect people to a greater historical understanding of our country, our neighbors, and ourselves.

1

Conversations

Experiences with Germantown's
Community of Memory

I n February 2010 I received an unexpected call. The chief of staff of one of Germantown's state representatives demanded that I come to his office and meet with the chiefs of staff of all the neighborhood's elected officials. A project that I was engaged in had raised concerns.

Germantown Speaks was a program to gather oral histories from community members. Five sessions had already taken place; in the next one, high school students would interview people who had participated in a 1967 protest at Germantown High School. That event was a pivotal moment in Germantown's civil rights history because the student activists were calling attention to the lack of African American history in the school district's high school curriculum. Many of Germantown's elected officials—including its city councilwoman, state representatives, and state senator—had been among the protesting students and had a close relationship with its leader, David Richardson Jr. Because of Richardson's role in the neighborhood's history and these personal connections, neighborhood leaders had a keen interest in what would be discussed at the next Germantown Speaks session. The gatekeepers of the memory of Germantown's civil rights generation, all now in positions of political power, wanted to make certain that this history project met their approval.

I felt as though I had been called to the principal's office, but I overcame my defensiveness, knowing that my partners and I were doing good history. I prepared some video footage of previous Germantown Speaks sessions that showed high school students interviewing elders recruited through some of the neighborhood's many churches. The students asked the senior citizens a series of questions about growing up in Germantown, covering everything from World War II and the Vietnam War to discrimination, a racially charged transit strike, gang fights, and jazz music. Trained by history professors in the practice of oral history, the teenage interviewers disarmed the reticence of the older interviewees in each videotaped session so well that lively discussions of the neighborhood in the twentieth century had emerged.

The situation made explicit something historians understand intuitively: History is political. If all politics is local, then local history can be especially political because it evokes intense, focused emotions that play out on the ground in real time as people defend the history they believe is theirs. The Germantown politicians seemed to be concerned about what history, and whose, was going to be discussed. Their concern was based on the attitude of Germantown's history community toward African Americans, who for decades after its founding had been excluded from membership in the Germantown Historical Society. Important twentieth-century documents and artifacts related to the African American community (such as details about Germantown's 1928 Harlem Renaissance event, described in Chapter 2) would not be found in its collections. Many people, including Germantown's political leaders, still harbored bitterness about the society's efforts in the 1960s to use Germantown's colonial history as the basis for an urban renewal project that would have displaced an African American neighborhood (see Chapter 3).

The memories of the African Americans who formed the politicians' voter base had not been included in the received public memory managed by the traditional history community. Not only was Germantown history considered unwelcoming to African Americans; some of Germantown's historic sites, notably gated mansions such as Cliveden, were associated with slave owners, though this fact was not presented to visitors until the mid-1990s. Had the history of Germantown been told only through its historic house museums and historical society, the African American experience would barely be reflected.

Could a public history program about a 1967 student protest help fill this gap in the historical record? Its leader became a politician held in high esteem among African Americans. Born and educated in Germantown, Richardson was a state legislator and mentor of the public officials now in

Figure 1.1
State representative
David Richardson at his
desk, 1973. Richardson,
a native of Germantown,
helped organize a student
walkout from Germantown
High School in 1967
to protest against the
lack of African American
history in the Philadelphia
public school curriculum
and other inequities; his
election to state office at
the age of twenty-three
marked a radical shift
in Germantown politics.
(Special Collections
Research Center, Temple
University Libraries,
Philadelphia, PA; photo
by Michael J. Maicher.)

legislative office. Because of their personal relationship with him, these
officials were protective of his legacy, just as they were likely protective of
the memory of the civil rights protest. A section of Germantown's Chelten
Avenue and a U.S. post office had been renamed in his honor after his
death in 1995 at the age of forty-five. Now I, a white historian from Cliveden, the slave owners' mansion, had come to explain why Germantown
historic sites were suddenly interested in the African American experience.

The video clips I had brought with me convinced the chiefs of staff
that the interviews would generate nothing embarrassing or disrespectful.
After my presentation, they recommended that their bosses take part in
the project and attend one of the sessions to answer students' questions
about the 1967 protest. Learning that their high school had played a role
in the civil rights movement had piqued the students' interest in history. The session went well, and, all in all, the oral history experience was
good for all stakeholders. The chief of staff who had called me to his of-

fice, Steven Kinsey, participated in other Germantown Speaks sessions and answered students' questions about his time in neighborhood gangs. (He is now a state representative, elected in 2012.) This multigenerational, collaborative partnership among historic sites, the high school, and senior citizens from area churches brought a variety of new perspectives to the contested terrain of Germantown history and allowed everyone to learn— together. It was not easy, as my experience in the state representative's office illustrated. The initial opposition gave way, however, because people were motivated to do good history and because leadership brought the collaborative project forward. This is the kind of work that needs to be done to make Germantown history effective.

This chapter shows the novel ways in which Germantown's public history organizations have addressed the neighborhood's racial tensions and the relevance of its historic sites. Apart from isolated attempts to make public history more inclusive, up through the 1990s the African American community had been largely kept apart from the traditional, antiquarian preservation efforts represented in the array of colonial- and federal-era houses that made up the Germantown National Colonial Historic Landmark District. The twenty-first century, however, saw the controversy about the President's House Memorial in Philadelphia's downtown historic district, the uncovering of more varied forms of evidence by professional practitioners of social and public history, and a clear (some would say "dire") need for historic house museums to attract different bases of support. New ways had to be found. As Germantown's public history was transformed from a defensive and reactive effort to stop change into a more progressive and engaging search for ways to manage it, each step of this evolution revealed new tensions in the processes of outreach, uncovering evidence, and forging partnerships: the building blocks of effective public history. In the 1930s Germantown had helped launch the Historic American Buildings Survey; in the 1960s Germantown students challenged the high school history curriculum to include more African American history. Surely it could once again find ways to reimagine how history can be made useful.

Any effort to make a new model of public history has to transform traditional ways of working. Changes in governance, interpretation, and outreach to neighbors were needed, but they brought new battles to Germantown. Building trust in public history, and interest in historic sites, is a full-time effort requiring the active involvement of multiple voices and varieties of leadership.

Assembling the Building Blocks
of Effective Public History

Cliveden and the Chews of Germantown

Cliveden was the home of the wealthy attorney Benjamin Chew (1722–1810). Built between 1763 and 1767 as an English-style summer retreat, it stands on a hillside, where it catches the breezes. Like other members of the colonial elite, such as James Logan and Judge William Allen, Chew built his estate in Germantown, six miles from Philadelphia, to escape the city's crowds and diseases during the warmer months. A generation later, Benjamin Chew Jr. (1758–1844) made this seasonal house the family's permanent home.

The elder Chew served as chief justice and attorney general in colonial Pennsylvania; later he was the executor of the estate of William Penn's children. He owned several plantations in Maryland and Delaware, along with the enslaved and indentured workers who toiled there. He earned money not only from selling crops but also from selling and loaning out individual enslaved workers. Census records from the 1780s and 1790s reveal that Chew had slaves at Cliveden and at his townhouse on Third Street in Philadelphia (demolished in the early 1900s) or leased them out to other people in the city.

The Cliveden property expanded and shrank during the time the Chew family lived there. Today the property encompasses 5.5 acres, with the house set back from Germantown Avenue. In 1970, after a fire destroyed Cliveden's carriage house, Samuel Chew V (1915–1989) realized that the family could no longer maintain the property and grounds. In 1972 Cliveden was turned over to the National Trust for Historic Preservation to become a house museum open to the public.

The National Trust was chartered by an act of Congress in 1949, to establish historic homes as house museums and to advocate for the preservation of places important to the story of America. Originally a government agency, the National Trust emphasized protecting buildings at a time when the National Park Service was in charge of preserving and maintaining landscapes, Native American lands, and battlefields. The trust became independent of the federal government in 1980 and is now a nongovernment, nonprofit agency that advocates for historic preservation tax credits, adaptive use of structures, and historic Main Streets, among many other related causes. Today it owns, operates, or is affiliated by contract with twenty-eight properties, including three presidential homes, American's oldest synagogue, and a Frank Lloyd Wright house. Cliveden stands in good company. Yet even though it bears scars from a Revolutionary War battle, contains priceless antiques, and offers a compelling story of its preservation, Cliveden is challenged by the economic realities that confront many house museums.

Cliveden, Inc., operates the property on behalf of the National Trust, which contributes no operating revenue (though it sometimes provides project grants for preservation and educational initiatives). While small compared with the National Trust's other sites, Cliveden's annual operating budget today hovers between four hundred thousand and five hundred thousand dollars, making it relatively large among Philadelphia house museums. It has an endowment (something most local historic sites lack) to help finance its mission to preserve and maintain its four buildings and 5.5 acres of land and fund its educational programs.

Cliveden's signature program, started in 1977, is an annual reenactment of the Battle of Germantown on its grounds. The event builds on a tradition started by C. A. Asher, whose Germantown candy factory helped promote a celebration of the 150th anniversary of the battle in 1927, when descendants dressed in their ancestors' clothing paraded through Germantown. (Reenactments had been staged in other parts of town in 1877 and 1912.) For the bicentennial of the battle, the Asher family donated funds for an event involving hundreds of reenactors and thousands of attendees. Even though colonial-era and Civil War battle reenactments have become popular since their reemergence in the 1960s and 1970s, an urban Revolutionary War reenactment remains somewhat novel. Today the battle takes place on the first Saturday of October and features over three hundred reenactors, who take over Germantown Avenue and attack the Chew mansion in front of thousands of onlookers (reenactors even fire out from the mansion). The battle represents only a few hours in the site's 250-year history, yet for many people it was the primary focus of Cliveden's history. The rest of its story remained hidden from public view until the twenty-first century.

Much more is known about the Chews of Cliveden, and even many of the soldiers who fought in the Battle of Germantown, than is known about the people whom the Chews owned or indentured. The history of the mansion and its contents, the battle, and the people who lived and worked at Cliveden from the 1760s to the 1970s were the subjects of continuing research from the opening of the site as a house museum in 1973. Yet the interpretation of the site remained focused on the battle, the Chew family's ownership, and the architecture and furnishings, because the Chew papers were not easily researched and combing through them was a massive undertaking. The family had accumulated 240,000 documents in archives that were turned over to the Historical Society of Pennsylvania in 1982. Until that point, researchers worked from scattered papers in disorganized boxes to produce lists for tour guides, covering dates, details about the battle, and facts about the architecture, the furniture, and the Chews themselves.

In 1974 Cliveden's initial long-range plan announced its intention to scour the Chew Family Papers and learn more about the family's plantation holdings. In 1998, a program for high school students called Suing for Freedom brought some of the stories about the household to the public. But the collection was not easily searched until a 2006 grant from the National Endowment for the Humanities provided resources to survey, conserve, and index the records. This research yielded results (described later in this chapter) that would change the interpretation of the site, its owners, and its workers.

Preservation and Managing Change

Germantown's connections to American history were preserved and presented in much the same way that most of Philadelphia, and the rest of the nation, practiced public history. The same impulse inspired the Mount Vernon Ladies Association to save George Washington's home in Virginia and open it to the public in 1860. They established the template for making houses connected to prominent figures and significant events in American history into museums celebrating colonial and revolutionary forebears.[1] A largely American phenomenon, house museums became ubiquitous across the country. They came into vogue in the 1930s, and again during a patriotic boom during the 1950s, the era of the Cold War that one historian described as resulting in a "false colonial" so widespread it was as if the 1950s modeled itself on Colonial Williamsburg.[2] Another peak came in the 1970s, as people celebrated the Bicentennial. Today an estimated fifteen thousand house museums in the United States make up by far the largest category of museums of any kind, and many of them struggle for relevance.[3] Philadelphia has hundreds of them, and Germantown has had dozens, including Stenton (opened as a house museum in 1899), Vernon-Wister House (in 1907), Grumblethorpe (in 1935),

Deshler-Morris (in 1948), and, much later, Maxwell Mansion (in 1964) and the Johnson House (in 1980), though today only ten remain open to the public.[4] Germantown's historic houses were tied to the economic fortunes of the neighborhood as well as to its history.

Most houses that became museums were built to last. Grand homes of prominent people are glorified for their architectural features or for the stories of the famous people who lived there. The histories of social movements and less prominent individuals typically were not associated with a specific building or place, let alone a splendid and well-constructed house museum. How would one represent the Underground Railroad, for instance, through a house or site, when the activities connected with escaping from slavery were not always documented, and the people who engaged in them were on the move or lived in the kinds of houses that did not last for generations? If Germantown's four centuries of history were told only through house museums, much of the neighborhood's history would be left out.

When Germantown lost its manufacturing and retail jobs during the mid-twentieth century, its population changed along with the economy, throwing the fate of many institutions, including house museums, into question. Large-scale factories, such as Philco Radio and Midvale Steel, left Philadelphia in the years after World War II, the centuries-old Germantown Academy moved to the suburbs in 1952, and the mainstays of Germantown's retail and entertainment corridor were overtaken by shopping malls and television. The neighborhood's population became majority African American in the late 1950s. By the 1970s, fewer people visited Germantown's colonial house museums, and most local residents saw little of their own history in them. At the end of that decade, however, the approach of the tercentenary of Germantown's founding as the first permanent German settlement in North America provided an opportunity to highlight the neighborhood's history and perhaps reverse the downward trend.

Historic Germantown Preserved (HGP) was launched in November 1979 to establish collaborative marketing and educational programming and enable volunteers at historic sites to plan events and tours for the 1983 Tercentenary celebrations. Many different parent companies and stewardship organizations were involved, ranging from local antiquarian "friends" groups and local colleges to established preservation agencies such as the National Park Service and the National Trust. Sites and organizations joined and left the all-volunteer consortium over the years, depending on their capacity to commit to its work.

The HGP group met monthly beginning in 1980.[5] They planned house tours and holiday decorating and, with help from the growing number of professional preservationists or curators working at Cliveden, Wyck, and the Germantown Historical Society, sought to bring visitors to downtown attractions such as the Liberty Bell and Independence Hall out to Germantown. Revenue from heritage tourism (on the Colonial Williamsburg model) had long been a goal, but it proved elusive, thanks in part to Germantown's many competing organizations and lack of collaborative programming. The Germantown Historical Society's high point of membership and attendance was in the mid-1970s, when it counted 650 members and a few thousand visitors a year. Cliveden's numbers remained steady for decades, with four thousand visitors a year (not counting uses of the site for big events such as the battle reenactment). If visitation was a key metric, it was clear that, beyond attracting tourists, Germantown sites needed to enlarge their base of support.

A decade later it was even clearer that the sites had to change if they were going to survive. The limits and increasing irrelevance of traditional colonial interpretation prompted some house museums to close. After intermittent attempts to make the Loudoun mansion a house museum, it was shuttered when a fire damaged much of the building in 1993; it has not reopened. Upsala, a large federal-era house (1798), was turned into a house museum after a fire nearly destroyed it in 1942. It was open infrequently, despite its prominent place right across Germantown Avenue from Cliveden, at the point where Germantown meets the Mount Airy neighborhood. Faced with high maintenance costs, an aging and insular board of directors, a small donor base, and annual attendance that had dwindled to single digits in 2001, the Upsala Foundation merged with Cliveden in 2005 (see Chapter 5 for its more recent fate). Loudoun and Upsala showed some people, at least, that unless Germantown's historic sites made changes, they might have to merge or close entirely. Facing these economic realities, Germantown's first house museum, Stenton, had already embarked on an ambitious collaborative education program to serve neighborhood children. The work of Stenton and Cliveden staff to build on that project's initial success is described later in this chapter.

Cliveden board of directors and staff realized that the site could not rely on tourism and that its traditional interpretation could not be sustained. Meanwhile, the National Trust had stimulated two initiatives with important implications for Germantown. The first was a national debate on whether there were too many house museums. Discussions in museum

journals and preservation trade papers went on for years and still reso-
nate.[6] The second initiative, set out in 1998, directed National Trust sites
to tell stories of plantation slavery wherever applicable (the trust operated
several former plantations). Cliveden set out to address both issues and
face the question of whether public history as practiced in Germantown
could thrive in the long term by reaching out to neighbors, forging partnerships, and doing good history.

Germantown's narrative began to change with the opening of the
Johnson House in 1980 (see Chapter 4). Beginning in the late 1990s,
there were overlaps in management and staffing between Cliveden and
the Johnson House and correspondences with respect to history and interpretation. The stories of slavery and resistance that made the Johnson
House an important symbol of the struggle for emancipation also showed
up in patterns of regional activity in the Chew Family Papers, then being
catalogued at the Historical Society of Pennsylvania. New stories emerged
and began to change the interpretation of Cliveden's history.

Historic sites use different plans to prioritize their various roles: gathering resources, preserving and maintaining the historic features of a
property, and so on. An interpretive plan covers all the elements that create an optimal visitor experience at a historic site, exhibition, or museum.
Until the twenty-first century, as noted, Cliveden's interpretation celebrated its connections to the battle and the Chew family's preservation of the
home, its architecture, and its significant colonial American furnishings.
Though it was not a secret that the Chews owned many plantations, it was
not part of what visitors to the museum learned. As Gary Nash noted in
2002: "Visitors to Cliveden . . . will learn a lot about its builder, Benjamin
Chew, attorney general and provincial councilor of Pennsylvania. But they
will learn little about the dozens of slaves employed by Chew at Cliveden
and on his Kent County, Delaware plantation."[7] Not only did visitors on
the tour learn nothing about the less savory elements of the family's history; they also were shooed quickly past the modern features of the house,
such as the bright green 1959 kitchen. Cliveden, once a house, became a
house museum that was a shrine to one brief period in American history.
To avoid becoming a failed house museum like Upsala, Cliveden chose to
make its history and its ongoing research into the Chew family plantation
records significant to a broader public.

In one of the many ironies of Germantown's public history, efforts to
connect with the public became more successful when historic sites began
to embrace many of the problems and inequities that have bedeviled Ger-

mantown since the early twentieth century. Rather than avoiding recent history, keeping historic narratives isolated, and burnishing a triumphant, celebratory narrative of the colonial period, Germantown's public historians reversed course and leaned into difficult topics and problem areas. Like the public officials who called me into the office in 2010, however, people had to be persuaded that practicing good history, including embracing historical narratives that did not always reflect well on the neighborhood, could be useful to Germantown's residents.

History Hunters

The unlikely leader of the effort to practice a more effective public history in Germantown was Stenton, built in 1730 and home to James Logan (1674–1751), a colonial statesman and the fourteenth mayor of Philadelphia, who as secretary to William Penn was responsible for running the colony of Pennsylvania in the early 1700s. Now owned by the city of Philadelphia, Stenton has been administered by the National Society of Colonial Dames of America in Pennsylvania since the late nineteenth century. The brick farmhouse and grounds became Germantown's first house museum 1899, under the leadership of, among others, Cliveden's Mary S. B. Chew. The Dames helped shore up the collections and the presentation of the house as an outstanding example of colonial architecture. They ran the house museum on a traditional model, with descendant volunteers and some part-time professional curatorial support, for many decades.

Stenton hired a professionally trained executive director in 1999, and the new leadership began to address issues such as declining attendance and detachment from the surrounding neighborhood. In asserting the relevance of its history, they had to reckon with the challenges posed by its location—behind a tall fence, near a dilapidated gun factory not far from Germantown Avenue. Working with its volunteer board of Colonial Dames, the staff launched a program of outreach to its neighbors. The annual Easter egg hunt attracts several hundred people on the Saturday before Easter. Building networks of affinity groups consisting of people who share an interest (in Easter egg hunts, music, or yoga, for instance) brings visibility to a site and encourages people to visit who might not otherwise come to a history program or guided tour. Affinity group initiatives combat the "malaise" of historic house museums by developing audiences who enjoy the historic properties for reasons other than history alone.[8] By opening sites to bird watchers and accommodating jazz concerts, morn-

Figure 1.2 Elementary school students encountering Stenton, 2015. The History Hunters Youth Reporter Program is an essential component of Historic Germantown's public history programming. (Courtesy of The National Society of the Colonial Dames in the Commonwealth of Pennsylvania at STENTON.)

ing yoga, after-school programs, and weddings, historic sites can attract a booming population of retirees. This "Golden Age" theory has influenced the tenor of the national conversation about house museums. The idea is that as the Baby Boom generation leaves the workforce, retirees and others will use historic sites for reasons other than their historical content or interpretation, bringing greater financial support.[9] Taking this approach, historic site leaders think beyond the cultural tourism model, define "interpretation" broadly enough to embrace "facilitation" along with the intellectual and social content of the experience, and include spiritual content embedded in historic places. Nationwide, organizations such Harriet Beecher Stowe Center in Hartford, Connecticut, and Jane Adams Hull House in Chicago present their historic house museums in ways for people to consider a call to action to address contemporary issues with their surrounding communities.

With new visitors and openness, however, comes the challenge of defining and illuminating historic features and the larger meaning of a place, preparing to respond appropriately when, for instance, people doing yoga at Awbury Arboretum or shopping at a farmers' market at Wyck ask, "What is this place?" Security concerns go hand in hand with inviting in the general public, often for the first time, and engaging them in the history and meaning of a place. To find solutions, build sustainable audiences, and demonstrate the relevance of the 1730 site to twenty-first-century Germantown, as well as attracting resources to preserve and maintain the colonial house and 2.5 acres, Stenton's leadership looked outside their own building and beyond their gates. Located technically in North Philadelphia in the Logan neighborhood immediately south of Germantown that is bounded by lands once owned by the family of James Logan, Stenton unlocked its chain link fence more frequently and opened more of the grounds to neighbors. Its staff also began attending community development corporation meetings in the Logan and East Germantown neighborhoods.

Community development corporations (CDCs) had their roots in the Special Impact Program, an amendment to the Economic Opportunity Act of 1964, which allowed federal funding for community development projects in poor urban areas. Historic sites did not typically participate in the activities of CDCs, but active involvement by house museums in efforts to bring economic improvement to the neighborhood was a critical step in the transformation of HGP's connections with the community. Participating in those meetings taught Stenton staff what the neighborhood needed and how historic sites might help meet those needs.

Stephen G. Hague, in addition to his duties as executive director of Stenton under the Dames, served a volunteer role as president of the HGP consortium. Hague's work with this loose consortium of sites, with their varied levels of professional staff, financial resources, and interests beyond their own gates, was strategically vital for Stenton and, in the long run, Germantown. Hague persuaded several Germantown sites to cooperate in developing history programs for teachers and students in the Philadelphia public schools. In the 1990s the School District of Philadelphia eliminated funding for schoolchildren to visit museums and historic sites. Hague pitched the collaborative project as a way to meet an agreed-on need: hands-on history education at actual historic sites. The concept was simple and sorely needed, but the cuts in the field-trip budget meant that tens of thousands of dollars would have to be raised to bring the students to the sites and train teachers and tour guides.

Hague built an advisory team of historians, teachers, and members of local neighborhood associations to develop goals for the project. He also

reached out to five Germantown historic sites to gauge interest in participation at an early stage: Stenton, Cliveden, Johnson House, Wyck, and the
Germantown Historical Society. A recently established initiative of the
Pew Charitable Trusts emphasizing heritage and preservation suggested
that foundation grants might support such a project. The first objective
was to secure a planning grant to build a curriculum around visiting historic sites and work with teachers to make sure it met their needs. The
project team then sought a larger grant to pilot the project for a year,
evaluate it, and refine it. There was broad agreement about the need for
such an educational project. The biggest barrier to change actually lay in
getting the sites to work together.

Giving schoolchildren a chance to experience historic sites was not
enough. For Stenton's initiative to succeed, each of the five organizations
had to be persuaded to work together on a deeper level than ever before.
Each site's board of directors had to approve the programming proposed
by the History Hunters leaders. First, they would have to agree philo-
sophically on what kind of program it should be. Wyck, a site whose leadership maintains connections with descendants of the original Quaker
family that lived there and identify with values of the Society of Friends,
did not want the program to be about the Battle of Germantown because
Quakers oppose armed conflict. Then some practical problems had to
be solved. For instance, the sites were not open on the same days of the
week. The Johnson House, staffed by volunteers, could commit only to
certain hours for school tours. Not all the sites had personnel trained to
run programs with fourth and fifth graders. Time and funds would be
necessary to cover training, and then there were the costs of the tours
and transportation for the students. Some of the historic sites wondered
whether the program's goals were worth the hassle. But meager attendance at some sites and intense pressure from funders for better results
to justify operating grants forced the leadership to recognize the need to
make changes and improve their educational offerings by joining up with
Stenton's idea.

The next hurdle was deciding what history content would be presented to the elementary school children. Jacqueline Wiggins, a professional
teacher with experience at historic sites, was hired to develop a curriculum, which became known as the History Hunters Youth Reporter Program. It included previsit materials for each teacher as well as a student
handbook to go along with the hands-on lessons at the sites. Wiggins, who

had worked at Cliveden as a paid tour guide and at the Johnson House as a part-time house manager, had developed a curriculum to unite the resources of the Germantown Historical Society with topics that the teachers wanted to cover. Wiggins's perspective pushed the subject matter in the direction of political history, specifically the history of marginalized groups, relating stories about the expropriation of land from Native Americans and revealing that Quakers had owned slaves.

The team members from Stenton were not comfortable with Wiggins's portrayal of the role of Stenton's founder, James Logan, in the management and extension of the Penn family's land holdings. They did not want students coming to Stenton to learn that Logan stole land from the Lenni Lenape Indian tribes of the Delaware Valley using the "Walking Purchase"—a historic arrangement that meant the beginning of the end for the region's native way of life. The agreement between the Penn family and Native American leaders, as brokered by James Logan, the family's adviser, called for white settlers to claim only the land they could cover in a day and a half's walk from an agreed-on starting point in September 1737. The proprietor and his agents hired three trained runners for the "walk," and they covered more than sixty-five miles in eighteen hours, violating the spirit of the original agreement. Rather than emphasizing the exploitation of Native Americans, the Stenton team suggested that the curriculum emphasize the variety of people Logan worked with to manage the government of Pennsylvania and the religious toleration on which William Penn's colony was based. Wiggins pushed back, but Stenton's advisers would not come around. Wiggins resigned from the project in 2002 and later filed a racial discrimination claim against Stenton with the Equal Employment Opportunities Commission. The case was settled out of court.[10]

The next History Hunters curriculum consultant stressed the program's literacy components, such as compiling family trees, investigating family history, and creating a series of questions for students at each of the historic sites involved. Wiggins's work made it clear, however, that difficult history had to be addressed directly. The History Hunters student activities now include the story of how James Logan of Stenton helped cheat Native Americans out of their land through the Walking Purchase. The debate about how this episode would be treated in the curriculum represents an early and important attempt to show episodes of Germantown's history that do not always reflect well on its inhabitants, especially the colonial leaders celebrated in its house museums.

History Hunters went on to win state and national programming awards. Ever since, the initiative has been a highlight of Stenton's successful fundraising campaigns and of its strategic advance as an organization. The stewardship of the Colonial Dames allowed Stenton's professional public historians to develop a program that changed how Stenton and other Germantown sites operated, most notably in its showcasing difficult chapters of its history. Despite challenges and roadblocks along the way, Stenton kept the historic sites engaged as a group. Since 2004, the program, funded by grants and major gifts, has served more than fifty thousand student visitors (nearly thirty-five hundred a year to each of the participating sites in 2016 and 2017). Sites respond to teacher evaluations with modifications to the program and new methods of training the guides who interact with the students. In 2016, the La Salle University Art Museum joined the original five to continue the program. The educational collaboration worked out well for Stenton and its partner sites, but could the idea be extended to help the rest of Germantown? Hague began to consider whether HGP could amount to something greater than the sum of its parts. If a handful of sites could work together successfully, perhaps a broader collaborative effort could result in even wider impact.

Planning for Greater Collaboration

Thanks to the success of History Hunters, the HGP officers secured a planning grant to address the feasibility of collaboration among all fifteen sites. In 2007 a grant from the Heritage Philadelphia Program of the Pew Charitable Trusts allowed Stenton to work with leaders of other Germantown house museums to explore greater systemic collaboration and find ways to ensure a secure future even for sites without professional staffs. Stenton's director, Stephen Hague, worked with me to guide HGP members in work with experts in community engagement, interpretation, and marketing that could help Historic Germantown site leaders establish more formal collaborative systems in programs, governance, and public engagement. Candace Matellic, a museum consultant, led a team that included the Philadelphia historians Steven Conn and Stephanie G. Wolf, the messaging consultant Barbara Daniel Cox, and a marketing firm in regular meetings with members of HGP. The strategy was (1) consider new organizational models for shared governance, including a new board of directors for the consortium; (2) develop a shared brand and marketing strategy to make it easier for people to think of Germantown as an entity, rather than a collection of individual sites; (3) craft a shared interpretive framework for the neighborhood's entire history, not just the colonial and revolutionary eras; and (4) commission a community impact study to understand what Germantown residents think about its history and historic sites.

The collaborative planning project of 2007–2008 challenged the sites as no other project had before.[11] A primary issue was what might be charitably called "coop-etition," the intense rivalry among the nonprofit historic sites for scarce resources, donors, and grant funding in a neighborhood that had never recovered from the Great Depression, in a city that had too many cultural organizations and only intermittent commitment to sustainable funding. And what funding there was usually went to larger sites and museums in other parts of Philadelphia. Some HGP sites had more resources, paid staff, and the ability to raise money; Cliveden, Stenton, and Wyck, for instance, all had some kind of endowment or rainy day fund. Fledgling sites were largely underresourced and run by volunteers. Not all the sites wanted to be a part of the effort, and even among those that committed time or resources, there was skepticism about what it would deliver to their specific organization.

Seeking to build trust, the leaders of the consortium went from site to site, speaking with individual boards of directors about the advantages of working together. Hague emphasized the potential benefits of deeper collaboration. When I served as his successor, beginning in 2008, I emphasized the realities. No site wanted to risk closing, Upsala's fate. Changes had to be made if the sites were to survive. Moreover, Germantown history depends on all the sites. If even one is struggling, the entire neighborhood's public history suffers. Together, as a group, the sites could make a case for greater attention and maybe even greater access to financial resources. The argument seemed to carry the day among people working at historic sites—but not everyone in the neighborhood even knew about those sites.

The leadership of the historic sites assumed that attendance was dwindling because people were not interested in history. The focus groups that were part of the grant project expressed a different view, stating clearly that the sites were off-putting and uninviting, and that colonial history, though interesting, was not compelling enough to make them want to visit again. The HGP community impact report also included surveys of residents, small-group interviews at historic sites, and meetings with public officials and community leaders. The input offered by the neighbors was illuminating. Comments included: "I never knew this place was open." "The fences and gates are really off-putting." "There's none of my history at your site." I realized that we public historians in Germantown had far too narrow an understanding of our work.

Cliveden is the largest and most visible of the Germantown sites. On Mount Airy Day, thousands of people come to Cliveden to celebrate the neighborhood in a large community festival featuring concerts and tables for neighborhood organizations and offering an opportunity to meet politicians. Surveys given out on Mount Airy Day 2008 asked what people thought of each of Germantown's historic sites. One item asked, "Have you ever been to—" followed by a list of sites. Of the hundreds of people who filled out the survey on Mount Airy Day 2008, 144 answered that they had never heard of or been to Cliveden—even though they were actually at Cliveden when they answered the question. Regarding Awbury Arboretum, a historic site whose gardens are free and open to the public, one person wrote: "You mean I can come onto this property and no one is going to shoot me?"

After getting over the shock of the comments, I sat down with my HGP colleagues. Our monthly meetings addressed key elements of the project, including the results of the community impact survey. We discussed the survey results with heavy hearts. We were working hard to develop meaningful programs for elementary school students, scouring for resources, and doing everything we could to fulfill our missions, and yet our Germantown neighbors did not know what we did, had little sense of who we were, saw the services we provided as unnecessary, and felt that we did not welcome them and might even wish to do them harm. Clearly, even in Germantown, which had come to be defined by history, much remained to be done to make history matter or be considered positively. A century of historic preservation had made little difference to the people I lived beside.

The historic mansions' green surroundings made them appealing in a dense urban neighborhood, and we learned from the evaluations that, for some, the property was as important as the buildings and the history. Many of the sites rest on large plots of land: Cliveden stands on nearly six acres, Grumblethorpe on three, and Wyck on four. Survey respondents commented: "The grounds are so beautiful, maybe let people enjoy the landscapes more." "Can I bring my kids on to the grounds to play?" Comments like these suggested that more affinity group programs based on the Golden Age model, such as yoga, concerts, and bird watching, would encourage people to use the grounds.

The public officials who were interviewed separately also had suggestions. Members of the clergy, City Council staff members, and people who ran senior centers all stressed the need for opportunities for young people. With school districts cutting budgets for field trips and after-school programs, neighbors would look positively on education programs at historic sites that offered activities for teenagers. Public officials thought it would be beneficial for historic sites to offer programming for students to learn about history, but perhaps they could also learn the skills that museum staff use, such as landscaping, website design, archival research, care for collections, and preparation of exhibitions. But the effort would have to start by providing safe ways to access the sites and their grounds so that visitors would feel welcome rather than threatened. These suggestions made sense. Open access, however, was not a normal operating model for most of the sites. Even the ones that were professionally staffed worried about vandals or graffiti. Boards of directors wanted to make sure access was supervised and attended with proper insurance coverage. Yet these concerns could be managed, my HGP colleagues and I felt, because the input from the neighbors and stakeholders, while stark, was sensible and valid.

Germantown Speaks

After reviewing and evaluating this community input and its own planning efforts, HGP took action. Rebranding was one of its first initiatives. In keeping with focus group survey comments, "preserved" was taken out of the consortium's name. In 2012 the renamed consortium, now operating with a full-time executive director, effectively merged with the Germantown Historical Society in order to keep the latter going.[12] Upsala and Loudoun had disappeared from the consortium's list of member sites; other institutions had joined—notably the Johnson House, whose history as an Underground Railroad station galvanized Germantown and showed that the neighborhood's history could reveal new stories.

Now called "Historic Germantown," the group applied for and received a multi-initiative program grant from the Heritage Philadelphia Program of the Pew Center to design and implement a series of projects aimed at making the neighborhood's historic sites relevant and changing the perception of them as off-putting and out of touch. The new projects, under the umbrella of Germantown Works, would address the agreed-on

Figure 1.3 A session of Germantown Speaks held at Germantown High School, 2010. Students and community members discuss the legacy of David Richardson and the 1967 school walkout; pictured at left, facing front, are Richardson's mother, Elaine; Edward Robinson; and Harriet Robinson. (Courtesy of Historic Germantown; photo by Karl Seifert.)

community needs identified in the survey results and community feedback responses. Using the common interpretive framework developed in 2007–2008, the initiative explored the ways in which commerce and industry had helped build Germantown over centuries. But when the project enlisted partners outside the historic sites, the effort to remake Germantown history took on a whole new meaning.

A smaller grant within Germantown Works called for historic sites, working with neighborhood churches, to enlist high school students to gather twentieth-century history from elders. (This is the oral history project called Germantown Speaks, described at the start of this chapter.) The churches had been selected through a strategic planning effort by Partners for Sacred Places, a preservation training organization that works with congregations in older communities. The unique collaboration of Germantown Works and Germantown Speaks continues to inform the ongoing effort to apply Germantown's history in effective ways.

Germantown Speaks implemented several of the key recommendations of the 2007–2008 planning grant in ways that showed how to think beyond colonial history and provide opportunities for young people. It did so without scaring any of the partners who were fearful of change, because it emphasized history education, as HGP had done. But Germantown Speaks also opened up new possibilities for more inclusive history. Students from Germantown High School were trained in oral interviewing techniques so they could lead group conversations. The conversations were filmed in a digital format and made accessible online. Perhaps most important, the program illustrated new ways to gather and learn the history of Germantown. It was very different from the kind of history usually collected, interpreted, and displayed by historic sites focused on the colonial era. Several churches and their congregants worked with staff from Stenton, Cliveden, the Johnson House, the Germantown Historical Society, and Partners for Sacred Places to discuss more recent events, some of which involved painful memories. The program marks the point when Germantown began to become a "community of memory."

The role I played in crafting this project taught me a great deal about the ways in which historic sites can work with community members to make history relevant. Katie Day, who has studied Germantown's churches and conducted numerous oral histories, worked with me several days a week during the fall of 2009 to train the high school students in interviewing techniques. The students were selected by Elisabeth D'Allesandro, an administrator at Germantown High School. Day and I trained the students in active listening and other ways to build trust with strangers, especially the elderly. The discussions were conducted in groups, with six or eight students interviewing ten or twelve senior citizens. To prepare the students, I reviewed with them aspects of the neighborhood's history that might come up in the discussions: challenging material about the 1928 event linked to the Harlem Renaissance, the racially divisive Philadelphia Transit Strike of 1944, and the Germantown High School walkout of 1967. They did not believe me at first when I told them about the strike and the presence of armed U.S. soldiers on the same bus lines that the students rode to and from school. We also discussed economics, World War II, and the Vietnam War, as well as their impact on the neighborhood. Over several sessions, Day and I gained the students' trust. We then scheduled meetings with the elderly interviewees. Teachers, professors, members of the clergy, and members of the Germantown Speaks planning project, including the people videotaping each meeting, stayed in the background and let the students interact with their neighbors and lead the conversations.[13]

Any doubts we had about whether people would want to discuss the recent past were erased immediately. Some interviewees brought their own mementos. (Among them was a sign from one of the six movie theaters that used to line Germantown Avenue.) The discussions were consistently lively, and the interviewees were eager to learn what interested the students about Germantown's history.

Oral histories can be an important part of community-building projects. Too often, however, even well-intentioned oral history programs operating without a discernible interpretive outcome, such as an exhibition or video project, wind up generating isolated and inaccessible sources—a collection of cassette tapes in the back drawer of an archive. Several factors made Germantown Speaks effective public history. Everyone involved came prepared, the students were organized and well trained, and the participants had a clear outcome in mind. The result was a set of videos that are archived on the Historic Germantown website.[14]

Every participant brought a different perspective. And thanks to our efforts to prepare the participants (including the public officials), we all learned something new at every session. For instance, at the second session, we learned about the daily impact of northern racism. Germantown High School integrated its swim team in 1962, becoming one of the first high schools in Philadelphia to do so. The problem, as recounted by one of the older members of the First United Methodist Church, was that when the Germantown High team went to swim in meets at other schools, it had to forfeit because the other schools did not allow African Americans to swim in their pools. Other community members talked about which movie theaters required blacks to sit in the balcony, separate from whites, and which of Germantown's grand old department stores allowed African Americans to try on clothes and which did not. Such experiences—only four or five decades in the past—prompted painful recollections that were shocking to the young interviewers.

The interviews also elicited pleasant recollections. The students learned where the jazz dances happened, which festivals were held in Vernon Park, and how much people loved the Wissahickon woods—a place that few of the students had experienced. At every session there came a turning point when the elders began to ask the questions: "What do you learn about the neighborhood's history in school?" "Where do you go to the movies?"

After each Germantown Speaks session it seemed as if we rose from the table with a slightly closer sense of community because of what we had learned, together, about the past. Germantown Speaks offered the neighborhood examples for how to become a "community of memory."

Some historic sites chose not to take part in this project. The staff of Historic RittenhouseTown and members of the board of the Maxwell Mansion, for instance, questioned how twentieth-century history mattered for the interpretation of their sites. Other institutions could not commit their small staffs to working with high school students. Nonetheless, the success of Germantown Speaks and other programs like it proved important. When Cliveden, in particular, faced the challenge of exploring its own heritage of slavery, soliciting active public input on its first-ever interpretive planning project, Germantown Speaks served as a model.

The President's House

Like Benjamin Chew, George Washington had a summer home in Germantown. During the 1793 yellow fever epidemic and again the following summer, Washington, then president of the United States, lived and worked at the Deshler-Morris House, where he brought his household, comprising family members and enslaved workers. Deshler-Morris House, owned by the National Park Service since 1948, is now a house museum.

The primary home of the first two U.S. presidents was in Center City Philadelphia, at 6th and Market Streets, now Independence Mall. That building is no longer standing, but a monument established there in 2010 marks where Washington and John Adams lived during the 1790s, when Philadelphia was the capital of the United States. The original building was demolished and covered over during the creation of Independence National Historic Park in the 1950s. Resurrecting the "President's House" in the twenty-first century led to a public effort to change the traditional narrative of Philadelphia's colonial history with a monument to the people who lived there when they were enslaved by President Washington.

This campaign began in 2003 after Edward Lawler, a citizen historian who was neither a history professor nor a museum curator, had published a report about the physical evidence for slave quarters behind the building.[15] Philadelphia's history museums and historical societies had not educated people about the state's and the city's connections to slavery. Few knew, for instance, that in 1780 enslaved people made up 6 percent of Pennsylvania's population, most of them living in or near Philadelphia. The fact that the former slave quarters stood underneath a proposed new pavilion for the Liberty Bell, the nation's symbol of freedom, was too provocative to ignore.

The effort to craft a memorial at a site that had been long since de-molished took several years and brought together local historians, black activists, and the National Park Service and other institutions in heated planning sessions. During meetings in October 2004, I watched as people shouted "Uncle Tom" and "George Washington is a rapist" at senior inter-preters of the National Park Service during an important forum when the National Park Service publicly acknowledged a "slave quarters" at Wash-ington's house.[16] Lawler's findings prompted outcries from historians at the Independence National Historic Park, who challenged some of his archaeological methods; from historians outside Philadelphia's established museum community (called the Ad Hoc Historians Task Force) who want-ed rigorous public presentations of the findings; and from black activists, led by the Avenging the Ancestors Coalition, who demanded that the Na-tional Park Service go much further than merely interpreting the site and offer a full public memorial to slavery in the United States on the grounds of Independence Mall. The Presidents House Memorial was dedicated in December 2010. The structure includes interpretive signage, timelines, and videos about Washington's entire Philadelphia household and the sto-ries of Oney Judge, Hercules, and other people he enslaved there.

The years-long process was noisy and complicated, even though it stemmed from the good intention to make known previously undertold sto-ries. Because of the pressure from the National Park Service, Philadelphia museums, and other traditional institutions, the process left unanswered such questions as how to gather competing viewpoints into constructive dialogue and how to establish a system for the vetting of content. The President's House Memorial and its limitations resulted from a crucial lack of intentional communication among all the parties to get to an agreed-on set of values. Even after millions of dollars committed to the project by the City of Philadelphia and federal investment secured by Philadel-phia's representative Chaka Fattah, the resulting monument, including a ghost-structure replica of the house at 5th and Market Streets, remains, to me, a memorial to contentious perspectives rather than a clear expla-nation of the sin of American slavery embedded, from the start, in the U.S. Constitution.[17] Others, too, have criticized the result, writing, "the President's House is broken" because of its faulty videos, lack of personal programming with visitors, and construction issues that have damaged im-portant cultural and archaeological resources.[18] One reviewer wrote, "The President's House is, in the end, an incredibly confusing place."[19] And, yet, though the result has its limitations, the process was worthwhile.

Philadelphia had covered over or whitewashed its colonial history to present a pristine view of the Founding Fathers long enough. Groups such as the National Coalition of Blacks for Reparations (N'COBRA) and the Avenging the Ancestors Coalition (ATAC) challenged Philadelphia's history institutions to uncover the city's connections to slavery and transform the sanitized version of history on display at the hundreds of historic organizations in the region. Members of N'COBRA and ATAC would later help Cliveden reckon with the Chews' history of slave owning.

Bringing the Chew Family Papers to the Public

Germantown Speaks involved people from all walks of life agreeing that they share a common heritage—a neighborhood's history—and discussing its good and bad aspects together. This was not quaint, idealized colonial history, nor were most of the stories exchanged reflected in the local historical society's collections or at neighborhood historic sites.

Germantown's collaborative projects gave the staff at Cliveden the confidence to talk about the full history of their own site. In the summer of 2009, just as Germantown Speaks was beginning, Cliveden went public with a call for perspectives on how to present Cliveden's connections to slavery and the Chew family's slave-owning history. Activists and historians had spent the better part of a decade pressing the National Park Service to acknowledge the enslaved men and women who worked for George Washington in the 1790s and establish a memorial to them on Independence Mall. Cliveden staff hoped to find a different way to learn from—rather than shout at—one another. Germantown Speaks provided a vocabulary and a way to discuss a painful past in order to achieve larger goals. As with Germantown Speaks, however, considerable trust had to be built in order to make Cliveden's history useful.

The Chew family owned Cliveden from 1767 until 1972 (except for a nearly two-decade period following the 1777 Battle of Germantown when it was damaged so severely from the battle that the subsequent owner, Blair McClenachan, gave up trying to fix the house and sold it back to Benjamin Chew). Family papers and records dating from the colonial period well into the twentieth century were amassed at Cliveden until the Chews donated them to the Historical Society of Pennsylvania, making it the largest single-family collection in the society's holdings.

Benjamin Chew and his son, both attorneys, seem to have thrown nothing away. The collection, which includes maps, receipt books, per-

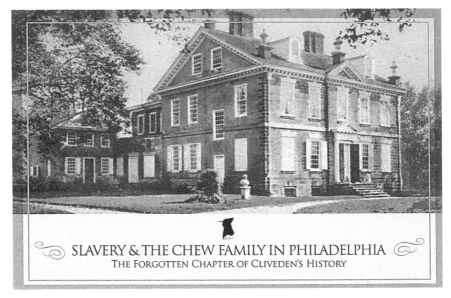

SLAVERY & THE CHEW FAMILY IN PHILADELPHIA
THE FORGOTTEN CHAPTER OF CLIVEDEN'S HISTORY

Figure 1.4 Postcard sent to community stakeholders, public officials, and institutional leaders, 2010. The card solicited input and direction for Cliveden's interpretive transformation. (Courtesy of Cliveden, a Historic Site of the National Trust for Historic Preservation.)

sonal accounts, and treaties signed by the elder Chew, as well as ephemera and more frivolous records, is an invaluable resource for scholars and historians. There are grease stains on some of the documents because a friend of one of the Chew daughters attended Queen Victoria's wedding in 1840 and sent back a record of the event, along with cake. Long letters describe séances in the house in the 1920s; the Chews believed the house to be haunted by the many people who had died there. Besides their own records, the Chews collected other important documents. Among them are a signed commission for the Mason-Dixon Line in 1767 and the oldest map of Pennsylvania, drawn in 1687 by William Penn's surveyor, Thomas Holme, who laid out Philadelphia as a "Greene Countrie Towne" with grid system of streets. It took several decades to assess the interpretive impact of this vast collection. A national grant awarded to the Historical Society of Pennsylvania in 2006 to clean, conserve, and index the massive collection, which now takes up seven hundred linear feet, facilitated research.

Cliveden's first director, Raymond V. Shepard, previously a curator of American furnishings, had earlier worked to uncover the record of its construction and contents. This research thoroughly rooted the interpretation of the site during the 1970s and 1980s in the colonial period, emphasizing the Battle of Germantown, the family, and the decorative arts. The research also noted the role of the Chew family, especially the Chew women, in early preservation efforts in Philadelphia during the late nineteenth century. Mary S. B. Chew (1839–1927), for instance, had helped preserve both Stenton and Independence Hall. Subsequent research efforts by later directors focused on the history of the family and the people who worked for them. By 1994, curatorial and education staff were aware of the Chews' plantation holdings, but details were scarce. It was known and made clear to visitors that the founder of the African Methodist Episcopal Church in Philadelphia, Richard Allen, was born into slavery on a Chew property. His mother, Sarah, was also owned by Benjamin Chew. Richard Allen, who would become an abolitionist leader and a bishop, purchased his freedom from either Chew or a subsequent owner.

A strategic planning document from 1994 reveals the staff's intention to gather more information about the Chews' ownership of slaves through further research in the papers.[20] A 1998 school program, "Suing for Freedom," introduced high school students to the story of Charity Castle, a woman enslaved by the senior Chew's daughter, Harriet Chew Carroll. Charity Castle sued for her right to stay in Philadelphia under the 1780 law stating that slaves brought into Pennsylvania would become free after six months. Only after 2006 would the newly searchable documents at the Historical Society of Pennsylvania make it possible to understand the breadth of Charity Castle's case and the involvement of prominent abolitionist lawyers advocating on her behalf. We know that she lost her appeal and was ordered back to Maryland but never went. Cliveden's papers cover only the trial, not the aftermath. Her ultimate fate is still unclear.[21]

In 2003 Kristin Leahy, a graduate student working with the National Trust for Historic Preservation, conducted the first dedicated investigation of the documents to learn more about the role of enslaved, indentured, and immigrant workers on the Cliveden property. That research turned into a small, temporary display in the Carriage House, "Invisible Hands: The Chews and the People Who Worked for Them," which greeted visitors to Cliveden with the stories of Charity Castle, Richard Allen, and indentured and immigrant workers known to have worked in service to the Chews or at Cliveden. The display remained until 2008. The continued indexing and cataloguing of the Chew papers by the Historical Society of Pennsylvania uncovered more information, promoted by the society on a blog page devoted to the processing and conservation of the collection.[22]

In the meantime, the merger with the failed Upsala Foundation in February 2005 had prompted a strategic reexamination by Cliveden's board of directors and produced a long-range plan designed to make the site more accessible to the surrounding neighborhood and, at least symbolically, to lower the wall and open gates that surrounded the property. Cliveden was determined to avoid Upsala's fate. Its new vision identified the surrounding community as its primary audience, with the tourist audience secondary. The 2005 long-range plan called for greater outreach into Germantown, attention to large preservation and maintenance projects such as roof replacements and environmental systems, and further research into the Chew papers, aimed at finding out the extent of the wealth derived from the Chew family's Delaware and Maryland properties. Without specifically directing the Cliveden staff to use the Chew plantation records to activate the site and engage the neighborhood, the long-range plan had set an agenda: Cliveden could be seen as a hub in a large wheel connected to the neighborhood, the city, and the region as a whole. The plan called for using these complex connections to engage people in a fuller understanding of the site's more than two-hundred-year history—good parts and bad—in ways that involved the rest of Germantown. Cliveden was no longer going be just about the battle, the house, or the Chews.

The Chew papers were found to contain provocative and revealing material. Though little was known about the 6 percent of Philadelphia's population classified as enslaved in the 1780 census, the Chew documents include stories about enslaved people escaping, purchasing their freedom, or otherwise taking matters into their own hands, even before the period when the Underground Railroad was commonly thought to have operated in the mid-Atlantic region. Other information (Charity Castle's court case, for instance) remains hard to interpret because the historical record remains incomplete.[23]

By 2009 documents had revealed the complex dynamics of the Delaware and Maryland plantations, including black overseers' complaints to Benjamin Chew Sr. of being beaten by enslaved workers on the Whitehall, Delaware, plantation.[24] Other records showed how the wealth represented at Cliveden was made off the backs of plantation laborers, and how marriages among elite families connected the Chews of the Civil War era to Confederate leaders. Such reports cry out for a fuller understanding of the intricate relationships on the plantations and in the houses where people lived, toiled, and raised families, all to make possible the lavish lifestyle of elite families like the Chews of Cliveden. The family papers

offered a way to gain greater insight into these lives, and just about everything at Cliveden could usefully be seen from broader, more diverse perspectives. But is soon became clear that the white, middle-class members
of the Cliveden staff, along with its largely white board of directors, were
not equipped to examine and interpret the papers responsibly. The President's House controversy was in the news; I wanted Cliveden to address
its connections to slavery in ways that avoided a similar uproar among
historians, the National Park Service, and the black activists supported by
the City of Philadelphia. That project had millions of dollars and plenty
of institutional support going for it. Cliveden had no such resources. (On
September 6, 2005, U.S. representative Chaka Fattah announced a federal appropriation of $3.6 million for the President's House site. This sum,
combined with the City of Philadelphia's commitment of $1.5 million,
guaranteed that the project would be completed.) And yet, after six years
all the intense discussions about the President's House had produced were
charges of race baiting, changes in management, and politically charged
condemnations of Philadelphia's continuing failure to reckon with its full
colonial history.[25]

A small grant allowed Cliveden to bring together historians, teachers,
and members of the neighborhood in July 2009 to share what we knew
about the Chew plantations and seek advice about how to interpret the
findings. A two-day conference, the "Cliveden Freedom Project," held at
Cliveden, included staff and several scholars who had studied Philadelphia slavery and were familiar with public history and the need to engage
broad publics, especially in the light of Cliveden's goal of making history useful to the surrounding community. Scholars, including Gary Nash,
Erica A. Dunbar, Emma Lapsansky-Werner, and Randall Miller, offered
helpful recommendations: Get the public talking about difficult history.
Don't prioritize the difficult history but see the elements of complexity in
daily life over the centuries. A site like Cliveden had free, enslaved, and
indentured workers on the property at the same time. What was it like to
experience the house and grounds on any given day, as a diverse workforce
maintained the property, provided food for its occupants, and managed
household operations? One panelist proposed reenacting episodes based
on material in the papers. If Cliveden reenacts the Battle of Germantown
each year, why not dramatic incidents from the Chew slave records as
well? The recommendations went to the Cliveden board.

Cliveden's board of directors were wary. They were inclined to follow
the leadership of the professional staff regarding the recommendations of

the Freedom Project panel, but they wanted to make some things clear before entering into a large interpretive planning process, especially one that involved local residents. The board members were concerned that the public process might in some way replicate the President's House situation and the acrimony and contention that surrounded it. To move ahead, the board, and the Chew descendants on it, needed to feel comfortable with the proposed strategy. Their uneasiness became more intense when N'COBRA contacted Cliveden's staff after the *Philadelphia Inquirer* published a front-page story on the Freedom Panel that included a picture of Cliveden above the fold.[26] N'COBRA members had definite ideas about what they expected from Cliveden.

Cliveden's staff invited N'COBRA members to the site in August 2009 to comment on the museum's internal planning for the interpretation of the Chew plantation records and their implications for understanding Philadelphia's involvement in plantation slavery. N'COBRA's members included Edward Robinson, a long-time educator and author of the Philadelphia School District's African American studies curriculum for elementary school students; he happened to live around the corner on Cliveden Street. N'COBRA wanted to film meetings and insisted on transparency for the process; they wanted at least one member of their group to attend every meeting Cliveden held and to be involved in drafting every grant proposal. N'COBRA members disrupted the proceedings at several of the Cliveden meetings, as they had at public meetings involving the President's House a few years earlier. The disruption seemed to me to have been orchestrated, but in a way that made it appear spontaneous. For instance, in October 2009 the Historical Society of Pennsylvania hosted a public event, "A Chew Celebration," to report to its members on the archivists' progress on the family papers. Members of N'COBRA interrupted speakers and demanded that the Chews and the Historical Society of Pennsylvania approve financial reparations for the people who were enslaved by the family. Specifically, they wanted the support of the Historical Society of Pennsylvania and the National Trust for Historic Preservation, owners of Cliveden, to support H.R. 40, a bill before the House of Representatives that called American chattel slavery a crime against humanity. These were not the voices that were typically heard at public history programs at the Historical Society of Pennsylvania and at Cliveden. New voices would be considered helpful, but the assumption of bad faith made it impossible to advance an understanding of the past and the present relevance of past injustice. Many attendees reported dismay at the lack of decorum; some Historical Society staff were reduced to tears, feeling that their program had been hijacked by N'COBRA. The Cliveden staff and board members who attended worried that other public forums could easily break down if not managed in ways that could harness the energy of interested parties and use it more productively.

The Cliveden board waited for the staff to recommend the next steps. I and other staff members approached funders and other historic sites that had a history of slave owning, as well as groups that had addressed the topic publicly. We were committed to finding a community-based approach that was open to the public and not driven by a single institution's internal agenda, and we believed that it could be done without the recriminations, hurt feelings, and public outcry that seemed to have bedeviled every phase of the President's House process. One funder put Cliveden's staff in touch with the producers of *Traces of the Trade,* a film that examines the excavation of slave ownership by the Brown family of Rhode Island. The producers warned us that an intentional process with public input would elicit painful memories from participants, with results that no one could predict. Without careful preparation and facilitation, public meetings could become unruly, as the Historical Society of Pennsylvania had learned in October 2009. The staff drafted a grant application that called for a public process, using approaches similar to those used by Historic Germantown, to gather input from public officials and other community members. This project, however, would include psychologists to help guide the meetings and allow everyone involved in the process to feel empowered to speak and be heard.

Cliveden's board members remained skeptical. It was one thing to interpret new aspects of the site's history but quite another thing to transform the entire meaning of Cliveden's legacy. "Why are we talking about slavery all of a sudden?" was a frequent refrain at board meetings. It was clear to me that though the staff was consulting with other professionals and proceeding with careful consideration of best practices, we had not prepared the volunteer board to move along at the same pace. Before approving the grant proposal, the board expressed the reasonable fear that too many viewpoints on the past would muddle Cliveden's interpretation. In the interest of allowing everyone a say, should claims that did not meet traditional academic standards get the blessing of a National Historic Landmark? The board feared that by involving N'COBRA and ATAC, we might be entering a co-authorship with partners whose ideas of historical truth were not acceptable to established historians. The board insisted on having one clear arbiter of the final drafts of the plan, and it was agreed that the Cliveden Education Committee would be that arbiter. This committee had expanded as the Cliveden staff addressed the Chew plantation records, growing from a few board members and elderly tour guides to a more diverse group comprising artists, teachers, interpretive planning consultants, business leaders from the surrounding neighborhood, and historians who had attended President's House meetings.

Just as the motion was about to be put to a vote, some board members expressed the fear that talking about the Chews and slavery might sully the family name or prompt protests against the site—or that we would discard the site's role in the Revolutionary War in order to emphasize the Chews' plantations and slavery. Were we inviting a public relations nightmare for a site that was struggling to be accessible to neighbors in a largely African American community? Since many other prominent families in Philadelphia owned slaves, including that of William Penn, why blame one family? Support for our grant proposal seemed to be about to go off the rails. Someone asked John Chew Jr., one of the Chew descendants on the Cliveden board, what he thought. A quiet person who rarely spoke at board meetings, Chew replied, "If this is the truth, Cliveden needs to be the place that tells it."[27]

John Chew had attended the Historical Society of Pennsylvania event that N'COBRA disrupted. He understood the anger people felt: "In an era when we have a black president and our country continues to suffer from the legacy of discrimination, maybe looking at this chapter of history together could be a way to help the situation." He and other members of the family asked only that the Chews be put into the larger framework of elite slave-owning families in the region—and the larger national issues that such history could help address. That was the summer when the president of the United States brought a police officer to the White House to have a beer and discuss why he had arrested an African American historian, Henry Louis Gates, in the Harvard professor's own home—a meeting that became known as the "beer summit." Clearly the United States still had a long way to go in addressing the nation's lingering history of racism. What better place to do so than one of America's great historic sites? What if Cliveden could do what President Obama did: hold its own summit to discuss race, history, and memory?

"*Clĭv-den*" or "*Cleyeve-den*"

The planning concept was approved by Cliveden's board and Cliveden received funds for a full-fledged interpretive planning project. We called it the "Cleyeve-den Project," referring to a long-running debate over the pronunciation of the estate's name. Though pronounced "Clĭv-den" (rhymes with "lived in") by the Chews and the staff (a 1772 document spelled the name with two "f's"), the site was known by Germantowners—young and old, black and white—as the "Chew Mansion on Clive-den Street" (sounded with a long "i"). Just saying the name revealed a telling disconnect between the historic site and its neighborhood, while telling visitors that they were mispronouncing it made for an off-putting introduction. This project would use the Chew plantation records and papers related to people who were enslaved by the Chews to bring in perspectives from the surrounding community. Through it, we sought to come to some kind of resolution, together, about what the gated mansion means to its surrounding community. Since we could not agree about how to say the name, maybe we could at least learn to be comfortable with more than one pronunciation.

The interpretive planning project began in the spring of 2010 and took more than two years of sustained research, community engagement, and organizational transformation to complete. It resulted in Cliveden's first-ever interpretive plan, which was approved in December 2012, a relatively long time (most plans take one year to complete). The first step in the planning process was awareness. Cliveden contacted public officials to let them know that the site staff would be addressing the Chew family's history of slave owning. Members of their legislative staffs and leaders of educational and social agencies were invited by postcard to a series of four programs titled "Slavery and the Chew Family: The Untold History of Cliveden." There, Cliveden's education and curatorial staff discussed their findings and learned from community members what they already knew about the subject and the site and what they wanted to know more about. Most people had never been to Cliveden, or had visited it only to attend a wedding, concert, or community meeting in the Carriage House. Few had been inside the mansion for a museum tour or to see the furnishings, so the public meetings included a tour. Public officials attended, including Germantown's city councilwoman, who was very interested in history. Each meeting included an opportunity for people to fill out surveys so the Cliveden staff could evaluate what they already knew and what they wanted to learn. More that 90 percent of those who completed a survey said they had no idea that there had been slavery in Philadelphia, let alone in Germantown. (To this day, at Cliveden programs and events, people express surprise on hearing about slavery in Philadelphia.) These responses suggested that we had a potential audience for education about Germantown and Philadelphia and larger patterns in American history.

Cliveden staff next launched a series of programs designed to involve more neighbors in the unveiling of the discoveries we made in the Chew Family Papers. This undertaking required that we rework the way Cliveden presented scholarship. Since the late 1980s, Cliveden had organized an annual training program for tour guides, the "Cliveden Institute," which involved arranging field trips and bringing scholars to Cliveden so the guides could to learn from the experts. Attendance had lately declined to no more than a dozen people, suggesting that the formula needed to be updated. Cliveden's staff now saw an opportunity to help the entire organization embrace its connection to African American history, and the education committee set out to create a truly public history program. Our first concern was figuring out what neighbors and stakeholders needed to know in order to interpret the Chews' slave-owning history and place our research findings in context. We also needed to know what scholars thought about the findings and whether they had suggestions about ways to contextualize them.

To address these issues, Cliveden took the staid Cliveden Institute formula and transformed the program into Cliveden Conversations, a series of facilitated discussions designed to bring together people of different backgrounds to learn from one another and share their opinions with Cliveden's staff. Teachers, neighbors, tour guides, museum professionals, and people interested in history were all welcome to speak together and with scholarly experts to give us a sense of what surprised them about the research into the Chew papers and help us determine how Cliveden should tell the stories that had been unearthed. Cliveden inverted the conventional process and did more listening than telling.

Even in the era of Obama's beer summit, it was difficult to bring together people of different races and backgrounds to discuss history, especially the history of slavery. Yet though the conversation can get heated and messy, open, facilitated discussions to gather multiple points of view about difficult events are the heart of effective public history because they create opportunities for people to learn from one another in ways they cannot learn alone or from a book. Here were descendants of slave owners and descendants of enslaved Africans coming together to discuss race, class, history, and memory in Germantown. The meeting place was packed, and the audience had a lot to say.

On February 1, 2010, a program titled "Can a White Person Tell a Black Person's History?" was taken over by personal passions. In attendance were several members of N'COBRA and some local historians who had helped ATAC organize citizen protests about the National Park Service's design for the President's House.[28] N'COBRA members expressed outrage that a slave-owning site would dare tell the stories of enslaved Africans: Black people needed to have their stories told by their own people. How could a historic site that was gated off from the neighborhood presume to tell those stories? Many anguished responses, all rooted in personal narratives, poured out. That first meeting demonstrated that without organized facilitation, meetings would continue to devolve into shouting matches with little forward progress. Cliveden did not have the resources to continue to hold such meetings, and the level of vitriol directed at the staff was taking its toll. I was told publicly that I had no right to interpret African American history. And though that was difficult to hear, I disagreed. Furthermore, I wanted people to know that an organization like Cliveden was prepared to change: to become a place where we can talk about slavery in constructive ways rather than descend into clannish sniping and identity politics.

Fortunately, several members of the interpretive planning team had experience in helping organizations address such a process. Shirley Parham and Barbara Daniel Cox, who were involved in the President's House project, recommended involving the most passionate and vocal people in our program: Try to get the protesters on the inside helping out, rather than merely obstructing the effort to embrace Cliveden's African American history. Other consultants, who had worked on the *Traces of the Trade* film, suggested that we pay more attention to language and avoid red flags such as the provocative title of the February 1 program. One key tip was to build concentric circles outward to develop an organizational readiness to address the varying viewpoints that our project was bound to attract. It was one thing to change a historical narrative by embracing new history, but quite another to get an entire organization to transform its way of telling history. Each institutional level—board of directors, staff, tour guides—moves at its own pace. Expanding Cliveden's interpretation required leadership, facilitated conversations, and a steady hand to ensure that everyone's viewpoint was heard.

The summer of 2010 saw a series of meetings, a Cliveden board retreat, and a project retreat for the entire team: staff, tour guides, consultants, board members, Chew descendants, and advisers from the National Trust. The project retreat brought together fifty-eight people at the Carriage House.[29] Thanks to skilled facilitation, people from all backgrounds had a chance to learn from one another. Clear rules about letting everyone be heard were laid out. Each person felt empowered to speak, and thus, the Cliveden custodian and the historian on the board of directors were able to express themselves on an equal footing. The project retreat ended with the participants, including members of ATAC and N'COBRA, signing a contract that stipulated values for the project going forward: "authenticity, accuracy, honesty, integrity, empowerment, and agency."[30] Essentially, we all affirmed that the Chew Family Papers had information value, social value, and cultural value, and that Cliveden's interpretation should embrace those values and tell the stories of all the members of the Chews' household and plantations in ways that respected their different experiences and perspectives. The presentation should avoid shame and blame and imposing a twenty-first-century morality on people from the past. And it should emphasize the Chew papers' stories about people: tales showing courage, personal agency, and ingenuity in finding elements of humanity within the horrific system of slavery. If Cliveden could tell the stories in a way that emphasized human beings rather than a dehumanizing system, the public would be moved and enlightened. Or, as one of the advisers, Ray Winbush, put it, "The lion will be king of the jungle, until the lamb writes the history. This project should be about telling history so that each perspective is valid."

The Cliveden Conversations resumed in the fall of 2010 with a series of four programs. Topics included updates on Cliveden's documentary research, a report on N'COBRA's work on reparations legislation, and scholarly presentations that put information from the Chew papers about, for instance, enslaved women, into a wider context, such as Philadelphia's role in the slave economy of the 1700s. Other Cliveden Conversations programs covered urban blight, mulatto poetry, African American storytelling, and Germantown's history of redlining and housing discrimination. Ray Winbush, a psychologist, led a discussion of the physiological impact of racism, showing how people could consider difficult historical subject matter through perspectives that were not merely historical. The preservationist Joseph McGill discussed his project of sleeping in extant slave

Figure 1.5 One of the first Cliveden Conversations meetings, 2010. Participants wearing name tags formed small groups to discuss new research and contribute ideas for programs. (Courtesy of Cliveden, a Historic Site of the National Trust for Historic Preservation.)

dwellings to draw attention to the preservation and interpretation of these spaces. (Cliveden's 1767 Kitchen Dependency was the first northern slave dwelling McGill slept in; see Chapter 5.)

The key to the Cliveden Conversations, as noted in the Introduction, is that people needed to feel safe, respected, and welcome to offer their viewpoints. Their insights have been helpful; they made suggestions about how to present programs and what to prioritize when making research known, and how to make the most of volunteer assistance, such as involving students to map the plantations. A Boy Scout leader said that he would bring his Eagle Scouts to help clean out the 1767 Kitchen Dependency, once slave quarters, now vacant. Boy Scout Troop 358 is the oldest African American troop in the country. Those Eagle Scouts had not known about slavery in Philadelphia, and here were its traces, at a historic site across the street from the church where the troop meets. By opening up its site in a community-friendly forum, Cliveden has forged unexpected partnerships, like the one with Troop 358, in ways that have served its mission of education and preservation well. Those Boy Scouts have completed ten

Eagle Scout projects at the site, and the troop feels a sense of ownership with respect to Cliveden. For them, the house and grounds are more than a place owned by the Chews or managed by the Cliveden staff. As for the Cliveden Conversations, this award-winning program continues, after nine years, to aid the interpretation of the site. As of spring 2019, forty-one Cliveden Conversations have been held, with over one thousand people participating.[31]

The dialogue-based method models a different experience of history—one where neither experts nor audience members profess to know all the answers and where we explore the questions together in order to get a more complete understanding than our own limited perspective would allow. In effect, the conversations model proclaims that facts are open to interpretation, making people more comfortable with the realization that there are different ways to pronounce "Cliveden." Conversations helped produce an interpretation of slavery that emphasized empathy rather than a list of details without context or humanity. Other sites that have grappled with how to interpret this subject, including Louisiana plantations and historic properties in New England, have found that some level of experience and empathy is necessary to process information about it. It is not enough to lay out what happened: A person needs to process the information with other people and with assistance from someone trained to cope with the resistance that typically accompanies a reconsideration of one's understanding about history. Julia Rose explores this process in a doctoral dissertation about Allendale plantation cabins on display at the West Baton Rouge Museum in Port Allen, Louisiana, that emphasizes history education as a common social experience, not merely a litany of facts: "Museum workers need to develop empathetic relationships with the historical characters to be able to more fully describe the lives of the free and enslaved at their historic site. One-dimensional representations, such as the historical names of enslaved individuals, might appeal to a museum worker who has previously refused to engage in changing the traditional site interpretation. . . . Key to developing an integrated and expanded site interpretation is allowing team members to first build one-dimensional representations on their way towards multidimensional representations."[32]

Rose's work offers practical hints for interpreters at historic sites, such as the "Five R's" for interpreting difficult history: People need a chance to *receive* the information; they may *resist* information that challenges their own understanding; learners will gain by seeing information *repeated* or reiterated in different ways throughout a tour; people need time to *reflect* on what they have heard and may have questions about it; and interpretation of difficult knowledge should offer chances for *reconsideration*, when people can offer feedback or their own responses.[33] More and more sites are finding ways to open up to the public about darker topics in their history. They continue to expand, even invert, their collections and interpretation to reveal how widespread the institution of slavery was—something that has been acknowledged at museums and historic sites only since the beginning of the twenty-first century.[34]

Cliveden's experience exemplifies the uncertainty of historical inquiry. We can never know everything about the past. Yet opportunity can be found within that lack of certainty, provided that people feel welcome and comfortable enough to join a journey of discovery as we uncover more information. Because of the sheer volume of the Chew papers, in 2012 Cliveden did not know enough of the history to produce a complete, comprehensive interpretation. And so, instead, Cliveden presented a series of questions: Victory or defeat? Person or property? Shrine or forum? Preservation or neglect? Posing these alternative viewpoints, on guided tours and in exhibitions, stimulated a healthy dialogue and left the visitor with some questions and some facts. Like the conversations, the tours demonstrate methods of interpreting all aspects of Cliveden's history as a shared experience.

An intentional process was needed: one with a clear sense of who would approve the final product, and one that involved and welcomed diverse viewpoints. Cliveden's interpretation has transformed the meaning of the site. No longer a shrine to the colonial past, or a memorial to the 1777 battle in the Revolutionary War, Cliveden has become a forum for openly discussing what we do know and what we do not know about the past and for continually trying to understand the struggle for freedom in the United States. Cliveden acknowledges that it does not have all the answers; it even welcomes both pronunciations of its name. Key facts remain unknown, such as the fate of Charity Castle, where Richard Allen was born, and the names of all the people who were enslaved at Cliveden but whom we can know only as numbers in a census record. Yet Cliveden expands and democratizes the public view of who matters by paying attention to all the people who lived, worked, fought, and died there, enslaved or free.

The project is bigger than any one perspective: bigger than that of Cliveden or the National Trust for Historic Preservation, bigger than that of the Historical Society of Pennsylvania, bigger than that of the Chews, the Boy Scouts, the reparationists, the funders, or Germantown itself. As a result, Cliveden's interpretation became a platform for new partnerships and new audiences, who could see their own stories in a broader, more inclusive light. The process was neither easy nor comfortable. During a project retreat, we gathered after an eight-and-a-half-hour-long meeting to hold hands and reflect on what we had learned. In that moment, which the organizers had planned as a soothing coda to the day's work, ATAC's historian, Shirley Parham, said, "I am amazed at how little white people know about African American history, but a variety of people really care about Cliveden."[35] To tell the whole story of a place like Cliveden, people have to lean in to such discomfiting truths. As Parham's remark affirms, one may not get closure or a sense of comfort from recovering details from the past.

Getting beyond "Building-ism" toward "Beingness"

New partnerships resulted from the expanded interpretation, generating two initiatives to ensure that details and perspectives that previously had been left off the record were placed directly into the public experience of the site. For the first initiative, updating Cliveden's National Historic Landmark status, we confronted the limits imposed by the rules of historic designation, recognizing that public history must move beyond "building-ism," the critics' term for the National Park Service's attention to the architectural features of historic places at the expense of people's stories. The aim of the second initiative, preparation and production of the play *Liberty to Go to See*, was to show how a building can become a place to experience a sense of history and explore difficult topics through dramatic arts.

To put its expanded interpretation on the public record, in 2012 the Cliveden staff rewrote the site's 1962 National Historic Landmark designation, extending the period of significance beyond the Battle of Germantown and blending the diverse social history of the site with the architectural history of the building. The renomination extended the original two-page document to thirty-eight pages.

Cliveden staff argued that the building showed the intersection of the wealthy owners and the people in service. To make their case, they worked with students from the University of Michigan who were taking a graduate course on the history of the National Historic Landmarks program. For their seminar, they received funding to write or update National Historic Landmark nominations, including Cliveden's, with greater attention to diversity. The students ran directly into the issue of building-ism and the narrow focus of the National Historic Landmarks program. Cliveden's updated nomination illustrates just how creative public historians have to be to make a case for national historic significance under the rules and guidelines that the National Park Service has been using since the 1960s.

Only 3 percent of existing National Historic Landmarks have been renominated, usually to extend a boundary or include new information brought forth by investigation or research. The graduate students expected to show Cliveden's importance to the surrounding neighborhood in the twentieth century, perhaps even into the twenty-first, and its role as a community hub. They wanted to make the claim that its significance went beyond its colonial history to encompass what it does today: serving thousands of people who see it as a community resource as well as a historic site. Working with the National Park Service, they tried to update Cliveden's national significance by showcasing its willingness to become a public forum, not merely reenacting the revolution but opening itself up to neighbors to discuss the history of slavery in Philadelphia. After the students submitted an early draft of the nomination, the Washington office of the National Historic Landmarks Program told the students that they had to tell the story through Cliveden's architecture. Somewhat daunted, the students worked with Cliveden's preservation director to make the case as well as they could.[36]

Cliveden's mansion, a stellar example of colonial Georgian architecture, and the Battle of Germantown were still significant in a national context. Despite Benjamin Chew's political offices and despite the 1962 National Historic Landmark nomination, however, the National Park Service staff did not consider the Chew family nationally significant. The students and the Cliveden staff felt that the best strategy was to focus on the new spaces that had been added to the tours and programs that highlight the new histories. Thus, the 1767 kitchen and the enslaved people who worked there and the staircase they and the Chew children used were features to address and not hide from view.[37] Visitors now experience these

Figure 1.6 The servants' staircase in the Cliveden mansion, 2018. The stairs leading to the second and third floors were largely closed to visitors until the site's interpretive expansion in 2011. (Courtesy of Cliveden, a Historic Site of the National Trust for Historic Preservation; photo by the author.)

spaces on tours and in programs that explore the complex life of the site over its nearly three centuries.

The nomination that extended Cliveden's National Historic Landmark significance to 1825 was presented to the National Historic Landmarks Committee of the National Park Service in May 2014. At the meeting, Joseph Ciadella, one of the Michigan graduate students, gave a brief report, and then Libbie Hawes, a Cliveden staff member, and I answered questions from the committee. The first keeper of the National Register, William Murtagh, moved to approve the nomination. After the presentation, he commented that, "as a native Philadelphian," he believes "Cliveden is pronounced only one way." After the committee unanimously approved the motion, Murtagh told me, off the record, that he knew how to pronounce the name only one way, adding, "but I understand the reasons for both."[38] Updating Cliveden's National Historic Landmark Nomination accomplished the first initiative.

The second initiative also involved several partners and showed that the building can speak quite well to the complex dynamics of its slave-owning history. Suggestions from the public at interpretive planning meetings and conversations events led to this history program that engaged the site through "beingness." *Liberty to Go to See* arose from a recommendation at the 2009 planning meeting that Cliveden stage dramatic episodes from the Chew Family Papers, much as it reenacts the Battle of Germantown on the first Saturday of October. In a remarkable collaborative partnership, begun in 2013, high school students from Philadelphia Young Playwrights worked with historians, Cliveden staff, and archivists at the Historical Society of Pennsylvania to develop a script. The title comes from a letter an enslaved man named Joseph wrote to Benjamin Chew, in which he asked, "May I have liberty to go to see my wife on another plantation?"[39] The young playwrights used the family papers to explore the different ways in which people in Cliveden's history sought liberty: asking for a divorce, running away from a plantation, or, like Charity Castle, suing for their freedom.

The playwrights workshopped drafts of the script at two Cliveden Conversations, including one in which Chew family members who knew nothing about their ancestors' history of slave owning participated in the discussions with the playwrights. Philadelphia's African American theater company, New Freedom Theater, produced a limited run of that play with professional actors. Audiences were limited to twenty people or fewer

Figure 1.7 Witnessing an altercation between a slave catcher and a runaway at Cliveden, 2014. "Liberty to Go to See" is a dramatic performance based on Chew family plantation records. (Courtesy of Cliveden, a Historic Site of the National Trust for Historic Preservation; photo by the author.)

because the performances took place in the Cliveden mansion. The first performances in 2014 were followed by extended runs in 2015 and television coverage by Philadelphia's public station, WHYY. The play has been performed each year since.

Liberty to Go to See brings dramatic arts into the interpretation of Cliveden. Many house museums have engaged new audiences with live theater, such as performing *A Christmas Carol* in a Victorian mansion, staged readings of "The Raven," or participatory murder mysteries. What makes *Liberty to Go to See* an engaging way to experience history is that the site-specific content forces people to consider what they might have done if they had had to make decisions about their liberty, as the residents of Cliveden sometimes did. Evaluations of the performances suggest that the difficult subject matter lends itself to dramatic use of the house and that the architecture becomes a sort of character. For instance, audiences move up the slaves' staircase for some scenes and eavesdrop on speakers, much as people might listen in on a conversation in another room of their own home. Using art to animate historic documents in the original setting adds a layer of tension and excitement to the historical experience; when performances are set in the actual rooms where the events took place, people participate in an intimate happening that provokes a feeling of "beingness."

Efforts to extend Germantown history beyond the eighteenth century have taken many forms in the twenty-first, offering several examples of effective public history. During the Upsala-Cliveden merger, a process that began in 2003, none of the historic site professionals used such phrases as "community engagement." Today, after the success of Germantown Speaks, the Cliveden Conversations, and other programs, many sectors of the neighborhood, in addition to the historic sites, solicit input from the broadest possible base. This approach shakes up what people consider "historic" and how historic sites in Germantown operate. While it takes a long time to build trust across institutions and to understand the personal passions that people bring to meetings, the lasting results make the investment of time and effort worth it. Building on the collaboration started with History Hunters and carried through Germantown Works and also Germantown Speaks, the past two decades of work make it clear that relationship building must continue and be iterative. Confirming Parham's observation, we had to admit that we do not know as much history as we should.

All the management challenges that went into the programs described in this chapter have yielded lasting benefits. Several programs, including *Liberty to Go to See*, have won state and national awards. Especially important was the Philadelphia Cultural Fund's recognition of Germantown's historic sites as a group for their efforts to foster economic and social progress. In 2012 the fund honored the Historic Germantown consortium with the Councilman David Cohen Award for promoting social and economic justice. The award reflects how the initiatives discussed in this chapter could lead to different business models and ways of working together, by interpreting history in a way that responds to, and respects, community needs. It honors the hard work of collaboration, the partnerships that brought forth new ideas, and the courage and willingness to engage new perspectives, and it speaks to something larger than the buildings alone: It validates the belief that reckoning with the past is a form of social justice and that making history useful can help serve the larger economic good in the neighborhood. In the twenty-first century, Germantown was able to turn the personal passions of history toward something truly public.

2

Amnesia

Negro Achievement Week, 1928

Even programs as powerful as *Liberty to Go to See* or the Cliveden Conversations can be forgotten in a place like Germantown. Negro Achievement Week is the example that makes the point. If somebody staged "the biggest event of its kind ever in Germantown" and no one remembered it, is it still part of history? The amnesia surrounding the 1928 celebration of Negro Achievement Week bears witness to the hard work needed to sustain a shared public history.

The weeklong gathering, held during Easter Week, April 15–22, 1928, took place at numerous Germantown venues. Nearly four thousand people attended its offerings: lectures, concerts, art exhibitions. It was sponsored by a branch of the Young Women's Christian Association (YWCA), but local cultural institutions, the Carnegie Library in Vernon Park, and several leaders from the business community participated, as they had done for previous Germantown pageants and history festivals. Collaboration has always been a difficult enterprise in Germantown, but what was especially noteworthy about 1928 is that Negro Achievement Week involved several racially exclusive institutions, such as Germantown Friends School, the historically black Cheyney State Teachers College, and the white, upper-middle-class Women's Club of Germantown. Apart from the YWCA, none of these organizations was known for interracial programs. In terms of interracial collaboration, the leadership of the YWCA pushed this program past anything Germantown had seen before.

The star power of the 1928 event is staggering to consider. Yet no trace of Negro Achievement Week can be found in the papers of any of Germantown's historic sites or collecting institutions. People in the neighborhood, including many of its historians, professional preservationists, and longtime volunteers at the Germantown Historical Society, had no idea that it had occurred, let alone that it was so nationally significant and culturally ambitious. When I began working with a group of teachers to plan a reenactment in 2011, I checked with two African American educators, both local historians: Edward Robinson and Shirley Parham. Neither knew about it. Fellow site directors in Germantown, including many African Americans, refused to believe that it had happened.

In January 1928 Caroline Shipley, chair of a YWCA program committee, wrote to W.E.B. Du Bois: "Our committee has been in existence several years. By reading and talking together we have been moved through a spirit of love to understand each other and our various problems together. I long that many others of both races may have the same experience. It is with this underlying motive that we are enthusiastically working together to give Germantown, although not a large place, the best Negro Achievement Week that we can arrange."[1] Two days later Du Bois, a founder of the National Association for the Advancement of Colored People (NAACP), replied, "I have great interest in your work and sympathy with the objectives."[2]

Another member of the YWCA program committee, a young mixed-race graduate student named Arthur Fauset, had invited Du Bois in October 1927. Fauset had moved to Germantown from New Jersey and graduated from Philadelphia's selective Central High School before pursuing graduate studies at the University of Pennsylvania. (He would become an authority on black history, anthropology, and folklore and the author of a 1938 biography of Sojourner Truth.) Fauset's studies brought him to the Y's Inter-Racial Committee, which was responsible for creating and planning Negro Achievement Week. His friend (later wife) Crystal Bird was also involved with the project. Bird, originally from Maryland, worked as a public school teacher in Philadelphia, then ran educational programs for African American girls at the YWCA before doing similar work for the Quaker-run American Friends Service Committee.[3] In 1938 she became the first black woman in the country to be elected as a state legislator. Despite their education and professional activities, as African Americans, Bird and Fauset were not part of the established historic community in Germantown, but in many ways they exemplified the upwardly mobile

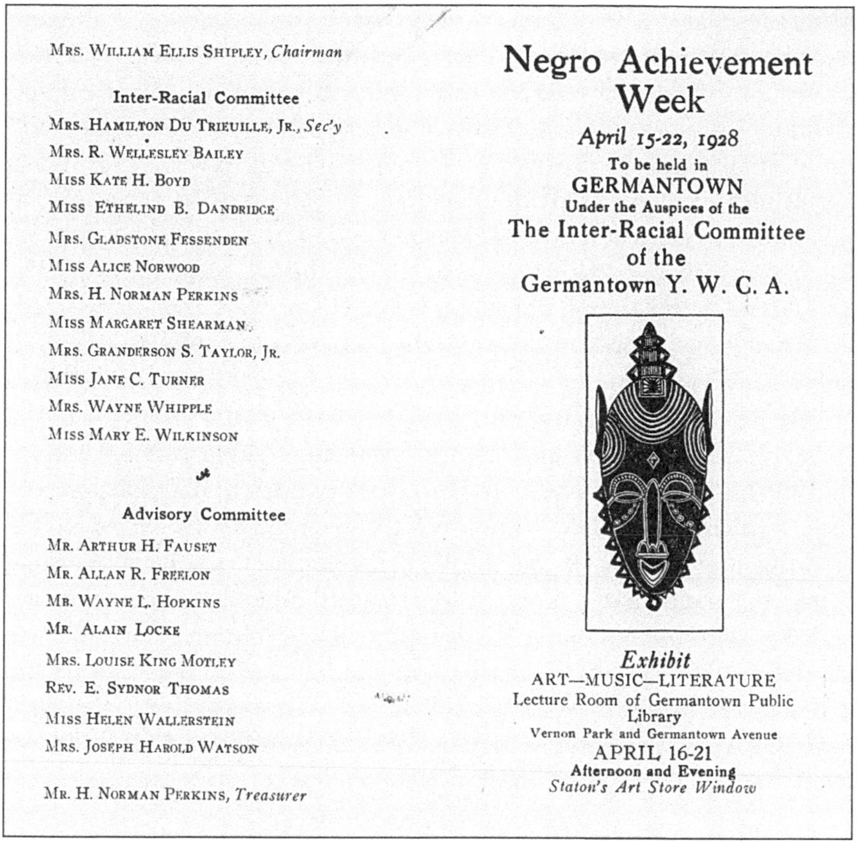

Mrs. WILLIAM ELLIS SHIPLEY, *Chairman*

Inter-Racial Committee

Mrs. HAMILTON DU TRIEUILLE, JR., *Sec'y*
Mrs. R. WELLESLEY BAILEY
Miss KATE H. BOYD
Miss ETHELIND B. DANDRIDGE
Mrs. GLADSTONE FESSENDEN
Miss ALICE NORWOOD
Mrs. H. NORMAN PERKINS
Miss MARGARET SHEARMAN
Mrs. GRANDERSON S. TAYLOR, JR.
Miss JANE C. TURNER
Mrs. WAYNE WHIPPLE
Miss MARY E. WILKINSON

Advisory Committee

Mr. ARTHUR H. FAUSET
Mr. ALLAN R. FREELON
Mr. WAYNE L. HOPKINS
Mr. ALAIN LOCKE
Mrs. LOUISE KING MOTLEY
Rev. E. SYDNOR THOMAS
Miss HELEN WALLERSTEIN
Mrs. JOSEPH HAROLD WATSON

Mr. H. NORMAN PERKINS, *Treasurer*

Negro Achievement Week

April 15-22, 1928

To be held in

GERMANTOWN

Under the Auspices of the

The Inter-Racial Committee
of the
Germantown Y. W. C. A.

Exhibit
ART—MUSIC—LITERATURE
Lecture Room of Germantown Public
Library
Vernon Park and Germantown Avenue
APRIL 16-21
Afternoon and Evening
Staton's Art Store Window

Figure 2.1 Program front cover: Negro Achievement Week, 1928. The Inter-Racial Committee of the Germantown YWCA advertised an ambitious historical and cultural event, organized in part to combat the rise of the Ku Klux Klan in the neighborhood. (Special Collections Research Center, Temple University Libraries, Philadelphia, PA; YWCA USA, designer unknown.)

African Americans who were beginning to make their homes there and in Mount Airy. Working with Shipley and others on the Inter-Racial Committee, they helped lure leading figures from the Harlem Renaissance to Germantown for a celebration of African American arts, history, and literature: the remarkable 1928 Negro Achievement Week for which Du Bois was a key speaker.

How was such an event forgotten for eighty years in a neighborhood that was steeped in history and had actively worked to preserve that history since the early 1800s? It seems inexplicable. The program was progressive: Though it followed traditional models (national and local) for a history festival celebrating an ethnic group, its organizers used program techniques that we use today, including evaluations and audience surveys. Its venues extended beyond the neighborhood to include Center City institutions, attracting both downtown and local audiences. Most important, the inspiration for its creation was modern. One goal was to recognize Germantown's growing African American population: The Great Migration from the South to northern industrial centers, including Philadelphia, was in progress. The other goal was to counter the growing presence of the Ku Klux Klan (KKK) in the neighborhood. History was being used to address and inform a present situation: the definition of an effective modern public history program.

Germantown's organizations, black and white and, in the case of the Y, interracial, used inclusion, civic engagement, and institutional and individual leadership to stage a program that was open to multiple perspectives, introduced new information and techniques, and assembled a wide assortment of partners so, in Shipley's words, they "may have the same experience"—and in the process showcase a community response to Klan activity. Negro Achievement Week 1928 reached beyond a narrow sense of "our people" to present a dazzling assembly of African American artistic and cultural talent for the broad public and craft a collaborative experience that would become the first modern public history program in Germantown, and perhaps in America.

Souvenir: Putting Black People into Germantown's History

In 1880, J. Gordon Baugh, an African American caterer, purchased a house in Germantown. When he died in 1912, his sons, Philander and J. Gordon Jr., inherited it. A year later, to commemorate the fiftieth anniversary of the Emancipation Proclamation, J. Gordon Baugh Jr. went through Germantown's streets to photograph its African Americans and the life that they had created with fifty years of freedom.[4] Baugh, who ran a printer's shop off Germantown Avenue on Duval Street, used the established template of the walking tour to celebrate his neighborhood and community. His souvenir pamphlet of photographs resembles a small booklet that the Germantown Historical Society had made in 1907.[5] Baugh showcases one ethnic group and chronicles its importance, much as the German American Samuel Pennypacker (a former governor of Pennsylvania) used the anniversary of Germantown's founding to celebrate the colonial founders.[6] And by using

Members of the cast of "Sleeping Beauty" produced during 1913 by
The Germantown Education Association which was organized in 1910 purposely
to encourage co-operation among our High and Other School Graduates.

Figure 2.2 Plate from J. Gordon Baugh Jr.'s photographic survey of Germantown, 1913.
Baugh documented the neighborhood's growing African American population and the
institutions, associations, and pillars of the community they had established in the fifty
years since emancipation. (Germantown Historical Society.)

photographs to document buildings, businesses, and other evidence of the
presence of "our people," Baugh was updating John Fanning Watson's use
of images and verbal descriptions to document life. His approach, however,
was much bolder than anything done in Germantown before.

Walking through one's neighborhood and taking photographs is ordinary today, but when Baugh walked from spot to spot in 1913, setting up
a wobbly tripod for a box camera and painstakingly framing each shot, he
must have been an unusual sight. His pamphlet, *Souvenir of Germantown,* opens with a poem, "Song of the Times," written in the style of a
Negro spiritual and presented in folk dialect: "They say bein' po's no sin
and povahty no discrace / But Lawd it's inconvenient, you feel so out of
place."[7] The photographs depict daily life, churches, neighborhood associations, and youth groups. They are captioned with phrases that reflect
pride that African Americans have come up from poverty and, over fifty
years of citizenship, have made a place in Germantown. One reads, "A
block partly owned and entirely occupied by our people." Further, Baugh

lists the jobs held by African Americans in the neighborhood and, even more boldly, the taxes they paid.

> Total assessed valuation of taxable property in the Twenty-second ward is $87,077,345.00. The branch tax office estimates that the Negro pays taxes on an assessed valuation of $120,000. It is, therefore, reasonable to assume that the market value is at least $160,000, and it probably cost him more to obtain it. . . . Eleven churches, estimated value $180,000 (5 Baptist, 3 Methodist, 1 Episcopal, 1 Catholic, 1 Presbyterian).[8]

The summary text reveals why Baugh presents those real estate figures: "The Negro population is made up largely of people from Virginia, Maryland, and Delaware and some may be here from several other states. Coming as most of them did, without money, friends, or anything to depend on except menial labor and no one to fire their ambition, their progress is good." The figures show that blacks, especially those who had come north, had proven themselves as contributing citizens in the bustling city.

Baugh rested his album on one other conceptual pillar: Germantown's connections to American history. The album contains references to the 1688 Germantown Protest against Slavery, with an image of the Quaker meetinghouse where it was signed, as well as to the 1777 Battle of Germantown and the Stenton mansion. But the sites associated with white colonial history are drawn in pencil. Only buildings associated with African Americans were photographed. Tellingly, in a work commemorating the Emancipation Proclamation, there was only one mention of slavery and none at all of Abraham Lincoln, the Great Emancipator. Instead, Baugh places black Germantowners into the historic narrative to show how they had established a sense of place. He shows their progress with pride. And he suggests a chronology that makes their emancipation in 1863 as important for the neighborhood as its founding in 1683.

Baugh's *Souvenir of Germantown* is a unique commemoration. It shows that Germantown's black population had their own identity, yet that identity was embedded in the neighborhood. There is no "black section" in Germantown, but Germantown's blacks were segregated in a more nuanced way. Though the African American residential neighborhoods were largely interwoven among the neighborhood's white residential areas, separate schools and separate community organizations were common. In particular, as mentioned earlier, four Young Christian Associations existed: two for whites and two for blacks. Baugh's survey reflects the separate pockets in which people gained their sense of identity.

Between 1920 and 1930, 7 percent of the black population in the South (approximately 554,000 people) moved north. A decrease in European immigration, due to World War I, and increases in production had created a labor shortage in Philadelphia and other northern industrial cities, pulling African Americans in even as hostile conditions in the South pushed them out.[9] After the war the labor shortage continued, because of quotas on European immigration. Between 1922 and 1924, nearly 10,000 migrants moved to Philadelphia each year.[10] From about 4,000 in 1880, the population of African Americans in the German Township grew to 20,000 in 1920 and about 33,000 by 1949.[11] Social agencies such as the YWCA and YMCA coped with these rapid changes in population, including the creation of more agencies, associations, and organizations. The 1930 census recorded a population increase of nearly 31,000 people in ten years. There were over 116,000 inhabitants of the Twenty-Second Ward, which included Germantown, Mount Airy, and Chestnut Hill.[12] A neighborhood emerged that was very different from the white suburb of a few decades before, with more Jewish, Catholic, and Italian residents, and a growing number of African Americans.[13] The demographic changes in Germantown between 1920 and 1930 reflected national trends in immigration and migration. Thus, they must be seen in a context of hopefulness by black Germantowners mixed with wariness by white residents.

Nativism, Separatism, and Commemoration

"Germantown-y"

As Germantown approached 1930, business leaders were feeling good. The business community trumpeted its New Town Hall (completed in 1925) as a center for the bustling community and its growing population. The Germantown Businessmen's Association celebrated its thirtieth anniversary in April 1928 with a rally and a banquet, including a speech by Philadelphia mayor Harry Mackey. Two years later, *The Beehive,* the newspaper of the Germantown Businessmen's Association, "published in the interests of the business, civic, patriotic, and historical societies of Germantown," would declare: "Germantown Presses Forward: No Business Depression Here."

Nativist groups in Germantown are almost as old as Watson's preservation efforts in the 1820s. The first meeting of the Native American party in Philadelphia was held in Germantown in 1837.[14] Among the neighborhood's established descendant-based groups were nativist lodges and hereditary societies such as the Junior Order of United American Mechanics and the Patriotic Order of Sons of America. Some of them delved into history: The Junior Order used the 1775 Concord Schoolhouse for meetings, and the Colonial Dames established Stenton as a house museum in 1899.

Despite changing its name from the Site and Relic Society to the Germantown Historical Society in 1925, the organization remained insular and devoted to the artifacts of the colonial period for decades. A speech given by its vice president, Cornelius Weygandt Jr., to the Art and Science Club of Germantown gives a sense of the society's take on the changing neighborhood:

> Why we should thank God for Germantown. Because it preserves so much of that better yesterday. That better yesterday was at its most secure and most comforting and enjoyable in the 80's of the last century. . . .
>
> Because it has so many historic sites and so many memorials of the various people that have made Pennsylvania. Here we have survivals of all our seven cultures: Holland-Dutch; Swedish, Finn and Lapp; British Quaker; Germans from the Rhine Valley; Scotch-Irish; New Englanders; and Virginians.[15]

African Americans, present in Germantown since the 1680s, do not make the list. Weygandt's speech to an audience of his peers, Germantown-raised, white, well-educated cultural leaders, reflects what the antiquarians were fighting to defend: their status using history. Weygandt proudly notes "historic sites and memorials," but only those of certain civilized peoples (including, oddly, New Englanders and Virginians as founders of Germantown).

If people could be left to live in their separate communities, Weygandt suggests, the right kinds of cultures will survive: "What did I mean by being 'Germantown-y'? I meant that we were individual; our own crotchety selves; non-conformists; indifferent to what other neighborhoods think of us; prone to flock by ourselves."[16] By staying within one's own group, and even burrowing further down into it, Germantown could be preserved as a special place.

Though given later, Weygandt's erudite 1940 speech was not far removed from other thinking of the 1920s and 1930s. The Germantown Klavern, with more than twelve hundred members, was the largest branch of the KKK in the city of Philadelphia in the mid-1920s and was active well into World War II.[17] "Most Germantowners did not burn crosses," Russell Kazal writes, "but the views expressed in their most extreme form by the Klan—the fear of new immigrants and African Americans as racial threats to America" created longstanding tension.[18] The KKK offered programs and community gatherings, like many of the other heritage groups.[19] The key difference was that at least some KKK events included cross burnings. Louetta Ray Hadley recalled seeing a cross burning by the KKK in her backyard in the Mount Airy section of German Township.[20]

Examples of everyday segregation could be found throughout Germantown. Movie theaters were segregated, and there had been "separate but equal" elementary schools since 1901. Even though many blacks were employed in restaurants or as caterers, few would have been able to eat in establishments on Germantown Avenue. There were different clubs for blacks and whites, and different churches even within the same denomination or faith.[21] Venerable institutions such as the Germantown Cricket Club and the Germantown Historical Society were closed to minorities.[22] And the Germantown Friends Meeting did not admit blacks until 1947. The racial preoccupations of Germantown's heritage and patriotic groups were part of larger, citywide divisions.

Economic decline and unemployment accelerated the trend and deepened Philadelphia's highly charged racial and ethnic divisions. In the late 1920s, one African American church even considered incoming black migrants a threat.[23] Amid such prejudices, however, as people of color made their way into Philadelphia and Germantown, they too used history to craft their own sense of place, as Baugh had in 1913.

Sectionalism

Compounding the divisions that racism and racial identity caused was a pervasive concern that each area of the city was pursuing its own goals in isolation, separate from other neighborhoods and separate from the city as a whole—a phenomenon labeled "sectionalism." Sectionalism and its tendency to create an overabundance of community organizations were recognized as a threat in Germantown as early as the 1920s. The secretary of the Germantown Businessmen's Association, George Bodine, a banker, cautioned: "'Tis hard to realize just how many organizations there are in Germantown."[24] Why not create a more centralized body to manage the many divergent organizations, societies, and clubs? The editors of *The Beehive* urged:

> Let Germantown learn the lessons of greater co-operation. . . . We do not mean to imply that the various sections of Germantown are in any way antagonistic to each other, but does a spirit of the closest cooperation prevail among the representatives of Germantown's districts? . . . *If the sections of Germantown have developed to such a great degree by working independently, how much greater would that development be if all the various business and civic organizations had added to the many movements necessary to the advancement of Germantown?*[25] (Emphasis in original)

Lack of coordination between intra-neighborhood organizations mirrored the divisions within the city as a whole. Municipal reformers and planners decried the absence of cooperation, while the tendency to self-segregate, as espoused by Weygandt and documented by Baugh, was becoming more and more evident.[26]

Mayor Mackey, on the thirtieth anniversary of the Germantown Businessmen's Association, preached the importance of working together, particularly because of the growing exodus of people and businesses to the suburbs. "United support of transportation plans will avoid sectionalism. Even though there are transportation improvements planned for certain sections, they are not for the sections of the city alone, but as part of a defensive program for the good of Philadelphia."[27] Bringing disparate groups together, keeping the sections of the city together, were necessary for the greater good.

Despite these exhortations, getting separatist organizations to work together was uncommon in a city as ethnically divided as Philadelphia, let alone a neighborhood that prided itself on its unique heritage, as Germantown did. One exception, and a sign that it might be possible to coordinate systemically across sectors and institutions, was the very ambitious Negro Achievement Week of April 1928.

Many organizations attempted to shore up the identity of their own people in the face of demographic change. The established, descendant-based historical community commemorated the 150th anniversary of the Battle of Germantown in October 1927. Many descendants of colonial-era families wore costumes, sometimes their own ancestors' clothing. The event included a small-scale reenactment of the Battle of Germantown at Cliveden. Hundreds lined up to tour the Cliveden mansion, which was still privately owned by the Chews and open to the public on only special anniversaries. These sesquicentennial events reinforced the attachment to the Colonial Revival of many of the descendants, and the Germantown events were more successful than the national Sesquicentennial Exposition held in Philadelphia the year before.

That citywide celebration of 1926 fizzled because of poor organization and actually lost money for investors. Germantown's 1927 reenactment of the battle, in contrast, was well attended and successful, proving that a history community based on descendants and a Colonial Revival theme could put on a big, popular, week-long event. This achievement reinforced the Germantown Historical Society's colonial focus and molded its approach to events for decades. Members of the Germantown Historical Society during this period, like other patriotic members of the elite, felt threatened by the changes going on in the city.[28] Celebratory history pageants papered over many conflicts by projecting an idealized American past,[29] while recreations of colonial settings simplified that past and showed its moral superiority over the twentieth century.[30] Thus, one of the legacies of Germantown's sesquicentennial was the installation of a replica of George Washington's ancestral home, which had been reproduced for the 1926 fair downtown, on a street in the Chestnut Hill neighborhood, adjacent to Germantown.[31] In a changing urban neighborhood, recreating the past in a controlled environment seemed like an attractive option to the antiquarian community.

When, in June 1928, the Colonial Williamsburg Foundation made public the plans it had made with the Rockefeller family to restore and reconstruct the colonial, prerevolutionary state capital of Virginia, many leaders of the Germantown Historical Society paid attention to the use of historic restoration for economic impact and tourism. The outsized influence of Colonial Williamsburg as a model would have a lingering impact on Germantown's conflicted approaches to history (see Chapters 3 and 5). The Williamsburg model invigorated Germantown's effort, propelled by what has been described as patriotic groups' attempts to capitalize on descendants' "special interest in the past."[32] Against this backdrop of separation, the boldness of the YWCA's interracial offerings that culminated in the 1928 Negro Achievement Week stands out.

"The Biggest Event of Its Kind
Ever Held in Germantown"

Out of the sectionalism described earlier, the ethnic tensions fostered by nativist groups, and the racial divisions within the neighborhood, there arose a high-minded approach to race that remains without equal in Germantown history. Of all the history festivals and civic celebrations held in Germantown in the twentieth century, the 1928 Negro Achievement Week stands out for its collaborative approach and the high level of African American talent assembled. Here was evidence of the ways in which groups could harness themselves together to create something larger than the sum of their parts. As the *Philadelphia Tribune* reported, "Never in the history of this community have Germantown residents been so stirred up as they were during the past seven days where Negro Achievement Week took place."[33]

As in other Germantown heritage festivals, the events of the week were hosted at venues throughout the neighborhood and listed in a program. But rather than an old-time town crier ringing a bell and crying, "Hear ye!" the program for Negro Achievement Week featured an African boule tribal mask on its cover.[34] Under "Opening Meeting," the brochure lists an address by Alain Leroy Locke, often credited with being the father of the Harlem Renaissance. Like several of the week's events, the opening night included a musical performance. The lecture and concert took place at the Germantown Theater in the neighborhood's main commercial district.

The following evening Harry T. Burleigh, a nationally known organ soloist, performed on the famous organ in Wanamaker's Department Store in Center City, accompanied by the Robert Curtis Ogden Association Band, which was listed as "an organization of Negro employees for educational, musical and spiritual uplift." The concert was broadcast live over WOO, Wanamaker's in-store station, and heard by an audience gathered at the Germantown Public Library. The next evening was "Art Night," with a program that featured William L. Hansberry, a professor of African history at Howard University, and the artist Laura Wheeler Waring, who had won the 1927 Harmon Foundation Award. That week Staton's Art Store featured posters and prints of works by African American artists, such as Waring and Henry Ossawa Tanner. Staton's was a picture gallery that dated from 1893, located at the corner of Coulter Street and Germantown Avenue, not far from Market Square. The Germantown Public

SUNDAY, APRIL 15th
Opening Meeting
Germantown Theatre, 4 P. M.
Dr. J. S. LADD THOMAS, *Presiding*
Speaker—DR. ALAIN LOCKE
Organist—S. VAN WHITTED
Chorus—RUSSELL JOHNSON, *Director*

MONDAY, APRIL 16th, 7:45-9 P. M.
Broadcasted Concert
Radio Station WOO
WANAMAKER STORE
Under the Auspices of the Robert Curtis Ogden
Association
The organization of Negro employees for educational,
musical and social uplift
Soloist, HARRY T. BURLEIGH
ROBERT C. OGDEN ASSO. BAND
Directed by Vernon Cuffee
ROBERT C. OGDEN ASSO. CHORUS
Directed by a noted Indian musician, Fred Cardin
Violin Soloist—LEON WISDOM
This Concert may be heard in
Germantown Public Library

TUESDAY, APRIL 17th, 8 P. M.
Art Night
In Germantown Public Library
MR. ALLAN FREELON, *Presiding*
Speakers—
LAURA WHEELER WARING,
Winner of 1927 Harmon Award
WILLIAM L. HANSBERRY,
*Professor of African History, Howard
University*

WEDNESDAY, APRIL 18th, 8 P. M.
Literature Night
In Germantown Public Library
ARTHUR H. FAUSET, *Presiding*
Speakers—
DR. ALAIN LOCKE,
Rhodes Scholar and Author
MR. LESLIE PINCKNEY HILL,
Principal Cheyney Normal School

THURSDAY, APRIL 19th, 8 P. M.
Community Meeting
Y. M. C. A.
5849 Germantown Avenue
DR. ROGER S. FORBES, *presiding*
DR. W. E. B. Du BOIS *"Contributions by the
Negro to American life"*
Cheyney Choir

FRIDAY, APRIL 20th, 8 P. M.
Germantown Friends School
Coulter Street and Germantown Avenue
ADMISSION 75c
STANLEY R. YARNALL, *Presiding*
Speaker, JAMES WELDON JOHNSON
"The Negro in Music, Art and Literature"
Violinist, CLARENCE CAMERON WHITE
THE WORK CHORUS
*Tickets at offices of Friends School
and Y. W. C. A.*

SATURDAY
*Special Exhibit Day For School
Children*
in the Germantown Public Library

Figure 2.3 Program back cover: Negro Achievement Week, 1928. The unique collaboration involved numerous local and regional institutions with nationally known intellectuals and artists at events throughout Germantown (see Figure 2.1). (Special Collections Research Center, Temple University Libraries, Philadelphia, PA; YWCA USA, designer unknown.)

Library held an exhibition on the contributions of African Americans to art, literature, and music.[35]

Wednesday night the program continued at the Germantown Library. Arthur Fauset was master of ceremonies for another presentation by Locke and a lecture on African American literature by the head of the Cheyney State Teachers College, Leslie Pinckney Hill. Thursday's event, held at the white YMCA, was titled "Community Meeting." W.E.B. Du Bois gave a lecture entitled "Contributions by the Negro to American Life," which was followed by a performance by the Cheyney choir.

Du Bois delivered a speech that he used on other occasions during spring 1928 and eventually published in the NAACP magazine *The Crisis.*

He directed his remarks mainly to people who had moved north during the Great Migration, and the address plainly called on African Americans to vote. Noting how southern states had disenfranchised black voters, he bemoaned the fact that blacks in northern states were not taking advantage of the opportunity for empowerment that voting provided. White people were willing to work with blacks, he acknowledged, but "throughout the world we have got to face the fact that it is the colored peoples in the world that are fighting for democracy today, and it is the white people that are standing for reaction and oligarchy and against those colored peoples."[36] Much as Baugh called for blacks in the North to embrace the opportunities offered by emancipation, Du Bois urged them to take full advantage of the right to vote.

Du Bois's speech addressed some of the most pressing concerns for African Americans of the day. Afterward, when Caroline Shipley reviewed the survey comments about the weeklong event, she wrote, "I have heard many comments on both sides concerning Dr. Du Bois's speech at the YMCA, favorable and otherwise. Some Negroes as well as whites felt that he was too caustic in addressing such an audience; that he reminded the whites too often of their injustice to the Negro. To me, Dr. Dubois' [*sic*] talk was a fitting close to the previous discussions of the week. The facts that he gave are some of the very facts that both groups need to know in order that they may work together intelligently." One survey respondent said that the community really was divided and suggested that programs like Negro Achievement Week might help to bridge the gap.[37]

The week concluded on Friday evening with the only event for which admission was charged (seventy-five cents): a concert performance and lecture at Germantown Friends School by Locke's colleague, the philosopher James Weldon Johnson, general manager of the NAACP and coauthor of "Lift Every Voice and Sing," known as the Negro national anthem. Presiding over the event was Stanley Yarnall, head of school at Germantown Friends—which at the time refused to admit African American students. As the *Tribune* reported, "Friday found the auditorium of the Germantown Friends School packed to capacity when James Weldon Johnson spoke on The Negro in Music, Art, and Literature. During the course of his address, Mr. Johnson took occasion to enumerate the positive and negative influences in the life of the Negro."[38] The composer and violinist Clarence Cameron White also performed.[39]

Negro Achievement Week was ambitious in depth and breadth. Judging from their reports, the host committee considered it successful in terms of both attendance and effectiveness. The final report was written by Beulah McNeill, a charter member of the Inter-Racial Committee and a member of the Colored Branch of the YWCA. Though details of attendance at each program are shrouded by the glowing coverage of the event, we know that 3,592 people registered to attend one or more individual programs.[40] The report to the event committee expressed the organizers' expectations that the program would lead to a "new heaven and new earth" for those who lived in Germantown. One survey response claimed that "it set the Negro community ahead 25 years!"[41] How did the events committee accomplish this feat in the divided Germantown of the late 1920s? The answer lies in years of interracial civic engagement on a local level and a national movement of black intellectuals.

Bringing the Harlem Renaissance to Philadelphia

The idea of celebrating African American heritage, which grew into Negro Achievement Week celebrations, came from Carter Woodson, a professor of history at Howard University.[42] Starting in 1925, Woodson brought disciplines together to call attention to and commemorate black people's role in the development of American life, industry, and culture, particularly in urban areas. The 1927 Negro Achievement Week, held in Chicago, highlighted the Harlem Renaissance and attracted interracial audiences "in an effort to promote the advancement of blacks in America."[43] The leading proponent of the Harlem Renaissance, Alain Locke, wrote: "I do not think it too much to say that through artistic achievement the Negro has found a means of getting at the very core of the prejudice against him, by challenging the Nordic superiority complex."[44]

Locke emphasized the racial, rather than the class, component of African American life and politics in the twentieth century, publicizing the emergence of the "New Negro" and a fuller picture of blacks' cultural contributions. This project would present African Americans as distinctly American but also reveal the uniquely African elements in their ethnic heritage. His message resonated in cities with substantial black populations, including those with a solid middle-class component. These residents were beginning to encounter obstacles, particularly over jobs, while also facing increased migration from southern blacks, which strained the cohesiveness of the black community.

Locke and Du Bois tried to use art and African identity as unifiers within the community as well as a means of promotion in the larger culture. A scholar of the period writes, "After the First World War, the rigid caste system in black middle- and upper-classes did little to help black migrants. With the mass movement to northern cities, black intellectuals shifted the focus of their thinking about the condition. 'Race Men' such as Carter Woodson and Du Bois hailed the historical and literary achievements of certain black thinkers, especially the writers in the Harlem Renaissance."[45] The so-called Race Men deemphasized, for the time being, the lack of rights and economic equality in order to demonstrate the value of the race within American society. They presented the achievements and contributions of African Americans to advance the idea of black people as Americans with a rich cultural heritage. This progressive approach to integration and education through art, literature and history would hold sway for just a short time: Soon, during the Great Depression, debates around race and class would split the black intelligentsia.

Both Locke and Du Bois had significant Philadelphia roots.[46] Locke (like Cornelius Weygandt Jr.) attended Central High School. Du Bois published his famous study *The Philadelphia Negro* while living in Philadelphia and working for the University of Pennsylvania as a researcher. Locke was a descendant of Ishmael Locke, an early teacher at the Philadelphia Institute for Colored Youth (the forerunner of Cheyney Normal School teachers' college).[47] Both Locke and Du Bois published often during this period about ways to provide "uplift" to African Americans. This approach to race was supported by the media and intellectual circles in the late 1920s, even in a city with many divisions, but there was a base of financial support as well.

Philanthropic organizations began to support African American artists around this time, moved by a desire, according to Mary Ann Calo, "to bring African Americans to the attention of the general public (briefly) in order to establish their creative capability and civilized impulses, thus seeking to raise the race in the estimation of the majority culture."[48] One of the more significant philanthropic organizations devoted to the cause of the "New Negro" was the Harmon Foundation, founded in 1922 by the New York City real estate tycoon William E. Harmon. In 1925 the Harmon Foundation established awards for achievement in music, religion, education, literature, the fine arts, industry and business, and science and invention. First place in each category carried a four-hundred-dollar award. There was also a five-hundred-dollar award for race relations. The foundation's first art exhibition was held in New York in 1926 at the International House.[49] In 1927 "The Negro in Art Week" was held at the

Art Institute of Chicago as part of the Woodson event. The year after that, with considerable support from the Harmon Foundation, Negro Achievement Week in Germantown featured Harmon award winners in art and music.[50]

Organizers combined Woodson's idea of celebrating African American heritage with artistic programs such as those sponsored by the Harmon Foundation to bring black contributions to cultural and civic life to the attention of mainstream, white audiences. Philadelphia newspapers in the late 1920s were filled with articles about black history, particularly in February. It was common to see articles about African art by Albert Barnes or orations about race in America by Du Bois in mainstream newspapers, along with references to the February birthdate of Frederick Douglass. Someone like Weygandt might well have attended an Achievement Week event, since he represented an audience that its planners were trying to reach. Why, though, was this effort held in Germantown and not another part of Philadelphia?

Interracial Civic Engagement

Groundwork for the 1928 event was the responsibility of the joint Inter-Racial Committee of the Germantown YWCA, a white organization, and the Y's Colored Branch as it was called at the time. The YWCA took a progressive stance on interracial activities, activities, and, according to Betty Livingston Adams, used Negro Achievement Week to respond to the local rise of the KKK.[51] Planning for the Germantown event began in earnest in 1925, but it had been discussed as early as five years before.[52]

The planning committee for Negro Achievement Week was made up predominately of women from the YWCA board, but it included three members from the Colored Branch. Two of those members—Caroline Shipley and Eva Bowles—had facilitated the creation of the separate branch. Shipley was the wife of a prominent Germantown banker and, though white, served as chair of the board of the Colored Branch for five years. In that capacity she worked closely with Bowles, an experienced teacher and social worker, who was the director of the Y's Colored Work Committee. Bowles saw the YWCA as a "pioneer in interracial experimentation."[53] Shipley and Mrs. Norman Perkins, whose husband was treasurer of the event in his capacity as vice president of the Germantown Trust, drew other members of the committee from the social service community and the boards of Germantown relief agencies.[54]

Figure 2.4 The Germantown African American YWCA's celebration of George Washington's birthday, 1928. Y members dressed up as George and Martha Washington for a tea party that offered a stark contrast to the Harlem Renaissance–themed event produced just weeks later by the Y's Inter-Racial Committee (see Figures 2.1 and 2.3). (*Philadelphia Tribune,* March 1, 1928; photographer unknown.)

African American heritage was emphasized in the Colored Branch's programming. When direction passed to its first black chair, Olivia Yancy Taylor, the branch held several black heritage events during the 1920s. Local groups using the branch for meeting space were encouraged to name their clubs after notable African American women. The Phyllis Wheatley Club and the Fannie Coppin Grade School girl reserves met at the Y, where programs involving speakers from Marcus Garvey's Universal Negro Improvement Association and a Pan-African Bazaar in 1920 were also held.[55] Many of these events had a decidedly political content, but they were coordinated for the branch's specific membership, with little publicity or outreach, unlike the 1928 event.

An image of the branch's Hospitality Committee illustrates the complexity of the issue of group identity. It shows prominent African American women dressed for a George Washington tea in February 1928, shortly before Negro Achievement Week.[56] The ten women are dressed as George and Martha Washington, wearing white wigs and colonial-era gowns and standing in front of a U.S. flag. The costumes were part of the women's patriotic identity, but they also remind us that the part of American history that was popular and promoted in Germantown was the colonial era. The women dressed as George and Martha reflect none of the independent strain of African American heritage Baugh captured in his 1913 photographs of Germantown's black community. Their costumes were an appropriation of the way members of the Germantown elite showed off their upper-class status. But they also suggest an effort by these women to claim their own primacy within the changing African American community. This response to new arrivals from the South was common after World War I.[57] The women in the photograph can be seen as expressing a desire and a willingness to participate in a shared history that was not available to them through exclusive heritage groups or a popular culture that ignored African American history. Perhaps, though, Watson would have approved of the way they took American history into their own hands.

Other organizations joined the black and white women of the Y to plan Negro Achievement Week. The exclusive, all-white Women's Club of Germantown—which used the historic Johnson House as their club headquarters—hosted a program titled "The Negro in American Literature."[58] Unacknowledged and probably unknown at the time was the role that building played in Germantown's African American history as a station on the Underground Railroad. Perhaps the club's inclusion in the Negro Achievement Week programming was born of proximity, since the Johnson House stood a block and a half from the Colored Branch of the YWCA. (The Y's location is a sign of the slow integration of middle-class African Americans into that section of town, since the Duval Street block was one of Germantown's most integrated and stable neighborhoods. The several leaders of the Colored Y who lived there no doubt walked past the Women's Club on the way to the Y.)[59] The Women's Club's hosting the literary lecture was the extent of the participation by Germantown's antiquarian historical community in Negro Achievement Week. Though the events involved a wide spectrum of collaborators, none was from the Germantown Historical Society.

Negro Achievement Week put forward national issues for local con-
sumption but did not present any programs on local history. It used the
established model of a week-long celebration and several business tie-ins
in a communitywide educational effort that was very much in keeping
with other Germantown history programs, such as the successful 1927
Sesquicentennial Week. Because of its scale and success, and the stunning
array of talent it attracted to various locations on Germantown Avenue,
however, Negro Achievement Week surpassed anything the history community had produced.

As a public history program, the 1928 Negro Achievement Week was
advanced for its time in its focus on collaboration and audience participation. It brought leading thinkers together, creating a lively forum to
address (sometimes indirectly) contemporary issues such as voting, civil
rights, and the presence of the KKK. Institutions and stakeholders lent
their support to craft, even in separationist Germantown, a shared experience that would allow them to address "various problems together."

"A Feast Long to Be Remembered"

Despite the involvement of leading institutions and nationally known intellectuals, media coverage in the local papers was relatively light. One reason
may be that the *Germantown Telegraph* was published by a board member of the Germantown Historical Society, Horace McCann. Coverage in
the downtown papers, such as the *Philadelphia Tribune* (the city's African
American newspaper) and the *Inquirer* was sparse; both merely parroted
the Y's press releases. *The Beehive*, however, saw Negro Achievement Week
as significant and featured a remarkable cover story on it. Its coverage reflects the true spirit of the week's program. Besides promoting the week's
events, the paper presented a profile of Germantown's African American
community and an account of the work of its social relief agencies.

The Beehive's cover story includes a report on the completion of an
ambitious project, a new swimming pool for the Wissahickon Boys Club,
a local youth club founded for African Americans in 1903. The opening
page cites the "New Negro," a concept central to the Harlem Renaissance
and the title of a 1925 book by Alain Locke: "Since the World War the
full significance of the New Negro Movement has dawned upon those
who think racially, and some of them are apt to think that a sudden meta-
morphoses [*sic*] has happened over night. Just as a child, after reaching a
certain age in its development, seems to stay there until suddenly evidence

of adolescence is seen, so this New Negro reached his adolescence from a group standpoint and, during recent years, has given evidence of this arrival by his expression, noticed especially along the lines of music, art, and literature."[60] The article describes many of the schools in Germantown that served the African American community. Though segregated, several were well-established institutions with a long tradition of educating black children: The Joseph Hill School, for instance, had been around since 1842.[61] This presentation of the civic and cultural work of African Americans in such glowing terms by *The Beehive,* an organ of the business community, was surely a sign of the flowering of Germantown's black community in the first three decades of the twentieth century.

Some individual responses to Negro Achievement Week from the black community were less enthusiastic. Nellie R. Bright, a member of the Colored Branch of the Y, for instance, voiced hers to the Inter-Racial Committee after the week's events. She spoke as an observer, and not a member of the committee: "It was a feast long to be remembered by all well-thinking people of both groups. I did wish, however, that the opening meeting had been held in more cheerful surroundings, that there had been standing room only, and that all of the music rendered at that time had been of the same rich beauty as that of the singing of the chorus. I stood looking into a shop window on Germantown Avenue, entranced by the mystic blues in Tanner's paintings, a voice at my elbow gasped 'look, they're colored people. I wonder who painted them.' When informed the painters were Negroes, the retort was, 'Gee I didn't know niggers could paint like that.'"[62] Bright hoped that people who took in the art would look on Negroes that they encountered with a greater sense of sympathy. Another observer expressed hope that such programs might bridge the gaps in a racially divided community. Mrs. J. S. Francis offered her view that "most of these speakers gave a good deal of attention to what is known as the Negro Renaissance, and talked at length of the growing group of young writers, particularly the poets." It was "most interesting to the white people."[63]

The impact of Negro Achievement Week in Germantown and its success in achieving its goal of uplift are difficult to measure, but the event captured imaginations in a way that makes the week remarkable in Germantown's history. The collection of top-notch artistic and musical talent, the intellectual firepower, the attempt at broad appeal with community tie-ins and wide-ranging institutional partnerships—all these mark the program as uniquely significant. Even though it was not explicitly about history, the week focused on the contributions of a group whose were not usually documented in public events.

The event reveals Germantown, despite its traditional antiquarian conservatism, as a place where progressive leadership and talent could be put to work. The people involved in planning Negro Achievement Week pushed the community forward in ways that were not characteristically welcomed. It says a lot about the African American community in Germantown, and about Germantown as a whole, that the event was held there. Chicago's 1927 event was held downtown under the auspices of citywide progressive groups and featured the symphony and the city's Art Institute. Philadelphia's Week happened not in predominantly black North Philadelphia or West Philadelphia, but in a neighborhood noted for its conservative institutions. Some of the elements that made Germantown seem so conservative—its preponderance of churches, segregated institutions, strong Quaker influence, and many nativist organizations—were the very ones that permitted the community's leadership, including its bankers and the Friends school, to work together to attract such notable speakers and performers.

In the six decades since the Civil War, the Germantown African American community had grown enough that members of the local elite and accomplished, dedicated outsiders could convince members of the neighborhood, some elite, others outsiders, that the message of uplift would land on fertile ground there. Certainly, the long legacy of social service agencies, with their innovative educational approaches, was an important part of attracting Negro Achievement Week to the neighborhood and making it a success—much more than any tie-in to the 1688 antislavery protest, the Battle of Germantown, or any other element of local history. The involvement of institutions such as the Germantown Friends School and Cheyney College, along with that of leading black activists, suggests a specific interest in Germantown as a neighborhood where nativist groups and the KKK could exist beside, though largely separate from, a large and growing African American community. The organizers' emphasis on cooperation derived from a liberal approach to race relations that was relatively successful in the 1920s but would be seen as limited by a subsequent generation of Germantown's black activists in the 1960s.

The initiative taken by the YWCA (and the YMCA) indicates the agencies' progressive, integrationist approach, born of a national vision for U.S. cities. It also indicates how a professionally led organization, acting in the interests of its community for agreed-on community needs, and encouraging leadership at all levels of the organization, can make a difference. None of these elements was in evidence within the established Germantown historical community.

Like other weeklong celebrations promoting an understanding of the past, Negro Achievement Week involved institutions across several sectors of the community: education, social services, religion, and business. And like the previous year's celebration of the 150th anniversary of the Battle of Germantown, it attempted to bring the community together in a coordinated way, with promotion and commercial tie-ins.[64] But unlike anything before or since in Germantown, the April 1928 programming reached beyond the usual narrow community focus to a larger understanding of a matter that had never been discussed at the community level—one that forced participating organizations to consider their roles in something larger than a celebration of Germantown. This matter was race, and that is why the importance of this event transcends even the ambition of the program or the merits of its execution.

In one week in 1928, Germantown achieved a level of cooperation and goodwill that might have provided a model for years to come in a community that was still highly segregated by class and ethnicity. Yet Negro Achievement Week was a success only for its time. It revealed that there was more to the present of Germantown than to the colonial past; it showed that Germantown's social service sector could put on an event that mattered. Why, then, did this event have so little staying power?[65] It is easy to attribute its disappearance from the annals of Germantown history as a condemnation of the Germantown Historical Society. If African Americans were not allowed to be members of the organization, the society was unlikely to make a place for African American art on Germantown Avenue. And if the neighborhood's many heritage organizations operated side by side with nativist groups, it would be a challenge to add events honoring the neighborhood's sizable black population to historical celebrations. Yet resistance from the old white establishment cannot be the only explanation, when even the staid Women's Club of Germantown offered its members a program about the Negro contributions to literature.

The lack of attention comes from a high-level contradiction: It was difficult to make sense of an event that was at odds with so much of what Germantown's press, history, and business communities understood about themselves. The YWCA and the YMCA worked continually to bring to a level of human understanding the changes that were taking place in Germantown, yet their ambition, in Shipley's phrase, "to understand each other and our various problems together" did not make for partnerships that were easy to maintain. The week's programming had elements of dialogue and presented novel and challenging ways to experience African American history and culture, but it was broad rather than deep. Being exposed to new and different perspectives did not, for most of attendees, translate into new findings about Germantown or new information that would let people make their own connections. In the end, the events did not have an impact that would make people talk about them decades later. A shared history anchored in Germantown's public memory could not be sustained without local institutional commitments to keep it going. Schools and colleges lacked the resources to commit to this kind of cultural and political project year after year—until much later, when Black History Month became a widely known way to draw people to African American history and culture.

Without an anchoring African American site, memorial, or institution other than the YWCA to sustain the collaborative work or commemorate the history, the event quickly faded from memory. Efforts to stage similar programs were sporadic and isolated. For instance, February 1929 saw a small "Negro History Week" event organized by a neighborhood association with members of the Black Y and the Jane Methodist Episcopal Church. By then "Negro History Week" lasted just one day.[66] African American students at Germantown High School tried to keep the spirit going: Baugh's son led the "Germantown Spur" club at the school and attempted (without success) to secure Du Bois's help to continue progressive commemoration of African American history.[67] Just two years after the 1928 event, a descendant of Germantown's Mennonite and Quaker community sought Du Bois's support for a monument to the 1688 protest, of which his ancestor was a co-author. Du Bois responded, "I think it would be a graceful thing for Negroes to erect a simple monument in honor of these men. Just now however the colored people are in such straits on account of the industrial depression that I feel nothing could be done. Perhaps it would be best to have the matter wait until 1938, which would be the 250th anniversary."[68] After the stock market crash, progressive uses of history became less prominent.

A memorial or marker for Germantown's African American history would have to wait until 1987. Until then, black life and achievement in Germantown would not be associated with a place. Without connections to local history, the dominant narrative prevails. And with no visible signs of black achievement in the built environment, the 1928 event amounted to a transitory gathering of speakers and temporary displays not meant to last. Negro Achievement Week was remarkable, and ahead of its time. It was not remembered because it ended up being too far ahead of its time, and too much about all people and not enough about "our people."

Calo notes that the Negro Achievement Week events held in New York and Chicago were not repeated either: "Attendance was high, but coverage in the mainstream press, generated by widespread publicity, tended to treat it as a sociological event, suggesting its primary significance lay in the fact that it happened at all."[69] What made all three events progressive was the involvement of African American artistic talent and scholarship. Unlike the events in Chicago and New York, however, Germantown's 1928 event was also progressive for what it said about the neighborhood's public history.

The Chicago programs took place in the Art Institute and the New York programs in International House—established institutions that were traditional venues for art exhibitions and concerts. With its sectionalism, its many associations, its parochialism, its adapted spaces, and its ad hoc coalitions, Germantown gave Negro Achievement Week 1928 a distinctly Germantown quality. The week's offerings brought forth such a collaboration of businesses, public institutions, schools, and clubs that, as in the 1777 Battle of Germantown, the whole neighborhood was involved. One study comparing the events in the three cities argues that "the significance of the Germantown event in Vernon Park was mediated by the fact that its programs were held in the public library rather than an art museum."[70] The implication is that the artistic impact was diluted because the lectures and exhibitions took place in smaller salon-style settings, such as the Women's Club. Unlike New York and Chicago, however, Germantown's 1928 event was progressive because of the way it addressed and overcame many of the problems inherent in public history: the tension between private and public, the question of who owns history, the hard work of collaboration among groups with different interests and organizational missions.

And this may explain why Negro Achievement Week 1928 was not remembered. It was "Germantown-y." The public nature of the week's events depended on the associations that were also committed to sectionalism and insularity, like an all-white private school and a women's club. No single institution stewarded the week's program or would keep its memory. It was developed by committee, the Y's Inter-Racial Committee, and its events were scattered around the neighborhood. That was the point—and that remains a central feature of public history in Germantown. It is decentralized, parochial, and locally rooted on a level that might be considered granular, even microscopic. Yet this design made the 1928 Negro Achievement Week more public, democratic, and neighborly. People who did not attend an exhibit or lecture could still catch the art in Staton's storefront window or hear the organ concert and chorus on the radio. The accidental learning that comes from public engagement is the way Germantowners experience the neighborhood's history. Some of Germantown's historic places remain hidden in plain sight for the same reason this very progressive gathering disappeared for seventy years: Germantown's problem of too many groups and too much sectionalism. But this problem also points to a solution: work that transcends individual group's self-interest to achieve something greater, as Germantown did for one week in April 1928.

Fest for the Quest

In 2010 I addressed the faculty and staff of the Germantown Friends School (established in 1845). I told them the story of the 1928 event and showed them a copy of the original program. My presentation inspired an audible gasp from the 150 attendees. They had no idea that their school had a role in a program connected to the Harlem Renaissance. None of them—including long-time Germantown residents, teachers, and neighborhood leaders who were knowledgeable local historians—had ever heard of the event. But part of their astonishment came from learning that Stanley Yarnall was involved. Yarnall, in their minds, was the man who kept the school from integrating its faculty and student body until 1947. I offered a challenge: What if we could reenact the event with students today?

Later that same year, teachers from Germantown High School met at Cliveden's Carriage House. I gave them a presentation similar to the one I had given at the Friends school and challenged them the same way. Germantown is known for its colonial reenactments—why not revive some of its twentieth-century history? Those public school teachers were excited enough to put together a team that would cross Germantown Avenue and collaborate with the Friends school.

The following April students from both schools, together with their teachers, produced Fest for the Quest. The students drew the title from a well-known poem by James Weldon Johnson, who had participated in the 1928 conference: "You are young, gifted, and Black. We must begin to tell our young, There's a world waiting for you, Yours is the quest that's just begun." The program ran three nights: a gospel night on Thursday, a dance on Friday, and a jazz concert on Saturday. Choirs and bands from the two schools performed in each other's auditoriums. The entire spring term curriculum for Germantown High School was devoted to the Harlem Renaissance. Its hallway was decorated with related art and biographical projects: One class recreated on the floor of the entry hall the mosaic that adorns the Schomburg Library in Harlem. The auditorium of the Germantown Friends School was packed on the same night when, eighty-three years earlier, people had filled the hall to hear James Weldon Johnson. This time, before listening to young people perform in a spirited jazz concert, the audience rose to sing Johnson's lyrics in "Lift Every Voice and Sing."

The challenges involved in putting together the 2011 reenactment were many. One of the most revealing: Soon after the Germantown High teachers decided to walk over to meet their counterparts at Sharpless Hall on the Friends campus a few blocks away for a scheduled meeting, my cell phone rang. One of the public school teachers asked whether I knew where Sharpless Hall was. I gave directions and asked, "Do you know where the campus entrance is?" The caller said, "No, none of the teachers has ever been here."

Similarly, on the first night of the Fest for the Quest, visitors from Germantown Friends School were seeing the public high school for the first time. They stood amazed at how beautiful the public high school auditorium was, a place where many elders from the neighborhood recalled hearing jazz for the first time, the site of many community meetings and events. Even though the schools were only six blocks apart, before April 2011 no teacher from either school had ever had an incentive to visit the other one.

The singularity of the 1928 gathering and its disappearance from the neighborhood's historical memory for eighty-three years illustrates the persistent unwillingness of Germantown institutions to share, connect, or collaborate on their own. The noninvolvement of the antiquarian historical community in the event was especially conspicuous. Events involving collaboration, connecting personal and collective issues in ways that intersect with current social and political situation, require leadership. In 1928 that leadership had to come from outside the Germantown historical community. But it did come, even if it proved impossible to sustain or recreate. The 2011 commemoration required the same thing: collaborative leadership that took people out of their comfortable sphere of regular activity to try something different.

In her thank-you letter to Du Bois, Shipley wrote, "I am wondering how in our work and in our daily lives we can create, cherish and use the power of love to arouse one another to the best advantage."[71] The 1928 and 2011 Harlem Renaissance programs in Germantown used civic engagement, partnerships, and multiple artistic and intellectual platforms to create something unique—a briefly shared but deeply affecting public history experience.

3

Authority

Which Germantown History— and Who Decides?

In 2005, working as a director at a historic site on Germantown Avenue, I helped a group of business owners establish a business improvement district there. A business improvement district, basically, places a tax on business property owners to pay for services such as promotion, sidewalk sweeping, and street beautification that will help attract customers. It is a twenty-first-century solution to many of the problems described in this chapter. At a meeting of the Central Germantown Council, a community development corporation that began operation in 1981, I had an opportunity to meet senior leaders of Germantown Settlement, another longstanding community development corporation. I introduced myself to Emanuel Freeman, Settlement's CEO. He looked me in the eye, pushed his finger into my chest, and said, "You historic mansions. You wanted to bypass us. You were going to give up on our community."

Taken aback, I wondered what would make a neighborhood elder express such hostility to a newcomer at his first meeting. The still raw emotions grew out of a series of events nearly four decades earlier that *Philadelphia Magazine* had referred to as "the Second Battle of Germantown." The 1967 "battle" (one of several contentious issues to roil Germantown that year) was the culmination of two decades of planning initiatives that sought to address economic decline, job loss, population change, and housing segregation. House museums were supposed to be a big part of the solution.

The decades after Negro Achievement Week 1928 were marked by the Great Depression, World War II, and the loss of Germantown's industrial manufacturing base. Germantown's public history must be placed in this social context before we can begin to consider why and how some civic leaders came to see the neighborhood's connections to America's past as an engine for economic revitalization. Their efforts in the 1940s and 1950s had implications for Germantown's public history for decades to come. These initiatives were efforts to remedy Germantown's economic plight by using its connections to American history to leverage some kind of economic benefit. But every drive to recreate Germantown as a tourist destination involved preserving and promoting a single version of history at all costs. Highly charged political challenges made the effort less about preserving or curating the past than about controlling which version of American history would prevail and whose Germantown would benefit.

Germantown's public history might have been used as a point of connection, a way to inform contemporary challenges and bring together different perspectives to solve them. Using history for economic and urban planning, however, worsened the divisions in the neighborhood. The nearby neighborhoods of Mount Airy and Chestnut Hill separated themselves from the economic fortunes of Germantown in the early 1950s.[1] Anchoring institutions such as Germantown Academy (founded in the 1750s) moved to the suburbs, with others poised to follow. Factories and large-scale employers such as Midvale Steel and Atwater Kent Radios had left shortly after World War II. Established retail stores such as Allen's, Rowell's, and Sears, Roebuck closed or moved away from the Germantown Avenue and Chelten Avenue commercial districts, crossing the city line to suburban shopping malls. Why would people want to visit Germantown now? And why would they want to stay? To answer these questions, Germantown's business and nonprofit leaders, in concert with city and federal agencies, tried to make colonial history their ticket to economic revival.

The most ambitious of the many plans to use Germantown's colonial past as an engine for recovery proposed to create an urban version of Colonial Williamsburg in Germantown's Market Square. This project would consume the Germantown Historical Society and members of the business community from 1946 on. Later iterations of this plan incorporated federal housing and urban renewal programs such as Model Cities. The lead architect of the Market Square phase was the Colonial Revival architect G. Edwin Brumbaugh, engaged by the Germantown Historical Society, while a later phase involving the city's redevelopment planners was led by the architect Henry Magaziner (1911–2011), whose name became attached to the plan debated in 1967. His vision called for "condemnation and restoration"—restoring Germantown by removing more recent features. History traditionalists, such as the white, socially prominent leaders of the Germantown Historical Society, backed Magaziner's plans over the protests of newly empowered groups, such as the descendants of Civil War veterans and the increasingly vocal African American political leadership, as well as historic preservationists and local artists.

In Germantown, as in big northern cities such as Chicago and New York, large-scale economic development projects provoked concern and renewed popular interest in historic preservation. In *The Death and Life of American Cities*, the New York citizen-activist Jane Jacobs describes how the urban renewal projects of the 1950s and 1960s posed grave threats to neighborhoods that involved the loss not only of historic architecture but of the networks and relationships that neighborhoods sustained, made up of the human activities, formal and informal, that occurred on city streets.[2] Demolition and development shattered social networks and healthy urban communities, denying people's need for historical connectedness. The urban planners and visionary architects who proposed the urban renewal projects, she writes, rarely took into account the enmeshed interactions of city life.[3]

In Germantown, Jacobs would likely have noticed the overabundance of certain resources, such as parks, clubs, activities, and architecture, in its diverse neighborhoods: so many quality-of-life factors with little connectedness or overall coherence. Narratives that decried change competed with narratives that celebrated change—as if it were an either/or situation—but there were few forums or networks to resolve the differences between them. In Germantown, and in Philadelphia generally, the process of urban renewal emphasized a narrative of decline rather than one of progress. There was plenty of life, yet it was lived in isolated networks in close proximity that did not interact nearly enough, in part because of segregated institutions and an exclusionary historical vision. Gentrification was not the problem; it was the lack of an open forum for making responsible decisions that could gain support from a workable majority of community members. Germantown's history was used in a way that prevented those processes rather than informing them. Germantown's very strengths—its history and its diversity—were deployed in a fragmented and sectionalized way that worked against the community's interests. The lack of overall connectedness distilled in this one neighborhood the kinds of heartbreaking losses that Jacobs saw in America's largest cities.[4] Unlike the interracial, multi-institutional effort that produced Negro Achievement Week, Germantown's postwar period saw many contested conversations taking place about history's role in the present, with few ways to channel the energies into constructive outcomes.

In this chapter we see how development plans that involved using white, colonial-era history and preservation to revitalize Germantown's economic fortunes polarized rather than unified the neighborhood's disparate groups. Jacobs presented the conflict between large-scale projects and livable neighborhoods and community building in terms of a city's death and life struggle. The development proposed for Germantown roused citizens to see their situation in the same way. The so-called Second Battle of Germantown prompted a kind of rancor never seen before in the neighborhood. Visionary projects intended to fight poverty and forestall white flight generated and inflamed grassroots organizations, adding to the overabundance of neighborhood associations while empowering the growing African American population. Black activists joined the opposition to the plans and took leadership of longstanding organizations with decision-making authority, such as Germantown Settlement. And the controversy was not soon forgotten, as Freeman showed when he berated me for what I represented: a historic house museum that reminded him of how history in Germantown overlooked his people.

The Community Audit: Germantown Portrayed

After World War II, Germantown's ethnic, racial, and religious groups faced diminishing employment opportunities and a housing sector that promoted division rather than inclusion. In 1948 Philadelphia City Council established the Fair Employment Practices Commission to enforce the city's prohibition of discrimination in employment based on race, religion, or country of origin. Mayor Joseph Clark (1901–1990), the first Democrat elected mayor in Philadelphia in more than sixty years, expanded its oversight when the reform-focused 1951 Home Rule Charter established the Philadelphia Human Relations Commission. Sadie T. Alexander (1898–1989), an African American civil rights attorney who lived in Mount Airy, served on the commission from 1952 to 1968 (she had earlier been named to President Harry Truman's Committee on Civil Rights).[5] The initiative included exploration of ethnic and religious discrimination through a Germantown community audit conducted by the Germantown

Figure 3.1 Benton Spruance, *A Visitor to Germantown,* 1935. Spruance's lithograph depicts Depression-era Germantown, with houses sliding from shabby to derelict with a skeleton in the middle. (Courtesy of Philadelphia Museum of Art; www.bentonspruance.com.)

Community Council. The council was a coalition of local civic groups, nonprofit agencies, and neighborhood associations founded in the 1930s and based in Vernon Park's Wister House; it served as one of several local coordinators for some of the federal initiatives covered in this chapter. In the end, the Human Relations Commission stimulated some successful mediation of conflicts arising from the migration of blacks into Germantown neighborhoods. For instance: "On Slocum St. in Germantown, the commission on human rights staff helped to form an integrated neighborhood committee after a new black family received a number of anonymous letters."[6] The Germantown Community Council also spearheaded a survey of "civil rights in Germantown by the citizens of Germantown," which involved thirty Germantown and Chestnut Hill organizations, churches, relief agencies, and even realtors.[7] The committee overseeing the survey answered to the council and included members of the YWCA and the YMCA, religious and welfare groups, and prominent individuals such as Benton M. Spruance, the noted Depression-era artist and lithographer, who served as chair of the council's human relations committee.

The civil rights survey was developed under the auspices of several national groups, including the American Jewish Congress and the Citizens

Council on Democratic Rights, and was modeled on a similar neighborhood survey done in New York City.[8] It required trained interviewers and was long, with sections pertaining to housing, family composition, and "additional questions on education to be asked of Negro respondents." Among these were the following: "Do you think there are any public schools which do not accept Negro students, or which only accept a limited number of Negro students each year? In schools your children attend are there any clubs to which Negro children are not admitted or limited? Has any member of your family been refused admission to any private school or college in the Germantown area?" Regarding housing, the survey asked: "Are there any sections in Germantown where it is difficult or impossible for Negroes to buy or rent homes?" There were items about residential conditions, though nothing about buildings' age or historic status. The survey also asked: "Are there any restaurants which will not serve Negroes? Are there any clubs or organizations that will not accept Negro membership?" Similar questions were reformulated for Jewish respondents to assess ethnic discrimination.

The survey results, compiled into the "Germantown Community Audit," were turned over to Germantown Community Council committees on housing, human relations, and zoning and planning. Germantown had been perceived as a genteel, white, Christian suburb, with numerous small black enclaves and too many organizations where ethnic or religious groups kept to themselves, interacting only in the retail business district.[9] The survey showed a reality that was far different and gave valuable insight into incidents like the one on Slocum Street. The neighborhood population in 1949 was more than one-tenth African American (10 percent according to the 1940 census, 13 percent in 1950).[10] That proportion rose rapidly over the next two decades.

Spruance found beauty in the aesthetics of Germantown's built environment without depicting it as "quaint." His wife, Win, was a Democratic committeeperson in Germantown and was friendly with members of Mayor Clark's staff.[11] But it was not political connections alone that made Spruance a good choice to manage the Community Audit and the work of forging greater community harmony. Trained at the Pennsylvania Academy of Fine Arts, he was chair of the art department at nearby Beaver College (now Arcadia University) until his death in 1968. He lived on Walnut Lane in Germantown with a studio located around the corner on Germantown Avenue. According to one biographer, "Spruance's choice of subject matter during the 1930s left few areas of modern life untouched.

The early conventional landscapes of his student years gave way to scenes of city life—crowded subways, apartment buildings, urban construction, busy street corners, and his Germantown neighborhood. He became absorbed with the human figure. He found subjects engaged in various everyday activities of work and play. Many works were also given over to the dynamics and perils of modern transportation. Autos in traffic jams, trains rounding curves, crossed bridges."[12] A 1935 drawing called *Visitor to Germantown* pictures three older buildings on Germantown Avenue.[13] One is derelict, with a "For sale" sign, while a skeleton sits in the doorway of the place next door. Spruance's art in the 1940s and 1950s depicted mystical and religious subjects: the eternal struggle between man and the forces attempting to demean or destroy him. "I do not think it sufficient to paint in innocent joy," he remarked in a 1955 interview with a Germantown newspaper. "Whether you're doing St. Francis or a face at the corner of Germantown and Chelten Avenues, the struggle between good and evil can be portrayed."[14] Committed to the neighborhood, he rendered images of it as it was—not focusing solely on the historic or idealized as had earlier Germantown artists, such as Joseph Pennell (1857–1926), whose dreamy renderings contrasted idealized antique streetscapes with ugly, modern city life.[15]

Another artist who used her creativity to bring attention to segregation was Marguerite de Angeli, who lived in or near Germantown for years and wrote and illustrated a children's book that dealt with the subject. De Angeli's books typically explore historical themes, such as the problems of immigrant children or Quaker history and education. *Bright April* looks at discrimination in Germantown from a child's perspective.[16] The book was considered progressive for its time in its use of language and true-to-life settings.[17] Many of its images show colorful, realistically rendered Germantown street scenes, filled with colonial architecture; the cover shows an integrated Brownie troop exploring the Wissahickon woods. Here was a creative use of features of the neighborhood to examine the effects of changing demographic patterns. If artists could portray the present-day built and social environment with delicacy and realism, Germantown need not be sealed off from contemporary life to keep it historic and beautiful.

The Community Audit approached discrimination with what Black Power activists would later call a characteristically liberal approach: deliberative, reformist, and slow. Germantown Community Council kept decision making largely in the hands of people linked to the Democratic Party and out of the hands of African Americans. Yet the audit was an attempt

BRIGHT APRIL

MARGUERITE DE ANGELI

Figure 3.2 Marguerite de Angeli, *Bright April,* 1946. This children's book by a sometime Germantown resident addressed integration in ways that the community's historical sites and organizations would not. (Marguerite de Angeli Family Trust.)

to coordinate Germantown's disparate social, civic, and religious groups and gather information about race relations. Throughout these efforts, the Germantown Historical Society stood apart, attempting to assert authority over a different set of vocal, competing interests. As Germantown coped with change, the traditional managers of its public history were going in many different directions, setting the stage for conflicts to come.

The Williamsburgification of Germantown

No project better illustrates the fragmented quality of Germantown history than the attempt to create an idealized colonial attraction in Market Square on Germantown Avenue, two miles from Cliveden. The Market

Square project began in 1946, when Leighton Stradley (1880–1956), president of the Germantown Historical Society, proposed the creation of a smaller version of Colonial Williamsburg to promote heritage tourism.[18] After two decades of real estate dealings, demolition, construction, and reconstruction, the Rockefellers' living history project at Colonial Williamsburg was by that time an established tourist attraction. The Virginia town had been dormant since it ceased to be the colonial capital, whereas Germantown was an active part of a major American city. And yet the desire to create "a miniature Williamsburg" in Market Square would motivate two generations of Germantown's historic stewards and give rise to a persistent myth about the neighborhood's missed opportunity (see Chapter 5). If a community in Virginia could build an idealized version of the past, the leaders of the Germantown Historical Society believed, they could too.

The project's conflation of history, economics, and myth would foster animosity in the neighborhood for decades. From the beginning it emphasized economic impact over historical accuracy. The square's historic features received only the narrowest consideration. The Germantown Historical Society had traditionally prioritized colonial and revolutionary stories; later periods were minimally addressed, and little scholarship was brought to bear on the historic preservation work in the neighborhood, with the notable exception of the work of the Historic American Buildings Survey a decade before. Even the society's magazine, the *Germantown Crier*, created in part to promote the Market Square restoration, tended to reprint early antiquarian writings by John Fanning Watson, Samuel Pennypacker, Jane Campbell, and Edwin Jellet rather than new research.[19]

Stradley, an attorney, led the initiative to revive Germantown's commercial zone around the square.[20] The National Park Service had recently acquired the Deshler-Morris House (the Germantown "White House"), which stands across Germantown Avenue from Market Square. "The Germantown Historical Society is planning to submit to the citizens of Germantown a project for the restoration of Market Square as it was in colonial times, somewhat according to the Williamsburg formula," Stradley wrote to a minister of the Market Square Presbyterian Church in 1948.[21]

The square itself is roughly the length of a small city block, offset from Germantown Avenue and surrounded by several office buildings and a church. It briefly served some of the functions of a market square in the middle of the eighteenth century, but Germantown's subsequent development was linear, with one main street and few intersections. Neither Market Square nor the later Town Hall one mile to the north ever served the function of a town square in the way that Vernon Park has. Moreover, minimal connections to the site's colonial roots remained, though plaques on the church signified that Washington worshipped there in the 1790s; only one building from before 1776 still stood along the square.[22] Though Market Square was the scene of intense fighting during the 1777 battle (where it served as the stronghold of British forces), it was best known to the community as the site of a grand Civil War memorial, a statue installed in the middle of the square in the late nineteenth century. "Restoring" Market Square to its colonial state would require moving that monument, setting the Historical Society on a course opposed to its proclaimed role of preserving public memory. Its willingness to destroy Market Square to save Germantown history by recreating a colonial atmosphere speaks to the urgency that Stradley and others felt. In the end, they would merely demonstrate that a section of a living, breathing city neighborhood cannot be sealed off and preserved.

The Market Square project ran through several decades, with numerous players and iterations. But its early years, from 1946 to 1949, encompass a period of great upheaval in Germantown's quest for identity. In the summer of 1948, Stradley wrote to property owners on the square to inform them of the plans. One of the project's adherents was Arthur Rosenlund (1900–1989), president of an insurance company, who planned to restore the Fromberger House, an eighteenth-century building that had been altered several times over the years. Rosenlund intended to move the company's offices into the square, taking advantage of the National Park Service's investment in restoring the Deshler-Morris House and capitalizing on the interest in colonial tourism.[23]

The Germantown Historical Society hired an architect from the firm of G. Edwin Brumbaugh and made the strained case that Market Square "was associated with more memories and incidents of colonial and revolutionary times than almost any other spot in the country."[24] Brumbaugh believed in the power of architecture to create an atmosphere that fostered the ideals of the early Republic. He enjoyed an excellent reputation in Pennsylvania (his father had been governor), as a restoration architect and as a designer of new structures in the colonial style. He connected the project with a recreation of Williamsburg in Germantown.[25] Plans were publicly unveiled in the first issue of the historical society's magazine, the *Germantown Crier,* in January 1949. Stradley's letter in the same issue explains that the society saw the project as an opportunity to use history for commercial benefit, "somewhat according to what's been done at Co-

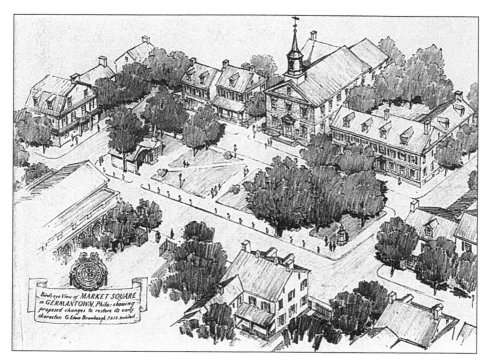

Figure 3.3 Architectural plan for proposed Market Square development, 1949. G. Edwin Brumbaugh's rendering removes a Civil War monument and depicts colonial revival landscaping and façades in an idealized and wildly inaccurate manner; the plan provoked heated opposition until the 1970s. (Germantown Historical Society.)

lonial Williamsburg." "We believe," he adds, "that our plan of restoration appeals to the love of history not only on our part but to a growing interest in history, especially colonial history, by a large percentage of American people." Subsequent issues of the *Crier* contain illustrations of the project, and an artist's rendering of the proposed design for the square graced the cover of the third issue. These public pronouncements revealed that the plan called for more changes in the historic landscape than Germantowners, including several members of the society, were willing to consider. The society was put on the defensive.

The plan to remove the Civil War monument raised the question Which history matters? Stradley asked the society's librarian, Edward Hocker, a published historian, to find evidence of what Market Square would have looked like in colonial times. Hocker provided some references, drawn from society scrapbooks (including Watson's), but he also expressed his concerns:

I wonder whether those who have from time to time proposed to "restore" Market Square to its condition in colonial times realize that this would mean: cutting down all the fine trees, plowing up the sod and removing the coping, making the place a bare open lot with footpaths worn across it, obliterating the work to which several generations of the Morris family gave attention to beautify the square. This monument may be hideous according to modern taste, but the tablets bear the names of all Germantown's Civil War soldiers and any attempt to tamper with it will arouse a storm among patriotic organizations.[26]

Referring pointedly to the Morris family, whose home was about to be opened by the National Park Service as Washington's Germantown White House, Hocker made it clear that no place can be frozen in time—and certainly not a site in a city neighborhood.

Meanwhile, Civil War descendant groups criticized the plan in terms that showed an understanding of how history has to make room for progress. William Emhardt of the Ellis Civil War Post, a leading Germantown merchant and longtime head of the Avenue Improvement Association, conveyed his anger privately and in letters to newspapers. He recounted how the entire square was crafted as a monument to the Civil War, not just the marker and the statue of a Union soldier: "The elms were brought from the Battlefield at Gettysburg and the oaks were all placed by interested individuals and named for them at a celebration at the time of planting." As for the Germantown Historical Society's version of history, he went on: "This is history we must forget. Let us return to dirt roads and dirt pavements, pumps and privies and eliminate modern sanitary fixtures, City water, sewage and gas, electricity, telephones, refrigeration, mechanized offices and really be colonial. What a pipe dream and who is the author? Who suggested that people would come a long distance to look at the Commons of primitive Germantown?"[27] Moreover, he noted, any comparison with Williamsburg implied tremendous costs. For the Virginia project, the Rockefellers had invested more than five million dollars.

In a letter prepared for the editors of local papers, Stradley addresses the criticisms but in a way that defines "historic" very narrowly:

> As to the removal of the war memorials, there is nothing sacrosanct about the monument and its location on Market Square. The Square holds no special place in Civil War History and the monument could

be placed to better advantage elsewhere. The plaque commemorating the Battle of Germantown could and should remain. The
trees could also remain without the slightest change. Our sole
purpose is to preserve the traditions and historical background of
colonial Germantown. A removal of the monument that we advocate would not detract in any way from their present position.

As to commercialism, this is merely a catch phrase with no
substance. There is no element of commercialism in our proposals.
In fact no one in our organization has any personal motive. We are
thinking only of Germantown and its best interests and we solicit a
reasonable consideration of our proposals by all interested parties.
There is no more commercialism in our proposal than there is at
Williamsburg.[28]

Forced to address the commercial interests of the project's advocates,
Stradley invoked Williamsburg as an example of activism in the community's interest. But Williamsburg was all about using historical reproductions
and reconstructed colonial buildings for economic benefit.

The Germantown Historical Society's bold attempt to create a colonial
attraction guaranteed that it considered "historic" only what was firmly
defined as colonial. This narrow definition sparked the ire of Civil War
descendants and raised the larger question of what restoring the past really means. Rather than curating and harmonizing the whole history of the
neighborhood—by connecting the Civil War monument to Germantown's
1688 antislavery protest, for instance—the society contributed to the dif-
fusion of the past, creating more factions and organizations as it narrowed
the sense of what and whose history matters in a centuries-old community.
The society's leadership came close to destroying a place dedicated to the
public's memory of the Civil War in order to manufacture an idealized
version of the colonial period. Owners of Victorian-era buildings refused
to sell, while the 1887 Market Square Presbyterian Church declined to
alter its nineteenth-century façade to fit the vision of a colonial market
square.[29] The plan typified the limits of the historical imagination in the
twentieth century and highlighted the deficiencies of Germantown's public history establishment. Worse, when the Market Square scheme was
combined with plans for a highway bypass that would divide the neighborhood between Vernon Park and Town Hall, it provoked fears of dislocation
and suspicions that historic preservation was rooted in conflicts of interest
and disregard for lower-income and black residents.[30]

Judge Harold Saylor (1892–1981), who became president of the Germantown Historical Society when Stradley died in 1953, believed that the protests against relocating the Civil War monument were getting in the way of the Colonial Revival vision for the entire neighborhood.[31] While the Historical Society engaged Brumbaugh to continue the pursuit of that white elite vision, Saylor invested in colonial architecture along Germantown Avenue, not just Market Square, and lent his stature as the society's longtime president to two economic development corporations. The first, Historic Germantown, Inc., was a holding company established in 1953. (It is not to be confused with the Historic Germantown consortium of historic sites founded in 1980.) The company set out to acquire blighted colonial buildings that came up for sale and adapt them for reuse. A dozen buildings on Germantown Avenue were bought and saved from demolition through his efforts.[32] The second nonprofit economic development group, Colonial Germantown, Inc., was formed in 1956. Saylor held a board position with Colonial Germantown, Inc., while president of the Historical Society. For the first several years, the leaders of Colonial Germantown, Inc., attempted to raise private and public funds to acquire real estate on the square. Within a few years, the Market Square project would be enmeshed with urban renewal politics and a series of plans for remaking Germantown.

Urban Renewal: Condemnation and Preservation

After World War II ambitious government programs were launched to combat blight and poverty in U.S. cities. Urban renewal programs intended to revitalize decaying inner cities failed because of divisions that could not be overcome. Sometimes the division was between private investment and public funding: Real estate developers (mostly white) and government agencies trying to solve housing and poverty crises were often at odds.[33]

Sometimes poor neighborhoods were demolished to make way for public housing, but because of the exodus of manufacturing, there were no new jobs for the residents. In *The Origins of Urban Crisis*, Thomas Sugrue describes this process as it unfolded in Detroit.[34] Arnold R. Hirsch declares that "rather than solve the urban crisis, urban renewal had set the stage for its next phase."[35] In Atlanta and other cities, effective coalitions between white economic interests and black political organizers attracted jobs and brought newly empowered groups into the political process.[36]

New Haven was also held up as a model for incorporating historic preservation and antipoverty programs,[37] whereas hubs of black cultural life in Charlottesville, Virginia, were eliminated, with devastating results.[38] Michael Wallace, focusing on preservation in cities, notes that urban renewal helped build a wider coalition for preserving the past and that the 1964 and 1967 riots in many cities were in some ways rooted in reactions against urban renewal and highway construction.[39] In Germantown, too, preservation and antipoverty programs would intersect. No poor neighborhoods would be destroyed—because the largest urban renewal project for Germantown was rejected.

Urban renewal in Philadelphia began as early as 1939 as an outgrowth of a movement to reform the political process and end Republican one-party rule but did not take off until a decade later. In 1951 Philadelphia adopted a new city charter and elected Joseph Clark as mayor. African American voters provided crucial support for the reform movement, bringing Democratic Party control to the city for the first time in generations. The political reform movement was closely linked to visionary but technocratic, top-down projects to rebuild cities. Philadelphia created the Planning Commission, led by Edmund Bacon, to develop big plans for specific sections of the city.[40] Slated for completion early in the twenty-first century, the urban renewal program called for housing projects, improvements in highways and transportation, and more parks, libraries, and shopping and recreation centers. Urban renewal was implemented most fully in University City (a section of West Philadelphia) and Society Hill (the downtown home of the Independence Hall historic area). In each instance the conditions for federal funding, whether it came from the Truman, the Eisenhower, the Kennedy, or the Johnson administration, required a major local player to coordinate the government investment.

For Philadelphia, the Redevelopment Authority was that instrument, and it, in turn, required a local agent to implement the federal funds.[41] In University City, the local conduit was the University of Pennsylvania, and at least one black neighborhood, known as the "Black Bottom," was destroyed during the 1950s and 1960s by the expansion of the university and the demolition of housing near it.[42] In the Society Hill neighborhood, the Society Hill Civic Association worked with the Redevelopment Authority and the National Park Service to craft a mixture of historic preservation and modern high rises.[43] Both were contested processes that ultimately modernized these neighborhoods.

As two Philadelphia historians note, "It was commonly assumed that Philadelphia's mingling of races and ethnic groups had in the past worked pretty well, but this assumption was questionable."[44] The city's divisions, so evident in the strikes and ethnic strife of the era before and during World War II, were even sharper during the postwar economic crisis, as Philadelphia lost its manufacturing sector and then its population and tax base. The struggle over federal funding caused deep rifts within the Democratic coalition, prompting changes in the power structure. Mayor James Tate, a Democrat, tried to empower local community organizations through the federal Model Cities program, until the Nixon administration cracked down hard on black community groups' participation in the process.[45] Throughout the city (including Germantown, as we shall see), those groups shifted away from the nonviolent protests of the civil rights movement to electoral strategies in an effort to gain more power over urban renewal decisions. As Wilson Goode, an activist who would eventually become Philadelphia's first African American mayor, declared in 1970, "Black priorities have moved from integration in the 1950s through the 1960s riots and civil rights movement to control of institutions in the 1970s."[46]

In the 1950s and 1960s, Germantown's traditional white leadership tried to insert the neighborhood into Philadelphia's overall renewal vision, sensing that its history, retail establishments, and dense population could supplement federal efforts planned for Society Hill and University City, and, in the process, adding a new chapter to its sense of separation from Philadelphia. A concentrated federal urban renewal program began in 1958 to rehabilitate several blocks of low-income housing in Germantown's working-class Morton neighborhood, due east of Germantown Avenue between the high school and the Pennsylvania Railroad.[47] The Morton project included no historic preservation and heritage tourism and involved none of Germantown's leading institutions. Yet "disputes over local community participation [had become] a regular feature" of urban renewal, and Germantown typified that pattern.[48] When discussions about a Colonial Revival Market Square aroused the ambitions of Germantown's elite business leaders, and they tried to expand the Morton project to include Market Square in acquisition and demolition plans, the rest of the community resisted. And since the Market Square plans were presented as preserving Germantown's colonial features, historic preservation was brought into the dispute. When Germantown tried to reshape its commercial core, it ended up reshaping its entire power structure.

Redevelopment and Public History:
Annapolis and Society Hill

Other places faced comparable challenges. Annapolis's mid-century preservation profile was similar to Germantown's: Both were declared National Historic Districts at the same time (1965); both have historic house
museums that were gradually adapted rather than purpose-built as museums; both have struggled to find a way to present elite heritage for tourism
purposes. In both, moreover, discriminatory practices produced uneven
results in terms of attendance or heritage-based economic tourism, and
involvement from people other than well-educated members of the elite
was discouraged. Closer to Germantown, the Old City/Society Hill section of Philadelphia showed how communities can overcome barriers that
prevent public history from thriving in an urban environment challenged
by aging building stock, postindustrial decline, and demographic change.
Annapolis and Society Hill are clearly not the same as Germantown: One
is a state capital, with state resources to shore up its heritage economy; the
other benefited from the National Park Service resources used to preserve
Independence Hall and other iconic places. Yet each had to figure out how
to remain relevant by addressing new historical information, responding
to challenges from previously marginalized voices, and finding different
ways of presenting the past for changing audiences.

In Annapolis, a robust group of community preservation organizations,
led by Historic Annapolis, worked with community groups and state authorities. Historic Annapolis, founded in 1952, did the work of advocacy,
documentation, and preservation. In Germantown, only the Germantown
Historical Society performed such tasks, with some assistance from the
Philadelphia Historical Commission. Germantown's historical community
did not have local regulatory authority or tools to deploy for preservation-based development, as Historic Annapolis did. No less segregated or
prone to power politics or cronyism, Annapolis found a balance between
neighborhood livability and the use of historic content, narrative, and architectural features to advance economic goals.[49] Historic Annapolis focused its earliest efforts on documentation and comprehensive surveys
and then used the results to leverage state and federal grants to acquire or
secure protected status for buildings and either incorporate the buildings
for tourism or return them to private or community use. Colonial Germantown, Inc., and the Germantown Historical Society seemed to feel

threatened by historical documentation. Too much information (such as testimony on the significance of Market Square's Civil War monument, with its trees transplanted from Gettysburg) had a way of stalling plans for creating a playground dedicated to the colonial period.

In Society Hill, the National Park Service was a partner in redevelopment, but other agencies, most prominently the Pennsylvania Historical and Museum Commission, also had a large role. Though the commission approved historic designations in Germantown, it was not involved in the kind of large-scale development to which Colonial Germantown, Inc., aspired. State officials, such as Germantown's state senator Israel Stiefel, helped with preservation designations but were not involved with building coalitions to promote local plans. Whereas Annapolis had both regulatory support and a historic neighborhood centered on the state capitol building, Germantown had few partners committed to building the coalition needed for large-scale heritage tourism development. Pennsylvania and Philadelphia did not see the revitalization of one neighborhood as a priority. It was not the state capital; even its connections to U.S. history did not rate as high as those of Society Hill, home of Independence National Historic Park and the nation's founding. Germantown had neither an equal claim to prominence nor a guiding authority that could lead the plan to implementation.

The Magaziner Plans: Concern for Germantown

Despite these drawbacks, the urban planners of the 1950s and 1960s brought leadership and imagination to Germantown, working to connect the neighborhood to regional, state, and federal projects. Unfortunately, however, the efforts to embrace a larger vision for the entire neighborhood only fragmented it.

The architect Henry Magaziner developed bold plans to address the issues Germantown faced. His plans and the urban redevelopment proposals that resulted from his work fueled the belief that only bold action would save Germantown from decline. Yet the very boldness of his vision turned potential supporters into adversaries.

Magaziner was a native Philadelphian who had many Germantown connections. He was involved in the preservation of Independence Hall and other historic buildings, and his distinguished career led to the establishment of the Henry Magaziner Award for Preservation by the Philadelphia chapter of the American Institute of Architects. Working in Germantown in the mid-1960s, he helped to save the Ebenezer Maxwell Mansion; in the early 1970s, he served on the board of the Germantown Historical Society. As head of the Germantown Community Council's Physical Planning Division in 1964–1967, he described himself as an architect who "since 1936 has given considerable thought to various sorts of schemes to restore to national prominence those portions of Germantown Avenue containing the historic house concentrations."[50]

While Colonial Germantown, Inc., sought to bring preservation-based economic development to a specific portion of Germantown in the 1950s, a group called "Concern for Germantown" engaged in discussions with Magaziner over broader, regional responses to urban challenges. A task force of citizens representing vital nonprofit institutions, Concern for Germantown brought leaders together at Wister House in Vernon Park to consider the strengths and weakness of Greater Germantown (that is, the whole German Township), in response to fears that institutions such as Germantown Academy would leave the neighborhood. By 1960 its working group included sixteen institutions, among them the Germantown Jewish Center, the African American Faith Presbyterian Church, and leaders of the YWCA, the public library, and Germantown Friends School—many of the same institutions that came together briefly for Negro Achievement Week in 1928.[51]

Magaziner's 1952 three-page study for Concern for Germantown, "Germantown Avenue in Germantown," launched his attempt to use government projects backed by ambitious progressive thinking to address fears that deindustrialization and white flight would change Germantown for the worse. Though first written as a brief concept paper, the study provided a template for subsequent reports, plans, and studies for the Philadelphia Planning Commission and its professional urban planners.[52] An expanded 1956 version by Henry Churchill, Jack M. Kendree, and Ty Learn for the Planning Commission and their 1960 study each included demographic trends and cultural resource assessments for the entire German Township, not just Germantown Avenue and Market Square. The professional urban planning in the 1956 and 1960 reports revealed in stark terms the recent decreases in population, by census tract and by public school enrollment, but cited evidence for a significant increase by the 1980s; they specifically charted a predicted rise in nonwhite registered voters.[53] Based on their projection of a coming population increase (which turned out to be unfounded), the planners focused on the postwar period's chief planning concern: accommodating the automobile.

Each report stressed Magaziner's call for bold action to meet three needs: protect historic attractions in ways that would enhance Germantown's greatest asset, its retail corridor; retain leading nonprofit and educational institutions such as Germantown Friends School; and alleviate congestion by channeling traffic away from Germantown Avenue. The initial 1952 study ultimately begat the larger proposals for a Belfield-Rittenhouse highway bypass, which Magaziner presented to the Philadelphia City Planning Commission in March 1964, setting the stage for the Second Battle of Germantown in 1967.

Magaziner's plans showed confidence that Germantown could recreate itself as a "regional center" for shopping. The plan radically redrew Germantown Avenue in order to use a restored Market Square as a support for the Germantown-Chelten shopping district on the south end of the avenue and create a northern historic area buttressing a newly created shopping district on the north end.[54] Building that district would require the relocation of seven historic buildings to a site near the Wyck historic house and garden, between Walnut Lane and Tulpehocken Street.[55] The new shopping district would combine "modernization and restoration," hiding modern stores behind restored façades: "The interesting old buildings would continue to be used as stores, which would be carefully conceived to blend harmoniously with the old buildings." Magaziner also called for a square around Town Hall, currently being used as a municipal services building—"for morale-building possibilities."[56] Between the stores and the relocated historic buildings would be a tree-lined pedestrian zone, with buses the only vehicles allowed access. Also proposed was the "Bypass": an eight-lane "traffic loop" around the Germantown-Chelten business district, where a few national stores such as Sears and J. C. Penney stood alongside Germantown's own Allens and Rowells, all holding on at that point, even as shopping malls were being built on the outskirts of Germantown. Multilevel parking garages would be built just off the arterial axis of Germantown Avenue. Magaziner's plans seemed to be trying to solve many pressing issues at once.

The plans had a visionary reach but were grounded in the influence of the Williamsburg model. Addressing traffic congestion and store placement, Magaziner wrote: "It would be possible to restore historic Germantown Avenue at the most interesting points. This could be done either by very restrictive zoning and voluntary cooperation, or if the funds were available, by actual condemnation and restoration of the old mansions with their grounds."[57] He pointed to the success of the river drives in Philadelphia's Fairmount Park, where dilapidated structures were torn down to fashion a continuous park, ornamented by historic houses and bounded by roads with cars whizzing past.

Creating a full parklike vista along Germantown Avenue "would produce a Philadelphia 'Williamsburg' of possibly greater historic importance than the Virginia Williamsburg, and more accessible to our greatest population centers."[58] Tearing down and rebuilding to get the desired result, or, as Magaziner put it, "condemning in order to restore," was the essence of the plan. The building blocks were there, and the vision for Germantown history was bold. The report states: "It took Herculean efforts to reconstruct a Williamsburg from what were little more than archeological ruins. Similar great efforts were required to collect from all over New England the buildings which today form Old Sturbridge, Massachusetts, and Mystic, Connecticut. By contrast here on Germantown Avenue, virtually nothing needs to be assembled nor newly constructed. The historic buildings stand here assembled, abounding in history, exuding architectural charm, ready to be made into a national attraction."[59] Under his plan, Germantown could outdo Williamsburg.

By that time the Williamsburg model had captured the country's imagination. Banks and insurance companies adopted "false colonial" as an architectural uniform, and vast areas of the East and Midwest remodeled themselves accordingly. There were Williamsburg-style drive-in restaurants, supermarkets, hotels, and gas stations.[60] Germantown's plan, thanks to its remarkable historical resources, would be fashionable and real. The long shadow of Colonial Williamsburg never went away.

Elite Germantowners' plans to rejuvenate Market Square promised to stimulate commercial and retail activities, long a strength in Germantown. The proposals of Colonial Germantown, Inc., and the Magaziner plans were before the public at this point, both calling for a radically altered downtown that would feature a restored Market Square and the relocation of several historic buildings. Here the Germantown Historical Society's nostalgic plan coincided with Magaziner's progressive one.[61] Despite the resistance of Civil War descendant groups and historians such as Margaret Tinkcom, planning for the Market Square project had slowly moved ahead. Some funds were raised through dues collected from businesses on Germantown Avenue, and efforts to promote the historic attractions continued, but major foundation support or public money in the millions of dollars was nowhere in sight. In April 1962 Colonial Germantown, Inc., reorganized itself, hiring a full-time director and broadening its scope to assist with urban development in Germantown.[62] Already a sponsoring institution of Concern for Germantown, now Colonial Germantown, Inc., endorsed Magaziner's proposal to the City Planning Commission that it extend the federal government's investment in Germantown to include a recreation of Market Square.[63]

The Magaziner plans tackled the issues facing the community with a comprehensive vision, assessing parks and recreation and school delinquency, as well as the economic and physical state of Germantown. It approached community revitalization holistically and with coherent design, addressing planning, economic restructuring, and volunteer engagement long before these became the core of the National Trust's "Main Street" approach to commercial corridor revitalization. And yet Magaziner's plan failed to engage a splintered community because that community was not informed of the full implications of a major roadway bypass.

Federal Funds for Renewal

In March 1964 the Philadelphia Planning Commission "received" Magaziner's plan. Since funds had yet to be approved by the federal government, the commission chose not to formally "accept" the plan, lest acceptance be mistaken for its own approval.[64] By September 1964 the federal government had approved more urban renewal funding, giving the Philadelphia Redevelopment Authority a green light to present the plans for public discussion. Peter J. McCahill, director of Germantown projects for the authority, recalling the Planning Commission's careful distinction between "received" and "accepted," sounded a note of caution because the plan called for closing off and bypassing sections of Germantown Avenue. "This changing of Germantown Ave.," he said, "is a rather radical and bold move."[65]

The plan's proposal for a full-fledged renewal effort rested on three faulty assumptions, the first about population growth, the second about the character of the residents, and the third about funding. On population growth, projections showed that Northwest Philadelphia would grow rapidly in the 1970s and 1980s, while other areas, such as the Mount Airy, Chestnut Hill, and Roxborough neighborhoods, would grow enough to offset any net loss created by the white flight from Germantown. According to the 1960 plan, "population increase will be the source of all problems—[it] will double by 1980. The pressure to fill up areas of low density such as Germantown and Chestnut Hill cannot be resisted. That is, by 1980

Germantown may have 150,000 to 175,000 instead of the 103,000 it has now."[66] The 1964 plan repeats these figures. According to Magaziner, "The population explosion could hit greater Germantown harder than most areas of the city," straining its infrastructure, housing stock, and traffic patterns.[67] Only planning could prevent these problems. Traffic and parking were a key part of this alarming scenario, and Magaziner and the planners proposed creative solutions. Yet Germantown's population did not explode as projected. Instead, it fell 14 percent between 1950 and 1980.

The second faulty assumption stemmed from a rosy and self-serving analysis of Germantown's response to its changing racial composition: "Germantown's vitality has been shown in the way it has met the recent racial change in some of its neighborhoods. Panic did not develop there as it did in many other areas. Rather, Germantown has worked through its problems."[68] Magaziner's hopefulness rested on what he describes as "uniquely Germantown-like" citizen-based redevelopment, citing the planners of Colonial Germantown, Inc. He praises the community for having "so alert and articulate a citizenry." "It has constantly been alert to zoning changes," he continues. "It has formed countless neighborhood civic organizations. It has fathered the Germantown Community Council and Colonial Germantown, Inc. It has many dynamic institutions. The resourcefulness is there. The wish is there."[69] Amplifying the wish was the support of the Germantown Community Council, at the time, and also support from Colonial Germantown, Inc.[70]

For Magaziner, the historic character of the neighborhood was obvious, and it was reflected in more than its architecture: "Germantown is one of America's oldest communities. It is also one of its most vital. . . . [E]ven though it has suffered decline as a business/commercial area, it still retains great potential for redevelopment as a strong regional center because it is neither a city nor a suburb, but retains the best features of both."[71]

Magaziner and his colleagues saw the many historic preservation groups involved in the community as an asset, and the plan could count on support from others, such as the National Park Service. For instance, he called on the state historical commission, the National Trust for Historic Preservation, and the Germantown Historical Society to ask state and federal groups to expand their presence in Germantown.[72] Magaziner looked beyond the colonial and revolutionary eras to note that "as early as 1688 Germantown protested publicly against slavery," hinting at historic preservation's role in the service of social justice.[73] Inattention to more recent developments with regard to race may have blinded the planners to the work that would be needed to secure support from black community organizers.

The planners working with Magaziner hoped that "a major foundation would provide funds."[74] This was the third faulty assumption. The Ford Foundation, Rockefeller Foundation, and Carl Schurz Foundation were suggested, for "a restored Germantown Avenue would be a wonderful way to teach history and to teach the lesson of European-American cooperation."[75] At the height of the Cold War and the civil rights movement, Magaziner made it clear that the plan would showcase the primacy of at least one of Germantown's ethnic groups and advance patriotic ideals.

"Only the big plan, one with centralized direction, will solve the little problems and the big ones as well. Bold thinking is what is needed," Magaziner declared.[76] The vision was artfully rendered and reflected a high point of wishful thinking by some of the best minds in the country about problems that had plagued Germantown for years, beginning with a main thoroughfare that had had too few intersections since the seventeenth century and was ill-suited to the demands of automobile and truck traffic. Not until the 1960s, however, did professionals and consultants weigh in on these commonly perceived problems and develop a strategy to address them. Magaziner and other planners thought that the right combination of approaches could give Germantown the same elegant mixture of history and modern amenities that Society Hill enjoyed—along with more significance than Williamsburg.[77] Leadership was required to bring the community's various groups together: "a coordinating agency for long-range planning though not another 'coordinating' agency." What Magaziner had in mind was not merely a neighborhood group to bring about what a Germantown Community Council slogan called "Unity in the Community" but more of a development corporation. "An agency in planning matters, with a staff," the planners explain, "would relate to planning overall and long range theory, leaving the local groups to work out immediate plans and problems." It would be "an organization that would study in depth the physical development of the area. Most planning studies are based on physical aspects of growth and change but no action gets taken unless there's money. It's possible for Germantown to attack this problem differently. Germantown is a part of a larger political unit of Philadelphia but it is large enough and varied enough and self-conscious enough to act as a political force. If focus for community action could be found, there is hope that objective planning can become reality."[78]

The money would flow to Germantown if one body could bring in the long list of agencies that Magaziner called for. In other words, the plan depended on attracting a few private funders. These funders never materialized. The question became: Which group will bring the plan into focus? And, specifically, which group can capitalize on federal dollars to remake Germantown?

Finding a Development Corporation

Without a guiding authority, any entity that brought Germantown's plan into focus had to sell the plan to the community. Magaziner believed that Concern for Germantown could handle the work of coordinating development activities but that a more centralized authority with capacity for staffing such an enterprise was essential as well. The various studies Magaziner and his colleagues drafted envisioned an agency with the power to execute the proposals and implement the plans, with political connections and facile enough community relations that it could "acquire and hold property for the mutual benefit of institutions involved."[79] A physical planning committee of Germantown Community Council, which Magaziner chaired, and Germantown Settlement were considered for the role of community development corporation, but the first was a loose advisory council rather than an incorporated entity, and the second dealt with housing and services, with limited experience in economic redevelopment on the scale Magaziner's plans required. Concern for Germantown receded from a leading role. In the words of William Will, director of Germantown Community Council: "In the urban renewal of those days, it took three to tango: A plan, community support for that plan, and a development corporation to carry it. Germantown had a plan and community support, but it still needed the corporation. Enter Colonial Germantown, Inc."[80]

The city agency steering urban renewal projects in Philadelphia, the Redevelopment Authority, typically worked with a community consultant. The authority engaged Colonial Germantown, Inc., which already had an established presence among Germantown business leaders, and its director, Jack Hornung (1932–2005), to provide technical assistance on urban renewal in Germantown.[81] The relationship with the Germantown Community Council did not work out as hoped, even though the two groups became inextricably linked. The board chair of each group was ex officio a member of the board and executive committee of the other group. Francis X. Delany, the former head of the council, wrote of the new arrangement: "At last the Council had a potential rival for community leadership. Colonial Germantown was a partner in theory, but an adversary in practice."[82] Hornung said, "We thought that by putting the president of the Community Council on our board we'd have a liaison, but it didn't work out that way."[83]

The attempt to get this bold plan through Philadelphia City Council animated Germantown and gave the community plenty to talk about. Many residents decided to fight against it.

"The Second Battle of Germantown"

By 1960 Germantown's economic downturn was clearly visible. The census trends described earlier persisted: The neighborhood's population had dropped, and white families were moving out, along with institutions such as Germantown Academy. As noted in the census records and studies by the La Salle Urban Center, Philadelphia's "black population in 1960 had grown to 27 percent of the total with significant increases in every neighborhood."[84] Big community festivals, always one of Germantown's great civic strengths, fell on hard times. Germantown Week went through several transformations after its late 1940s high point. A version called "Vernon Fair Week" in the 1950s highlighted all the community's ethnic and civic groups, but in 1963, Delany lamented, "the ailing Vernon Fair finally died."[85]

The demise of Vernon Fair was but one of many signs that times had changed. The battle to revive Germantown by physically reshaping it would engulf the community and forever alter the landscape, though not in the ways the planners intended. Public opposition to the plan became the biggest civic event of the period, far more engaging to the community than any public festival.

Opposition to the Magaziner plan focused on the bypass in ways that reflected how complex the urban renewal project had become. In 1965 and 1966, Delany wrote, "Plans and meetings about plans were almost as numerous as neighborhood groups."[86] The competing viewpoints cannot be characterized in terms of black or white, old guard or newcomer. Opponents came largely from residential block associations, both white and black, notably the West Side Neighborhood Council, Wayne-Harvey Neighbors, Price-Knox Civic Association, Neighbors of Germantown Heights (formerly Penn Area Neighbors), and East Mount Airy Neighbors. Wister Neighborhood Council was formed to oppose the bypass.

Citizens for Renewal Now was started by an optometrist with the backing of Colonial Germantown, Inc. The coalition that formed and continued to grow in opposition—consisting of historians, social agencies, working-class groups, and residents, both black and white—was fragile because its members had little experience working together and all parties did not have access to the same information. Even to call it a "coalition" overstates its cohesiveness. The Germantown Businessmen's Association came out in favor of the plan, but the Germantown and Chelten Retail Businessmen's Association rejected it. Even though opposition to the urban renewal plans was, for Germantown, effective and broad-based, the coalition would break apart almost as soon as the plan was defeated for good in 1972.

Wallace describes how "traditional preservationists had a lot of trouble establishing an alliance with black constituencies, even apart from black reluctance" to work with white groups.[87] To some professionals, "historic" meant "beautiful"—and poor people's housing and places of worship were not necessarily considered pretty. But even this was more complicated in Germantown. Tinkcom's assessment of Market Square insisted on telling the full story of the square: its gritty commercial and industrial history as well as architecture not associated with the colonial period, including the Civil War monument.[88] Yet some conflicts might have been avoided or softened had Colonial Germantown, Inc., been less heavy handed. Its members controlled a large block of advertising in the *Germantown Courier,* creating the impression that it was trying to censor and disenfranchise opponents.[89] This impression is expressed in a letter to the editor: "I look for the Courier to present the best and fairest coverage possible of all sides of the issue and instead I find slanted news coverage and editorials with innuendo and name-calling. So with chagrin I flee the Courier's 'promotion' efforts and seek the facts in the dailies."[90]

The strategies used by preservationists and curators did not work well in black communities. As Wallace writes, "There was seldom overwhelming support for preservation in black communities. Many were ill-disposed to preserving places indelibly connected with white supremacy or poverty."[91] In Germantown, the legacies of bigotry and division throughout the centuries were a stumbling block.

Many factors at play during the 1950s, 1960s, and 1970s caused urban renewal to fail in Germantown, but a key component was the resistance of the African American community. Understandably so: Twelve African

American churches and many working-class houses stood on Rittenhouse Street (once known as Poor House Lane) in the path of the proposed bypass. A 1969 newspaper article reported that the Redevelopment Authority would acquire forty-three nonresidential buildings and fifty-three residential structures in order to demolish them.[92] The Northwest Philadelphia chapter of the National Association for the Advancement of Colored People opposed the roadway. These campaigns underscored for African American residents the need for black control of decision-making processes. Because the plan was driven by Colonial Germantown, Inc., many in the community would associate the divisiveness with public history. The lack of input, however, not historic preservation itself, was the chief reason for black opposition to urban renewal in Germantown—along with the fact that the urban renewal process, as noted earlier, projected a narrative of decline. The meaning of "urban renewal" had shifted from improved housing and social services to displacement and highway construction. The clash between Germantown's black community and the planners precipitated a radical change in tactics.

For blacks, by 1967 representing more than 40 percent of the population in Philadelphia and a majority in Germantown, the issues that mattered were education, poverty, employment, and housing. Seeking greater input into plans for the commercial corridor went hand in hand with educational reform and antipoverty efforts. Local control meant securing decision-making power in the bodies that brokered federal and state funds: political offices and social agencies such as Germantown Settlement. As Michael deHaven Newsom suggested in 1971, "Adequate planning for black input at the initial stage of a project would, of course, remove the necessity of disruption."[93] The Magaziner plan did not take that into account or make any dialogue-based effort to build support among the black community, and even if the goals of Colonial Germantown, Inc., had not been strictly preservationist, the "Colonial" in its name gave the strong impression that one version of history was siphoning off funds that should go to the entire community. The outcome became a lesson about the need for buy-in that would have to be repeated frequently in Germantown. After 1972 Germantown's black leadership had far more say about how local decisions got made than did the leaders of the Germantown Historical Society. Even then, however, changing the relationship between the black community and historic preservation to support a greater sense of shared history was a challenge.

The history of the 1960s in Germantown could, on one level, be told as a story of a community in decline that refused to go along with consultants and planners acting on behalf of a government that had rubbed its leaders the wrong way. The development, presentation, and rejection of the Magaziner plan, however, reflected another aspect of Germantown: the increased involvement of professionals, who now, like business and civic leaders, had access to power. The articulateness to which Magaziner referred was most evident in the growing influence of neighborhood and civic groups, which Germantown had always had in great number. The various community groups and the consultants and professionals hired to speak on their behalf were now numerous and empowered, leading to a variety of competing agendas that not even a civic organization like the Germantown Community Council could manage. Lack of coordination on the planners' side, however, was not the sole explanation for their failure. In council director Delany's summary: "Confrontation replaced consensus." The council even dropped the slogan "Unity in the Community."[94]

In 1964 the Magaziner plan called for spending a million dollars to create the modified bypass as part of a seven-million-dollar plan that would build a pedestrian walkway on a portion of Germantown Avenue near the Chelten Avenue shopping district and relocate some historic buildings into a small section of Germantown Avenue between Walnut Lane and Tulpehocken Street, right where the old black YWCA had been located. By 1966 the Redevelopment Authority had issued its proposal to spend more than ten million dollars to put much of Magaziner's plan into effect. The authority used a traffic study to support the need for the bypass, which had been modified from eight lanes to four between Vernon Park and Town Hall. The proposal included pedestrian walkways and green space. It did not include the Market Square restoration but, rather, called for the square to be redesigned to emphasize historical continuity, with more trees and contemporary buildings to make it more attractive.[95] A full recreation of a colonial atmosphere was not recommended. One reporter observed that "nothing like that is going to be financed with [federal urban] renewal funds."[96]

Everything hinged on the bypass. When this plan was presented to the community, the opposition was intense though fragmented. Neighborhood organizations, made up of both white and black residents, insisted that the traffic problems were overstated. In July 1967 the Germantown Community Council president Robert Boynton complained that "insufficient study has been made for the bypass and that it won't solve the problems that the planners say it will solve."[97] Two months later, *Philadelphia*

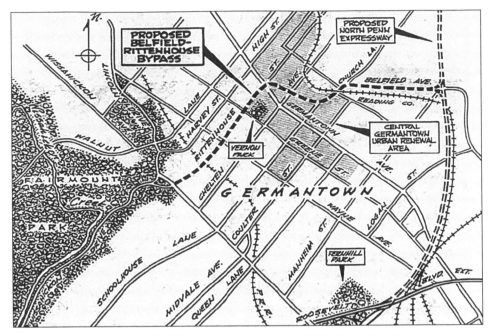

Figure 3.4 Proposed Belfield-Rittenhouse Bypass map, 1967. The route called for removing dozens of homes and churches to create a multi-lane road to accommodate automobile traffic to serve historic tourist attractions and retail shopping as part of the vision of Colonial Germantown, Inc. (Used with permission of Philadelphia Inquirer. Copyright © 2018. All rights reserved. Map design by Francis Pontari.)

Magazine ran its cover story labeling the uproar "the Second Battle of Germantown."

Not only had Colonial Germantown, Inc., failed to insert its Market Square project into the urban renewal plan, but also the plan as a whole angered and offended influential members of the community. The opposition included professionals, such as the architectural historian Margaret Tinkcom, who stressed that the full life of the square superseded one narrow and idealized interpretation of it. (Tinkcom served as historical adviser on the 1966 Redevelopment Authority proposal.) The Germantown Community Council was no longer working productively with Colonial Germantown, Inc. Engaged by the Redevelopment Authority to build public support for the Magaziner plan, Colonial Germantown, Inc., had alienated important sectors of the community. Colonial Germantown, Inc., had deliberately avoided constituent cultivation. Hornung believed that "you can't be democratic and get things done"[98]—this from the representative of a group that one newspaper described as "organized by some of the businessmen and institutions in Germantown to look after the interests of the community."[99] Hornung's view, shared by Rosenlund and other commercial leaders, became clear to the wider public when the plan was put before Philadelphia City Council in 1967.

The spring and summer of 1967 offered neighborhood forums a chance to see and discuss the Redevelopment Authority proposal. At numerous community presentations, the process of building broad community support was getting under way, but now there was a defection from within Colonial Germantown, Inc. Robert Anderson, one of the few board members who actually lived in the German Township (in West Mount Airy), rallied the "Citizens Committee" to oppose the final Magaziner plan for central Germantown, now projected to cost $10.6 million. "The deterioration of the Germantown business section is due to the Germantown businessmen themselves," James DeAnnis, president of the West Side Community Council and a member of the Citizens Committee, charged. "The streets are so filthy and so filled with trash that nobody wants to shop there. If the businessmen would only get together and improve their buildings, it would bring people into them. If I want to buy a new suit I sure don't need a four-lane highway to go buy it."[100] The Citizens Committee rounded up residents and small business owners, white and black, who believed (correctly) that they had been deliberately shut out of a process that would ultimately serve the interests of a few, most notably the leadership of Colonial Germantown, Inc.[101]

The Germantown Community Council had originally endorsed the 1964 plan, but, as the "Second Battle of Germantown" article points out, once "they eventually got the traffic study from the City of Philadelphia . . . they began to doubt a proposed bypass was the answer to traffic and parking problems."[102] Hornung used the Planning Commission's traffic study to forecast dire consequences. As reported in the *Inquirer*:

> "This traffic, if unchecked, would 'clog up' central Germantown, which Colonial Germantown, Inc. envisions as a pedestrian-oriented 'regional center,'" [Hornung] said—but the GCC [Germantown Community Council] trained all its fire on the bypass. The bypass would require demolition of too many homes, and its cost could be better applied to other uses. [Robert]Anderson spoke for many when he said, "We feel that the taking of all the homes on the south side of Rittenhouse from Germantown Ave. west to Wissahickon

Ave. is not in the best interests of the community. In other words, we're trying to say simply that if a roadway is to really serve a community well, sometimes homes have to go, but in this case, taking the homes just lessens the housing in Germantown."[103]

The Germantown Community Council finally voted against the Redevelopment Authority plan. In response, the Philadelphia Planning Commission made clear that its version of Magaziner's plans was all or nothing. When the Redevelopment Authority's community representative, Carol Buhr, resigned in protest in 1967, it became evident that the planners were not relating to the community effectively. At the time it was said that Buhr "agreed that the people weren't taken into the confidence of the authorities and that this is what the fracas [was] really all about." *Philadelphia Magazine* described the situation as "the classic case of the community worker who's supposed to convince the public that a plan worked out for special interests is for them and then begins to side with the public."[104] The very process of fighting the plan was bringing together a new generation of politically active Germantown residents. New members on the multiracial Germantown Community Council also began to address concerns facing black residents, such as police brutality and lack of input into education policy.

Both sides offered testimony at loud and rancorous sessions in City Hall. In a telling detail, as four hundred Germantowners set out to attend the hearings at City Hall, groups against the plan gathered in Vernon Park, while supporters left from Market Square.[105] In October 1967 the plan was voted down in City Council.[106] Technically, it was amended to include more study and community input; effectively, it lost and would never be revived. The City Council resolution calling for the plan to be resubmitted to the community for their input was "believed to be the first legislation ever enacted in Philadelphia specifically recognizing the right of citizens to be involved in planning."[107] The opposition had won the first round, showing the power of the neighborhoods.

The planners also lost the second round, when the federal government, in the form of the Department of Housing and Urban Development (HUD), declared, in effect, "no roadway, no urban renewal." This loss led City Council to quickly call another vote in order to submit the Redevelopment Authority Plan intact—the same plan it had voted down in October—in the hope that federal funds would be forthcoming. But now the response from Germantown's anti-bypass neighborhood associations was even more combative, as they argued that the roadway funds would be better spent on recreation, services for the aged, and other community improvements. They noted how the bypass had changed what the community thought it was going to get. Mattie Humphrey, a member of the Wister Neighborhood Council (formed to fight the bypass), told a newspaper reporter, "The road is unnecessary and destructive to the human part of the community. The original plan called for new housing and parking but the housing has been eliminated in favor of the roadway."[108] As the Germantown Community Council "vowed to continue the fight,"[109] in the words of its former director, Germantown's Democratic councilman David Cohen (1914–2005), elected in 1967, condemned the "divisive roadway." Going against Democratic mayor James Tate, Cohen called the plan a "tragedy" for the people of Germantown.[110] Joseph Yarbrough Jr., working with the Wister Area Committee to bring eight neighborhood organizations, half of them from Germantown, to Washington to argue with HUD officials for a greater role for grassroots organizations in urban renewal, now called "neighborhood development."[111] Yarbrough worked on the staff at Germantown Settlement and lived in the Wister neighborhood. He opposed the bypass but hoped that federal support for other programs would be forthcoming. A news account from 1970 cited his prediction "that as a result of citizen involvement more attention would be given to housing and rehabilitation."[112]

The Germantown Community Council, four neighborhood organizations, and several individuals in the path of the bypass filed suit against HUD and the Philadelphia Redevelopment Authority in October 1969.[113] The case came to an end with the federal funding cuts of 1969 and 1970, and the bypass plan was officially stopped by a U.S. District Court in 1971.[114] By the end of the year, the Vietnam War had altered federal priorities, and urban renewal budgets were slashed. The Germantown plan was put to rest in 1972.[115]

Had Magaziner's plan been implemented, the bypass would have divided Germantown much as the Vine Street Expressway split Philadelphia's Chinatown. Many of Germantown's historic features would have been forever altered. Working-class houses of the colonial and Victorian eras would be gone, along with many places of worship. The construction of large, multistory parking garages would have marred the landscape. Relocating seven historic sites to a pedestrian plaza would have created a concentrated area for public history, but, in the age of television and shopping malls, it is not clear that this new district would have attracted more visitors or competed with Valley Forge or Independence Mall as a tourist destination. Descendant groups, led by the Germantown Historical Society, supported the plan, but their short-term victory might have left Germantown with much to undo and without a sense of place. Gone would have been the enmeshment so important to Jane Jacobs: the interplay of the varieties of urban life, people interacting with each other amid trees, parks, and businesses. Much of the "human part of the community," including its historic buildings in their original settings, would have been sacrificed in order to bring in carloads of tourists to see distorted recreations of a single version of Germantown's story, the bygone colonial period.

Black Power Activism and Electoral Success

Many of the civic associations that proclaimed victory in the battle against the Redevelopment Authority plan had emerged or matured in response to racial change.[116] German Township had added to its already overcrowded landscape of civic and neighborhood organizations between 1950 and 1968. Of the fifty-three civic organizations recorded in that period, thirty-one were less than four years old, including several that were founded to agitate either for or against urban renewal. The population had decreased while the number of organizations rose.[117]

Though there were scattered attempts at grassroots planning in Germantown, the nearby neighborhoods of East and West Mount Airy became case studies in forward-thinking approaches to managing a changing neighborhood. These efforts have been the basis for social science studies demonstrating successful accommodation of sizable demographic changes without violence or accelerated decline. The success of the West Mount Airy Neighbors in combating discrimination and keeping predatory real estate agents from driving down property values is well documented.[118] This pathbreaking neighborhood association started in 1959 with the goal of maintaining integration.[119] Mount Airy came into its own during the 1950s and 1960s and separated itself from the fate of Germantown by maintaining stability through concerted neighborhood organization.

Black Philadelphians had endured Ku Klux Klan rallies in their neighborhoods in the late 1920s and significant Klan membership in the region into the 1940s.[120] During the 1944 Philadelphia Transit Company strike, when union drivers walked out to prevent the employment of blacks as trolley and bus drivers, armed federal soldiers were brought into the city to keep public transportation moving. In the 1950s and 1960s, crumbling housing stock and de facto segregation, combined with the city's declining job pool, left blacks with few options. The city charter had been amended in 1948 to forbid discriminatory language in real estate advertising, but could a legal process controlled by whites guarantee equality for blacks? As urban renewal plans worked their way toward political reality in Philadelphia City Council, black community groups also addressed the plight of Germantown High School and police crackdowns on area gangs, with the overarching goal of achieving greater decision-making power over issues that affected the black community. As white flight began to have an effect on city elections, African Americans gained political power, but change was slow in coming, particularly in with respect to school reform and housing.

David Richardson and the Germantown Protest of 1967

David Richardson Jr. and other Germantown activists were young but effective, mentored by veterans of the civil rights movement from North and West Philadelphia, notably Wilson Goode and Hardy Williams.[121] Richardson was a staunch advocate of Black Power, promoting unity in order to achieve control over local affairs. Bringing ideas about black empowerment into neighborhood activism, he proved very successful in organizing disparate African American community groups to protest against police brutality and school district policies, extending the Germantown tradition of advancing "our people" to the black community.[122]

History played an important role in Richardson's goals and strategy.[123] On November 17, 1967, calling for more black history and black studies courses taught by black teachers, Richardson led a walkout of two hundred Germantown High students. The protest had been coordinated with other city high schools, including South Philadelphia and Bok Vocational. As the Germantown students marched down Germantown Avenue toward Center City, students from Simon Gratz and other schools joined them. They all headed to the school district's Main Administration Building, where they clashed with police. In the fracas, Richardson was arrested. After the 1967 protest, he founded Young Afro-Americans (YAA), which formally organized his efforts to calm fights at Germantown High dances and, with similar groups like the Brickyard Youth Council and the Groovers, mediated conflicts between local gangs. YAA also pushed for reforms at Germantown High. In 1971, during a strike by the Philadelphia Federation of Teachers, Richardson developed the Germantown Area Schools Project as an alternative educational program for neighborhood children.

At its core, Richardson's work was about unifying a fragmented black community in order to have greater input into decisions affecting them.

For him, it started with education, including the teaching of history. Perhaps if the memory infrastructure had been more inclusive, the push for black studies in Germantown schools would have been less combative.

After the Bypass

The traditional leadership of Germantown was now forever changed. The rise of more active residents altered the composition of the Germantown Community Council, leading to internal challenges to its authority to speak on behalf of the community. A black caucus had formed within its board of directors in late 1968. In May 1969 the chairman of the caucus presented problems confronting the black residents of Germantown and stated that if the council did not address itself to those problems by August, "the black members would see no reason to continue with the council."[124] This challenge produced a co-directorship, with one white and one black board chair sharing administrative control, an arrangement that lasted two years. By 1970 the council was more diverse than it had ever been, with its thirty-eight members split evenly between black and white and representing a cross-section of neighborhood groups. Germantown Week changed again. It was now the Germantown People's Festival, a bi-cultural concert series designed to call attention to the deteriorating physical and social condition of Vernon Park.

A letter from the Germantown Community Council to the Philadelphia Health and Welfare Council in 1972 speaks to the oppositional stance to regional planning taken by some in the community. Though the topic is social services and funding for the poor, the message applies to the community's approach to planning and preservation: "We are opposed to a regionalism defined and imposed by national and state agenda. . . . It is important for a citizen-based planning agency to develop social planning out of the common concerns and imperatives and experiences of its constituent communities and to advocate such planning to the public authority."[125] But what happens when those "common concerns and imperatives and experiences" are voiced by multiple organizations without a concerted vision? The letter reflects a stubborn parochialism amid pressing needs and the willingness of Germantown's disparate leaders to accept pyrrhic victories over federal and state plans rather than achieving real change based on their own goals.

In 1975 Colonial Germantown, Inc., held its final meeting and disbanded. The venue, appropriately, was the Germantown Cricket Club, a famous Colonial Revival structure built for the community's elite. The organization had run deficits and had trouble retaining board members.[126] The professional developers working on behalf of an antiquarian vision for Market Square had lost out. Colonial Germantown, Inc., had done a fair bit to spruce up the square, and it had saved a dozen historic structures that might otherwise have been lost, but it failed to generate a larger renewal of Germantown Avenue.

The Germantown Community Council ended officially in 1973. Germantown's sense of itself as independent from Philadelphia had become a barrier to its becoming part of federal programs to develop the economy and overcome a decades-long decline. Opposition to the Magaziner plans created a semblance of unity.

New Leadership

What was left after the demise of Colonial Germantown, Inc., and the bypass plan was a consensus among black activists that liberal approaches to civil rights in northern cities were ineffective. Rejection of the bypass signaled the beginning of success for Germantown's black leadership. Earlier civil rights efforts, such as the YWCA's Inter-Racial Committee and the community audit, typified white liberal attempts, even if they involved prominent African Americans such as Sadie T. Alexander. They were also tied to Democratic machine politics.

Federal initiatives of the 1950s and 1960s, whether Eisenhower-era urban renewal projects or the Johnson administration's Model Cities program, stressed local political control, acting through community action committees. In Philadelphia the Democratic Tate administration (1962–1972) saw reduced federal investment in cities, but the idea of control by local politicians and community action committees persisted. It gave administrative control over such federal grants to local social service organizations, such as Germantown Settlement.[127] Under the Nixon administration, the rules were changed so that local politicians controlled decisions about the programs. Investment in the cities was no longer forthcoming. Black community organizers concluded that meaningful reform could not be left up to Washington as long as African Americans were not in a position to influence those decisions. In the late 1960s Philadelphia activists who were inspired by the Black Power movement and who aligned themselves with the Democrats pursued political power as a strategy for defending and advancing the movement's achievements.[128]

By 1970 African American community organizers were pushing for

greater representation in elected office. Hardy Williams had been elected state representative and one year later ran an unsuccessful yet highly
visible citywide race that received considerable attention and elevated the
promise of electoral power. The future mayor Wilson Goode managed
Williams's campaign. David Richardson, Goode and Williams's protégé,
ran for state representative in 1972 against a three-term Irish Catholic
realtor, Francis X. Rush. Richardson's electoral victory was stunning. He
carried his district by 15 percent, with such high voter turnout that three
of his assistant campaign aides were elected ward committee chairs at the
same time. He was twenty-three years old.

Germantown Settlement

That same year, Germantown Settlement, the neighborhood's largest social service agency, changed from Quaker control to control by African
Americans, led by Emanuel Freeman, the person who challenged me at
the Central Germantown Council meeting in 2005. Established in 1884
by Quaker women as a free kindergarten for the children of Irish and
Italian immigrant laborers, Germantown Settlement expanded into a social service agency that operated a library and children's programs and
advocated for better housing. Its white clientele had mostly fled Germantown by the late 1960s. By 1972 it had come to be seen as a high-minded
agency where white people distributed resources to black people, as it did
during the Morton Area Redevelopment in the 1950s. Richardson and
Freeman emerged from the black community that Germantown Settlement had served, both inspired with an entrepreneurial passion to change
the neighborhood.

   With Richardson in office and Germantown Settlement under the
growing influence of its black board members, including the twenty-four-
year old Freeman, African Americans now had more influence over local politicians' decisions about poverty and housing programs. Many of
the social, educational, housing, and antipoverty programs supported by
Germantown's representative in the state capital, including the Germantown Area Schools Project, were now run out of Germantown Settlement.
During the 1970s and 1980s, Richardson and Freeman made that agency
the chief conduit for channeling state funds into Germantown to support
Richardson's vision for the black community. Agencies run out of Germantown Settlement ultimately included the Greater Germantown Housing Development Corporation and the Central Germantown Council.[129]

Germantown's many other youth-serving and antipoverty groups, and programs run by churches, had a hard time getting around Germantown Settlement when they applied for funding from state and city agencies.

Getting Richardson, Freeman, and others into positions of power, and securing the decision-making authority of Germantown Settlement for four decades, represented a success for Germantown's African Americans. These developments produced leadership and stability for a large portion of the population that had been lacking it. This success, however, did not bring any greater leadership or focus to the rest of Germantown's multiple groups; it only enhanced the power of one. The idea of "Two Germantowns" in conflict would persist well into the twenty-first century.

Germantown Settlement declared bankruptcy in 2010 after numerous lawsuits and liens. Its leaders' tactics recalled some of the mistakes made by the members of the Colonial Revivalist old guard before the Second Battle of Germantown.[130] The leadership of Colonial Germantown, Inc., was too self-serving to win the popular support needed to accomplish its larger vision, while Germantown Settlement became more involved in skimming off the top of federal funds than in delivering services.[131] A reporter for the local public radio station wrote of its demise:

> Over the course of two decades, public funding under Germantown Settlement's umbrella totaled as much as $100 million. Tax liens were surfacing by 2004, but Settlement delved into housing and commercial real-estate developments and opened one of the city's first charter schools. Five years later, legal claims against Settlement stretched into the tens of millions of dollars and the charter was shuttered amid financial concerns that spurred a federal probe. Settlement was forced to sell off its remaining assets after the HUD-ordered foreclosure of two low-income senior-housing facilities in Germantown and all city funds to the agency were halted.[132]

The combative interactions and polarizing approaches of the 1950s and 1960s cultivated in the neighborhood an either/or style of leadership that foreclosed opportunities to work together for economic revival, let alone for a shared public history. Germantown by the 1970s had a majority African American population, and African Americans had significant decision-making power over social services. Center in the Park formed in 1968 to provide services to the elderly. The Neighborhood Interfaith

Movement formed in the 1970s to fill the void left by the Germantown Community Council; its coordination of religiously based youth education and job training programs continued into the twenty-first century. These successes did not yet extend into the sphere of public history or community memory. Without some representation of the black experience, Germantown's public history lacked the integrity to serve the entire neighborhood.

———•———

Basing hopes and plans for Germantown's economic revival on its colonial history must have seemed a reasonable bet in a time of Cold War–enhanced patriotism, when Colonial Williamsburg set the standard for interpreting public history. But could any public history program have brokered a dialogue among all of Germantown's stakeholders during this period? The traditional historical community was split between the Market Square colonial team and the people who wanted to preserve the Civil War monument and nineteenth-century improvements. The emerging voices of preservation professionals and a new generation of African American leaders rejected the vision of Colonial Germantown, Inc., outright.

The rise of black political leadership in Germantown coincided with, and was fueled by, the community's rejection of the bypass. A revitalization program based on a version of public history did not involve enough of the public to succeed. Failure to consult with African American community groups was proclaimed as a reason for the bypass's rejection. White residents as well as black residents rejected a closed process that redrew the neighborhood without consulting the people who lived there. The ability of the neighborhood's white elite to assert its power over the community was at an end. Above all, the period introduced black leadership for the neighborhood's decision-making bodies and an ethos that stressed black unity rather than access to white support.

Eventually the neighborhood's history would publicly include its African American community. The process of revealing Germantown's connection with the Underground Railroad brought together preservationists and African Americans and shone a spotlight on Germantown's nineteenth-century social activism rather than the colonial period. One building, and the community's experience of it, offered a way to rewrite Germantown history. The next chapter traces the Johnson House's evolution from a private home to an exclusive Women's Club to a National Historic Landmark on the Network to Freedom.

4

Integrity

*Making the Johnson House
the Heart of Historic Germantown*

By the start of the twenty-first century, the lack of an anchor for Germantown's African American history could no longer be ignored.

A person sitting at the bus stop on the corner of Washington Lane and Germantown Avenue, site of the Johnson House, can see a lot of history. A stone near the roof of the schoolhouse across the street dates the building to 1775. Next to the school is a burying ground that dates from 1693. A marker lists the names of the Revolutionary War soldiers buried there, including five labeled "unknown": Records suggest that the five were most likely people of Native American or African descent.[1] Directly across from the bus stop is a brick building with a "Built in 1761" sign. In front of the Johnson House is a marble stepping stone from the horse-and-carriage days. A steady stream of cars and city buses runs along and across the Belgian block stone paving, over rails once used by the 23 trolley.

From 2004 to 2006, I served as director of the Johnson House Historic Site. Working on that corner—sweeping up trash, shoveling snow, or giving tours—I noticed many people waiting for the bus there in silence. Every so often, though, one would pass the time by walking around, looking over the fence, and perhaps even reading the blue historical marker on the lawn. The marker states that the house was a site on the Underground Railroad during the 1850s. From time to time, someone would feel compelled to say out loud, to no one in particular: "Did you see this? This

THE JOHNSON HOUSE

Built in 1768 for John Johnson. This was home to three generations of a Quaker family who worked to abolish slavery and improve living conditions for freed African Americans. In the 1850s the house was a station on the Underground Railroad. Here and in smaller buildings on the property, men and women escaping slavery found shelter on their way to freedom.

Figure 4.1 Johnson House state historical marker, installed 1995. Evidence of the site's connection to the abolitionist movement and the Underground Railroad was uncovered in the 1980s. (Photo by the author.)

place was on the Underground Railroad. Really? I've waited for the bus here how many times? And I never saw this?"

Until the 1980s, or maybe even until the historical marker was installed in 1995, no one waiting for the 23 bus would have any way of knowing this history. Had it not been for Germantown's citizen historians, only a handful of people would have known about the role of the Johnson House as a station on the Underground Railroad.

In this chapter we explore the blend of fact and legend that made the Johnson House a National Historic Landmark on the Underground Railroad. We also see how the received historical narrative about a place can change. The Johnson House was involved in the Battle of Germantown and for many years was included in historic house tours because of its association with the battle. Having avoided demolition in 1980, it was declared a National Historic Landmark in 1997—not for that revolutionary connection but because it was a station on the Underground Railroad. Very little has been published about the Johnson House, so it is necessary to summarize the story and then tease out the trail of evidence that built the case for its national significance. As people outside established academic, government, and institutional history organizations became interested in their heritage and explored wider forms of evidence and novel techniques to uncover the past, they also pressed for monuments and museums that reflected new discoveries about old places like Germantown. The Johnson House shows how narratives change and how the memory infrastructure of a location evolves, expands, and brings new evidence into the process of how things get remembered and preserved, and why.

The efforts to make the Johnson House a historic site that illustrates or commemorates an episode of Germantown's African American history modified the established public history of the neighborhood. The rewritten narrative, which would supplement, rather than replace, the existing one, turned the house into a site of opportunity and agency, and not merely a nostalgic symbol for a bygone age.[2] The efforts to make the Johnson House a National Historic Landmark tested the limits of Germantown's public history and provided a stimulus for a more effective history. Johnson House filled a gap by showing a new story without destroying the former one. It restored part of the larger narrative of Germantown, extending it beyond the colonial history that had been used to set the neighborhood apart from the rest of Philadelphia.[3]

Germantown had not stopped trying to restore its colonial heritage, but new evidence about the past and a broader range of ways for the public to experience and understand it expanded the definition of "historic." When, finally, a house museum began to tell a chapter of African American history, the neighborhood's history gained an integrity that it had been lacking. A historical narrative that had been dismissed as irrelevant to the majority of its population overcame its limits. There is no better place to understand the complexities of Germantown's public history than on that corner of the avenue, where, hidden in plain sight, the Johnson House emerged in the late twentieth century as a new historic site.

History of the Everyday

New ways to consider Germantown's history emerged from several streams. A combination of new scholarship on slavery and abolition by academics, documentation by architectural historians, and detective work by passionate nonexperts drove the historical profession as a whole to embrace a broader social history.[4] The result was a larger canvas on which to present

American history in general. Preservation activities began to change when the results of the study of social history at the university level were applied to public history. The "new social history" used statistical and demographic analysis to look at history from the bottom up, rather than from the perspective of men or of the elite or in terms of military or political power. It was informed in part by structuralist and Marxist examinations of power structures and what got left out of the official story. It was also informed by intellectual honesty and an intention to convey a fuller sense of the past by analyzing topics such as diet, disease, and poverty. And it used methods and sources outside the official records, such as shipping lists and the memoirs and diaries kept by those who had typically been left out of received historical narratives.[5]

During the late 1960s and 1970s, Gary Nash and other historians examined the largely undertold history of Philadelphia's free black community, the largest in the United States before the Civil War.[6] Colonial histories explored non-elite perspectives, including those of lower-class Philadelphians.[7] A more detailed picture of Philadelphia's immigrants emerged.[8] The Philadelphia Social History Project, begun in the 1970s at the University of Pennsylvania, applied social science techniques to examine aspects of human behavior and relationships. Its director, Theodore Hershberg, expanded into subjects such as employment, social mobility, and urban growth.[9] (Hershberg also taught the first African American history class offered at an Ivy League university.)[10] While critics felt that the project overemphasized computation and never produced the full synthesis of urban history that it promised, it remained extremely influential, producing numerous dissertations and extending the reach of historical research.[11] As an outgrowth of this new research, the Philadelphia Social History Project provided historic sites with more evidence and new perspectives, affording the basis for telling a fuller version of history. Eventually, the content brought forth by these new forms of scholarship had the potential to allow wider audiences to see Germantown history as relevant to their own lives.

The new social history also made room for exploring sites and their context. If there were new stories to tell, historic buildings could be looked at differently. Living history sites such as Howell Farm in New Jersey and Conner Prairie in Indiana rejected the practice of using dressed-up reenactors to relive the role of ancestors; instead, interpreters revealed the workers' lives on a nineteenth-century farm. Similarly, beginning in 1988 the Lower East Side Tenement Museum in New York City brought scientific rigor to its mission of preserving and telling the life stories of immigrants who passed through the nineteenth-century building. This was preservation with an eye toward the kinds of stories that the original leaders of the preservation movement had avoided—those of newcomers to America. In the past, sites with connections to patriotic events had been favored. Certainly that had been true throughout the twentieth century in Germantown. Then, in the 1960s and 1970s, social historians began to argue that history as presented had served primarily elite narratives and taken a conservative approach to the material remains of the past that neglected most of the story and, even worse, discouraged the rest of the population from engaging with history to gain a fuller understanding of the past.[12]

The challenges of crafting a shared history continued to confront Germantown, but now opportunities suggested themselves. Rather than having too many descendant-based groups celebrating the story of their people, the historic buildings of Germantown allowed the recovery of the stories of all sorts of different groups and their respective histories. The "power of place," in Delores Hayden's use of the term—the "power of place to nurture citizens' public memory, to encompass shared time in the form of shared territory"—had been problematic for Germantown because so little territory had been shared and so much of the preservation work of the twentieth century had separated sites of memory from nourishing social networks in the community.[13] The "power of place" had divided as much as it unified. Could drawing more attention to different histories offer the neighborhood what it needed: a less contested historic territory? Germantown's problems—too many institutions, a sense of separation from downtown historic sites, and a melancholy longing for an idealized past—would challenge and engage new people who became interested in Germantown's history.

Robert Ulle, a graduate student from the University of Pennsylvania's social history project who happened to be Mennonite, applied strategies based on demographic and social history to Germantown. His research into African American churches focused on the growth of Germantown's black community since its founding in the 1680s. The results of Ulle's work informed the activities of the Germantown Mennonite Historic Trust, which saved Historic RittenhouseTown and the Johnson House from demolition in the 1980s.[14]

Stephanie G. Wolf analyzed Germantown families and produced a unique in-depth social history.[15] Her *Urban Village*, primarily about the colonial period, focuses not on the houses or the 1777 battle but on family and social and economic life in the village of Germantown. She illustrates what its various ethnic groups brought to Germantown, a transitional neighborhood where people arrived, established themselves, and left, only to be replaced by another group trying to make a go of life in Pennsylvania. Wolf's conceptual framework uses anthropology, demographic analysis, and sociology to look at historical familial and business relationships.[16]

Ulle and Wolf helped to establish continuity between Germantown and the rest of the region in ways that broadened what Germantowners considered "historic" and pushed the local antiquarian historical community as well. The Germantown Historical Society's newsletter, the *Germantown Crier,* began publishing works by professional scholars: Margaret Hope Bacon examined religion in Germantown, Margaret Tinkcom documented its colonial buildings in order to designate them and save them from demolition, and David Contosta covered all of German Township, including Chestnut Hill. The history of the everyday helped Germantown's historical community, professional and antiquarian, extend its thin base of support in the neighborhood. When people from outside established circles contributed their energies, new opportunities emerged.

Citizen Historians and "Criterion P"

One bright April day in 2005, twenty students from Mennonite High School in North Philadelphia came to the Johnson House to assist in an archeology project called "Beneath the Underground Railroad." The eleventh graders became the latest in a long line of citizen historians who have helped the public look beneath the surface and see the past in a different, sharper light. "Outsider history makers," as Benjamin Filene calls them— not necessarily descended from elite founding families or trained in academic history—have a long tradition in Germantown.[17] They bring their passionate curiosity and help shape what gets remembered. Germantown's African American history would be much less rich without them.

In Philadelphia, from John Fanning Watson's *Annals* to Edward Lawler's discoveries about the President's House, citizen historians have done more to push the boundaries than many of the collecting institutions or historic sites.[18] Often the passion that ordinary citizens bring to learning more about the past raises important questions that challenge what is presented by established museums and historic sites. Their methods may be prone to error, as when they rely on a single source or on oral traditions without corroboration; sometimes their conclusions fall short of the solid detective work of conservation scientists or preservation professionals. Taken as part of a larger body of evidence, however, the work of outsiders can inspire further scrutiny and enable fuller investigations that lead to a greater understanding of the past. National Park Service historians informally consider the passion of motivated citizen historians to be one aspect of "Criterion P."[19] The other *P* is political influence. That passion of outsiders and the contemporary political situation play crucial roles in this chapter. Germantown history gained new chapters and a new sense of urgency when passionate outsiders helped address the lack shortchanging of African American history in the neighborhood and the region.

Germantown, with its many house museums, ended its attempt to create a miniature Williamsburg in 1975 when Colonial Germantown, Inc., held its last meeting. Yet the neighborhood still had no monuments or historic markers for black people when the publication of Alex Haley's *Roots* in 1976 and its enormous popularity as a television series in 1977 prompted African Americans all over the country to explore their personal connections to American history. Charles Blockson, Louise Strawbridge, and Edward Robinson worked outside Philadelphia's established museums and university history departments to do research, identify gaps in the historical narrative, and advocate for ways to fill them. Working independently, they brought African American history to broader publics in the neighborhood and the region. Blockson explored his family's connection to the Underground Railroad. Louise Strawbridge interviewed Germantown's African American seniors about their experiences in the twentieth century, often publishing her work in local newspapers. In part because of his close relationship with his nephew, state representative David Richardson, Edward Robinson emphasized African nationalism and was instrumental in drafting a new social studies curriculum for Philadelphia schools.[20] During the 1970s Robinson helped build an intellectual framework for understanding the Black Power movement in terms of the African American heritage in Philadelphia and especially in Germantown and Mount Airy. As he made the rounds of high school auditoriums and church groups, Robinson contributed to a political milieu for teaching history and fostered an interest in exploring the heritage of Germantown's black community. Blockson, Strawbridge, and Robinson brought their personal curiosity to their subjects; they began to connect dots and reveal connections that had not been seen before by either the antiquarians or the academic historians.

Strawbridge, an artist and a descendant of an established Philadelphia family, worked for Center in the Park, a home for senior citizens, in the 1980s. Center in the Park was founded in 1968 and moved to the site of the old Carnegie library in Vernon Park in 1986. Strawbridge was coordinator of the center's activities, and much of her work was based on oral histories collected there. She became a regular visitor to the Germantown Historical Society as she tried to put these stories into context. Many of the participants in the program were African American, and her unfamiliarity with the black community led her to scour the archives for source material. There was not much. One of her finds was J. Gordon Baugh Jr.'s 1913 *Souvenir of Germantown*. With the help of the seniors at the Center in the Park, Strawbridge published an annotated version of Baugh's commemorative booklet in the 1983 and 1984 issues of the *Germantown Crier*, replacing Baugh's terse captions, such as "place where our people bought butter and eggs," with the names of the businesses or homeowners in the photographs. The project rediscovered a world long gone and represented some of the Germantown Historical Society's first public steps in an effort to document the neighborhood's African American history.

Strawbridge's oral history project at the Center in the Park led to a series of programs recording the African American community's experience of Germantown in the twentieth century.[21] The findings included details of social and residential segregation based on the reflections of graduates of the neighborhood's many schools and youth clubs. Originally, Strawbridge recounted, "I was not prepared to hear about growing up in such a segregated—and prejudiced—world."[22] Soon a fuller picture of the all-black Hill School, known as the "Colored School," emerged, along with accounts of the early years of the Wissahickon Boys Club and the vibrant black branches of the Young Men's and Young Women's Christian Associations. Published in the *Crier* and in local newspapers, Strawbridge's work established a documentary record of the African American community.

This work shaped the memory infrastructure. In a 1987 ceremony that brought together many graduates of the Joseph Hill School, a marker was installed on the site where the school had been.[23] It was one of the first markers to identify an exclusively African American site. More important, it commemorates a local touchstone of everyday working-class life that is now gone—not some signature event or nationally prominent figure. An even more ambitious project that grew out of the oral histories was the *Philadelphia Courthouse Mural*. The artist, Douglass Cooper, illustrated and often quoted episodes narrated by seniors at the Center in the Park.

The panoramic work, completed in 1995, covers eighty years of the city's history, including wartime work at the Navy Yard, churches and clubs, and civil rights protests in the 1950s and 1960s. It also illustrates some of the isolated black neighborhoods within Germantown, working a kind of subjective mapping into the artwork.[24] With the oral histories made visible and tangible, Germantown's African American community was extending its own sense of place into the memory infrastructure.

This level of history gathering served Germantown well because it led to a reconsideration of established claims for the neighborhood's national significance.

During the late 1970s the Germantown Historical Society applied to extend Germantown's National Historic Landmark District to include more buildings in the Mount Airy neighborhood, many of them not from the colonial era. In 1977 the National Park Service approved that extension of Germantown's National Historic Landmark District. Yet even the updated nomination of 1977 shows how much Germantown's sense of separate identity depended on the colonial period: "The American Revolution and the winning of independence greatly influenced Germantown. Most important the post-Revolutionary years speeded up the Americanization of Germantown. General political, economic, and social events destroyed the community's remnants of isolation, and its unique character receded into history."[25] Making a case that Germantown's public history helped bring people into the American narrative was a new way of understanding the neighborhood's many varieties of "our people" as sharing a larger, common heritage.

Germantown's unique character derives in large measure from its continual wrestling with the meaning of the past one hundred years. To understand Germantown, it is not enough to know what happened in the past; it is important also to know how its history was constantly being rediscovered. Shortly after the nomination to extend the district was approved, the Johnson House would become the center of a movement to declare it, and its connections to nineteenth-century African American history, nationally significant. Not only had Germantown's uniqueness not "receded into history"; through its ability to reshape the public understanding of the past, it had added another fascinating episode to U.S. history. The work of outsiders continually helped to expand public memory and our understanding of the past; now they would help establish in Germantown a National Historic Landmark that stood for African American history.

Expanding the Memory Infrastructure

No episode in Germantown's preservation history better exemplifies the evolution of public history than the Johnson House Historic Site.[26] Expanding the public memory infrastructure by establishing the house as an Underground Railroad station was a culmination of all the threads explored in this book—and yet it also illustrates the challenge of getting Germantown to overcome its legacy of divisions and embrace a shared history.

The Johnson House campaign brought together the community's history of social activism, the vibrancy of its politically powerful black community, and the evolving historic house museum field in an effort that preserved the house and made it the heart and soul of historic Germantown. Both facets of Criterion P were involved: passionate citizen historians and a political moment when Germantown needed a prominent emblem of African American heritage. And that building, slumbering on the corner of Germantown Avenue and Washington Lane, where it was long known as a colonial site and the former home of a women's club, came to be seen as a place where blacks found safety on the road to freedom and a symbol of people working together.

Like much of the history of the Underground Railroad, the Johnson House story rests on a blend of fact and tradition. The case for establishing it as an Underground Railroad landmark likewise mixes historical evidence and embellishment, some of it elucidating the contradictions that are typical of Germantown history. The Underground Railroad itself, though mentioned in scattered sources in the late nineteenth and early twentieth centuries, was rarely studied, much less promoted publicly, until the 1970s.[27] Charles Blockson and Robert Ulle, coming from different perspectives and working independently, spearheaded the drive to research the house, secure funding, and arrange limited tours there. Their detective work shows in the continual progress of the public history as a discipline.

Germantown had been overlooked in the annals of Philadelphia Underground Railroad history. It is not mentioned in Baugh's *Souvenir*. A scholarly history of Philadelphia in honor of the city's tercentenary asserts, "Both Philadelphia and neighboring Phoenixville were important junction points on the routes that slaves followed northward."[28] Germantown's discovery of the Underground Railroad started with an unlikely source: an obscure novel titled *The Riversons: A Tale of the Wissahickon*.[29]

The book's author, S. J. Bumstead, was from New England but studied medicine in Philadelphia. He had some correspondence with Hiram Corson, a member of a leading abolitionist family from Plymouth Meeting and Norristown, in Montgomery County, several miles from Germantown.[30] Why this aspiring physician was writing fanciful novels is unclear, and his account may not be accurate or provable. The question is worth considering here because the novel was the primary evidence for giving the Underground Railroad a larger role in Germantown's public memory.

The novel tells the story of the Riversons, a Germantown family who operated a mill along the Wissahickon Creek and ran into tough times in the mid-nineteenth century. Old Colonel Riverson had died and left his family's mill holdings in a perilous state, forcing his children to work in the mills of nearby Manayunk to fend off creditors. It is not hard to see the real-life people and settings behind the fictional characters. Many references to Germantown's Mennonite churches and Quaker schools are undisguised. "Trexel, Lorgan and Co." recalls Drexel, Morgan and Company, a major bank in Philadelphia and New York. The Riversons themselves seem to be a composite of industrial families of the Wissahickon, such as the Rittenhouses, and some antislavery families of Germantown and Norristown, such as the Johnsons and the Corsons.

Young Marian Riverson's habit of walking in her sleep at night through the Wissahickon Valley causes public alarm. Often she comes back with gold coins in her hand, arousing suspicion. Is she robbing people, or perhaps selling herself, to help the family pay off their creditors? A friend, Dr. Sydney Ransom, finds out that her sleepwalking takes her to caves in the hills along the Wissahickon. Exploring, Ransom meets people who transport freedom seekers to the caves in a Dearborn wagon; there the escaping slaves hide before moving on to abolitionist sympathizers in Germantown. (A Dearborn wagon had a roof and sometimes side panels that could conceal riders.) The path of their escape runs from Norristown in the west across the Flat Rock Dam on the Schuylkill River, through the Wissahickon Valley, across the Wissahickon at Crease Lane, and on down Township Line Road (now Wissahickon Avenue) to a signal that shows the location of the caves in which they hide. As he becomes more familiar with the caves, Ransom figures out that Marian Riverson is sleepwalking each night to the cave where the old colonel hid his gold. The family uses the gold to pay their debts, Marian's reputation is restored, and she and Ransom are wed. Descriptions of Underground Railroad activities amount to only a small portion of the narrative.

The novel is mentioned briefly in a paragraph in a 1926 issue of the old Germantown business journal *The Beehive*. This item, titled "Lost Cave in the Wissahickon," reports that a local man, William Shingle, had talked about caves along the Wissahickon Creek, including one where a dog had been lost. He went on to relate a Germantown tradition that "such a cavern existed and was used in the Civil War times as a hiding place for runaway slaves who came in on the underground railway." Shingle's description of the path taken by the fugitives matches the one described in *The Riversons*. The article concludes: "There is in existence a little-known novel, *The Riversons,* says Mr. Shingle, written by Umstead, who lived in RittenhouseTown. It was written before the Civil War but attracted little attention."[31] Though the article gets the author's name and the chronology wrong (the novel was written well after the Civil War), the importance of this casual reference cannot be overstated.

The Bumstead novel and the *Beehive* article matter because Charles Blockson used them as the primary evidence that the route to freedom from the South ran through eastern Philadelphia, then northwest to Germantown, up to New Hope, Pennsylvania, across the Delaware River to New Jersey, and north to New York and Canada. Blockson was a teacher in the Norristown School District who began to research African American genealogy after reading William Still's 1872 history *The Underground Railroad*, from which he learned that his ancestors were involved with the Underground Railroad.[32]

Beginning in the late 1970s, members of the Mennonite congregation in Germantown also made some important discoveries. Until 1980 the Johnson House was run by the Women's Club of Germantown and used for card parties and dances (the actress Grace Kelly had a birthday party there). After 1980 the house was in danger of being lost until the Germantown Mennonite Historic Trust bought it for a dollar. The Mennonite historian Melvin Gingerich noted that its builder was an early Mennonite minister and the Dutch-German architecture was important to Mennonite history nationally. Members of the local historical community, including the curator of Wyck and the executive director of the Mennonite Historic Trust, lived in the Johnson House at various times as caretakers. Ulle's research into black community churches in the 1970s set the stage for a deeper understanding of the house.

The 1768 Dutch Colonial farmhouse was built by Jacob Knorr, the same woodworker who built Cliveden, the Germantown Mennonite Meeting, and other local buildings. Samuel Johnson (1777–1847) and his wife,

Jennett Rowland Johnson (1784–1876), occupied the house after 1805. They had ten children, all of them members of antislavery organizations in the Philadelphia region.[33] Rowland Johnson was perhaps the best known. He was a leader in the Longwood Yearly Meeting of Progressive Friends, later a "station master" in West Orange, New Jersey, and a vice president of the American Anti-Slavery Society. He and his brother Israel Johnson founded the Junior Anti-Slavery Society of Philadelphia when they were twenty and eighteen years old, respectively. Abolitionist activities brought them and the other Johnsons and their large extended families into contact with national figures in the movement, such as Lucretia Mott and William Still. In a letter to his brother Ellwood, Israel Johnson describes the violent opposition to an 1838 antislavery meeting at Pennsylvania Hall in downtown Philadelphia, which resulted in a riot and arson: "The whole building was in one sheet of flames!!! The light was so great that they saw it very plain at Germantown."[34] Family members' exact role in antislavery circles is not well known. Perhaps their considerable wealth allowed them to avoid commercial, religious, and political repercussions in a largely Democratic and proslavery Philadelphia.

It was easy to show that the Johnsons were abolitionists. Proving that they were Underground Railroad station masters was a bit trickier. Family traditions going back 150 years suggested all manner of activity, such as meetings with agents at the house and even narrow escapes by fugitives through the roof during slave patrols. Many local secondary sources bear some of this out. One mentions that a Johnson traveled "a thousand miles to track down and rescue a family of poor free blacks that had been kidnapped from their home in Sussex, Delaware by the infamous slave traders of that day."[35] Sussex County was the home of Jennett Rowland Johnson's family. Some later accounts put the Johnsons at an important intersection of Underground Railroad traffic by describing them as wagon drivers for escapees on the route from Chester County, through Norristown to Germantown to points further east.[36] Blockson suggests that the Johnson family held meetings in Germantown attended by William Still and Harriet Tubman. The reference to abolitionist meetings at the Johnsons' home is important, since there are records of such meetings being held nearby.[37]

Germantown in the early 1800s was undergoing a transformation from quaint village to developing commercial district and seeing an increasing variety of religious and political activity. It had been home to several nativist groups in the 1830s and 1840s, at the same time the Underground Railroad was operating there.[38] The story of Margaret Brooke illustrates abolitionist activity in this period.[39] A slave catcher stole her from a Germantown farm in 1837, where she worked as a paid servant, and the following year a group of Quakers purchased her freedom for four hundred dollars from a Baltimore slave owner. We know that in 1840 Israel Johnson tried to integrate the local Friends meeting.[40] And the railroad line often used by the Vigilance Committee, the Philadelphia-Germantown-Norristown Railroad, could easily spirit people from 9th Street in Philadelphia through Germantown and Norristown, both centers of abolitionist activity.[41]

Questions remain, however. Exactly how was the Johnson House used for abolitionist activity? How many runaways did the Johnsons or their relatives actually help on their road to freedom? The Johnsons are not mentioned in Still's *The Underground Railroad.* As in any research on the Underground Railroad, precise documentary evidence is hard to find. Nonetheless, the family's connections to important communities—abolitionist, Quaker, business, school, and extended kinship network—provided areas worth pursuing.

The Johnson House, as noted earlier, stands at an important intersection, where Washington Lane and Germantown Avenue meet. At a time when there were very few cross streets because farmers did not want to divide their land, Washington Lane was a vital passage from the mills of the Wissahickon Creek past Lucretia Mott's house (and the African American community at La Mott, as well as Camp William Penn, established in 1863 to train units of the U.S. Colored Troops), and on to farms in Montgomery and Bucks Counties. The Kirk and Nice funeral parlor, the Concord School, the Washington Inn (a tavern hotel), and several other businesses, most related to making or selling leather goods, stood among the properties of the Johnsons and neighboring families. It was an active corner. Promising leads about who may have come through Germantown have tended to stem from the immediate neighborhood.

Johnson House owes its National Historic Landmark status to childhood recollections that helped clarify the relationship of the house to the rest of the neighborhood. Edward Johnson (1847–1919) in a memoir of his 1850s childhood, for instance, describes how the house was used:

> My cousin could not understand how so many different colored people were in the back garret. It seemed to her a different family was there every time she went up to it. They would be there at night and gone in the morning. One of my earliest recollections

was being wakened early in the morning by furious knocking at the back door. My father answered it and coming back said that a big colored man, a slave was there, with a note which said he was trying to escape and please to give him food and clothing and help him to the next station. I remember giving him his breakfast; getting the Dearborn wagon; putting him in the back part; covering him with straw and a piece of carpet. We then drove back Washington Lane several miles to put him on the right road to some Quaker farmer in Montgomery County whose name was in the note and whom my father knew. We afterward heard through the underground channels that he got safely to Canada where he was free.[42]

Edward Johnson was the son of Ellwood Johnson (1823–1907), who became the owner of the house on the death of his father, Samuel, in 1847.

B. Frank Kirk was a Germantown fixture in the late 1800s, running the family business, the Kirk and Nice funeral parlor, which was founded in 1769 and labeled itself the oldest funeral home in America. He was the nephew of Charles Kirk, described by William Still as a "helper."[43] The Kirks were a prominent abolitionist family in Norristown, and they lived and worked close to another noted abolitionist family, the Corsons.

The funeral home stood across the street from the Johnson House. Frank Kirk later told a newspaper reporter, "I remember wondering why so many families of black people lived in the attic of the Johnson house one night and then the next morning were gone."[44] The references to the "back garret" and the "attic" are important, as they refer to an attic above the kitchen where there is a potentially significant piece of physical evidence: a two-foot by three-foot hatch opening onto the roof. Johnson family lore had long held that people hiding in the attic once had to sneak out onto the roof and hide there to avoid a slave patrol.[45]

Kirk also recalled meetings of important abolitionists:

Germantown, in old slavery days, was a station of the "Underground Railway" for the escape of fugitive slaves. Many a barn in Germantown and many a house too would be used for sheltering these people. . . .

On one occasion there was a meeting of the secret officers of the Underground Railway. I happened to be home that night and my father introduced me to the big guns. Among the number was

Figure 4.2 Johnson House, north elevation with hatch door, 2018. The hatch door on the roof, visible on the right side, near the chimney, was reportedly used by freedom seekers to escape from law enforcement during the 1850s; once hidden, it was revealed by a 2009 restoration project. (Photo by the author.)

William Still. . . . Another prominent director at that meeting was Harriet Tubman, who made nineteen journeys from Maryland and Virginia to Canada, leading nearly five hundred colored people from the chains of slavery to freedom, some of whom lingered in Germantown and are living with their children here today. The heads of many Quaker families in Germantown were at that meeting and gave substantial aid to help along the good work. The directors of the Underground Railway ran a big risk in their work but they were working for a good cause, and took chances that men in other businesses would not have dared to go into. All these men and women were not only abolitionists, but they were all temperance people and every one church members.[46]

Were there also abolitionist meetings at the Johnson House? These records suggest a role without necessarily defining it. And the many unverifiable sources give rise to other sources, including novels, memoirs, and family lore, fertile ground for myth making. The examples in this chapter suggest that even stories can be linked to documentary evidence and suggestive connections. For instance, Blockson has identified "Johnson Hall" as the site of meetings with speakers such as Harriet Tubman and Frederick Douglass.[47] Business directories of Germantown offer no record of a Johnson Hall. Could the Johnson House be what was meant? The Frank Kirk and Edward Johnson accounts just cited name Pomona Grove or Pomona Hall as a meeting site. Pomona was a home directly across the street from the Johnson House on the same block of Germantown Avenue. Is it possible that Harriet Tubman came to Germantown? The presence of Lucretia Mott within the Johnsons' circle increases the likelihood that she did, since Mott reported taking Tubman around to meetings and churches in the late 1850s.[48] It is plausible that a community where well-to-do families with shared political sympathies had helped purchase someone's freedom in 1838 might also pull together to donate money to the Vigilance Committee and other supporters of Underground Railroad activities.

Confirmation of the Johnson House as an Underground Railroad station grew out of historians' use of a broad variety of sources. This use of multiple sources is true of all Underground Railroad research, since illegal activity and clandestine operations make for scant documentation. In the context of the Germantown historical community, however, it represented a wider approach to sources than had been used before. Family letters, memoirs, and papers provided some clues, as have stray accounts, such as that published in the 1926 *Beehive.* Members of the extended family lived in areas known to be involved in the Underground Railroad. Letters from family members discussed Philadelphia abolitionist activities, though not the hiding of runaways. Israel Johnson's stirring description of the events surrounding the burning of Pennsylvania Hall in 1838, probably the low point in Philadelphia's antislavery history, was seen in a different light. Edward Johnson's 1909 memoir became crucial to establishing a link between the house and its use as a safe haven. The family papers contain an undated list of names, seemingly an invitation list, which includes members of the abolitionist community and their families, such as Lucretia Mott, John Needles, and Samuel Nickless.[49]

Census data and property records were especially helpful in establishing connections to antislavery efforts and historical continuity between the 1768 house and activities in the 1840s and 1850s. Originally the Johnson family holdings extended for two square miles, all the way to the Wissahickon Creek, the site of dozens of mills and a link to the river traffic connecting Germantown to Norristown. The property was the site of a farm and a tannery. Its many outbuildings included a hat shop and a cobbler's shop, which used the leather produced at the tannery. Among the many people who lived and worked in this area were the Anderson family and individuals named Elijah Baynard and John and Lucy Douglas (also spelled "Dugles"). Baynard is mentioned in a couple of later newspaper accounts as an Underground Railroad agent who brought people through the Wissahickon Valley from Norristown to Germantown (sometimes hiding them in caves). He also made hats on Justus Johnson's property, nearby on what is now Tulpehocken Street.[50]

Ulle connected these sources with other data, producing a richer (though by no means complete) depiction of the neighborhood in the period than had been available before. In 1850, for instance, 42 percent of the African American residents of Germantown (50 out of 118) were born in slave states. In 1860, the percentage was lower even though the black population was higher (38 out of 143).[51] Ulle compared these census figures with property records of the time, noting that eight people of color are listed as part of the households of the Johnsons of Germantown and elsewhere. They were listed as paid servants on census data from 1850 through 1880. Most members of Germantown's sparse African American population lived near three locations, one of which was the intersection of Washington Lane and Germantown Avenue. The second important source of information was the direct result of Philadelphia abolition efforts. In 1838 and 1847 the Pennsylvania Abolition Society conducted a census of the free black population. These records, intended to give a fuller count of the city's established free black community than the federal census did, present a unique picture of life in the city, though with little description in the Germantown section.[52] Ulle compared these records with reports of court cases (including that of Margaret Brooke from Maryland) that suggested other records existed that could supplement the picture derived from the census records. Susan Lewis, described by Charles Kirk as a person helped to freedom through purchase by Quaker families, was a party in one such case that suggested connections among disparate parts of the Philadelphia region connecting in some ways with Germantown.[53]

This research firmly established the Johnson House as a station on the Underground Railroad and inspired further stewardship activity. The Johnson House opened for tours in the 1980s, and a local board of directors was formed. The board hired part-time staff in 1997. The Johnson House now had a significance that was entirely separate from its period of construction, its role in a revolutionary battle in 1777, and its colonial-era architecture. This development goes to the heart of historical continuity and shows how a historic building can evolve in public memory as the public rewrites its meaning. A similar reevaluation lies behind the examination by Cliveden, Stenton, and other sites of their nineteenth-century histories and the legacy of the Chews and Logans as slave-owning families in the Mid-Atlantic region. Cliveden began to illustrate the history of the family's servants, including Irish immigrants, and its numerous plantations in Delaware and Maryland.

Ulle's work inspired him and other researchers to look at other sources in different ways. Edward Johnson's 1909 memoir and B. Frank Kirk's reminiscences were the kind of antiquarian recollections of olden times that filled issues of *The Beehive* and other Germantown papers. But scrutinized and subjected to deeper analysis by Ulle, Blockson, and others, these sources explained and connected to previously unexplored aspects of Germantown history. Even old, forgotten novels, they realized, might offer information.

Confirmation that one eighteenth-century building, the Johnson House, could be interpreted so differently when viewed in a nineteenth-century context led staffs and researchers at other sites to explore the full life of the historic buildings of Germantown. Two examples are noteworthy. The Concord School, a 1775 schoolhouse, is across the street from the Johnson House. Teacher lists and other records indicate that a fuller rendering of the neighborhood's history is in order. One treasurer's record book indicates the presence of a "black student" in 1847. In May 1857, two dollars in rent was paid by "a colored family." When Philadelphia began offering free public education in 1840, teachers rented the schoolhouse. It is possible that, in this predominantly Quaker section of town, educational opportunities were offered to poor or minority students,[54] in keeping with the practice of many Quaker schools for the poor that opened in the 1840s and 1850s. Furthermore, records indicate that the school paid William Still five dollars in 1869, well after the Civil War, when Still was a steward (with Israel Johnson) of organizations involved in the care of freedmen and freedwomen. (This was three years before the publication of his seminal book on the Underground Railroad.) The schoolhouse research has not yet turned up a list of students, but a collection of old books in the school that have students' names scribbled on the pages holds the promise of filling in some gaps.

An inventory of the schoolhouse collection that involves gathering the names inscribed in the books is ongoing. Perhaps these names, when cross-referenced against census data, Still's book, documents related to the property of the Johnsons and their relatives, and other neighborhood records, will reveal Germantown residents of African American descent who came from slave states and remained in the area.

Placing a Value on History

The integrated effort to save the Johnson House and turn it into a museum grew out of the same kind of effort that more than a century earlier had gone into organizing and running the Underground Railroad in Germantown.[55] The Mennonite Historic Trust promoted the connection between the Johnson House and African American heritage in the neighborhood, and its powerful message of whites and blacks working for a shared goal. Staff from the Mennonite Trust, staff and board members from Cliveden, community members, and African American professionals convened a working group. In 1997 a friends group led by the African American sorority Delta Sigma Theta, using Cliveden of the National Trust for a pass-through of grant money, formed a nonprofit corporation to lead preservation and planning efforts. With funding from the William Penn Foundation, the effort to rewrite the history of the Johnson House and present a new version of its old history within the context of the African American history of Germantown was now under way. The Johnson House also became an active member of the Historic Germantown Preserved consortium of sites. Supporters from the neighborhood were recruited, and a co-stewardship agreement was drafted, providing for the Mennonite Historic Trust to own the site for five years but for the Friends of the Johnson House to manage it until the end of the term.[56]

The Johnson House matters for three important reasons. First, it showed that public history can be rewritten and the public understanding of a site can change. The fact that the building was preserved in the first place allowed it to be researched more thoroughly and reinterpreted. That preservation is, in part, a legacy of previous efforts—by the Women's Club, for instance. Second, the Johnson House is the culmination of a long process in which the historical profession in Germantown came closer to its own neighborhood environment. A historic site that speaks to the role of whites and blacks working together to make life better for people conveys a positive message. Finally, the whole project represents a triumph of Criterion P, with passionate nonexperts working together with aspiring and veteran historians to expand the neighborhood's memory and restore a missing piece of its narrative. Germantown's political situation in the 1970s and 1980s demanded it. If history was to matter to Germantown, and if the political leadership was to see any value in Germantown house museums, the neighborhood's African American population needed to see themselves represented in one.

Highlighting the role of passion and politics, however, is not the same as saying that political pressure made the Johnson House a National Historic Landmark on the Underground Railroad. Instead, the process shows the ebb and flow of public memory. Outsider historians created an interest in African American history that supported a call for a monument to that history. The leadership, population, and connection with grassroots informants with the passion and advocacy of outsider historians such as Blockson, Strawbridge, and Robinson captured the attention of a generation. The Bicentennial and *Roots* had inspired a deeper examination of their own and their neighbors' backgrounds and heritage and led them to ask whether existing historic landmarks reflected it. The gaps in Germantown's public memory were being rectified.

The story of the Johnson House's designation shows effective public history at work. The effort activated long-dormant stories, sought an understanding of key questions from multiple perspectives, and allowed people to take an active part in new discoveries. The Johnson House Historic Site had been empty, but it had remained standing long enough that people could find new meaning in it. It played an essential role in creating a fuller narrative in Germantown and Philadelphia. Some of its preservation value lay in the information that the Johnson House story contained, which now casts a new light on life in nineteenth-century Germantown and on the history of abolitionism and social activism. The site, now staffed largely by part-time guides and volunteers and overseen by a primarily African American board of directors, continues to be one of the most visited sites in Germantown. Its compelling story inspires art and music projects by neighborhood groups.

The work of the eleventh-grade archaeologists from Mennonite High School produced twelve hundred artifacts in 2005: small pieces of plates, bowls, pipes, tools, bone fragments, and food leavings, remnants of the everyday activities of the Johnson family and, perhaps, people who stayed in the house or its outbuildings. The high school archaeology project uncovered foundation walls of buildings that previous studies by preservation architects had missed. Professional archaeologists took the students to the laboratory to take part in analysis of the artifacts so they could learn more about what they had dug out, sifted, and sorted. Students then guided staff as they constructed a small exhibition on display. The project, titled "Beneath the Underground Railroad," brought together new histories of the everyday with the passion of outsider historians to show more of Germantown's history in different ways. In Germantown, as in many other communities, outsiders have a way of moving the past forward to the great benefit of public history.

Johnson House and Its Value to Germantown

The archaeology project showed the information value of the site, and ongoing research on the best way to stabilize and preserve the building is ongoing. A 2005 "Save America's Treasures" grant brought in money to repair the roof, rehabilitate the outbuilding, and remove deteriorating plaster and repoint the exterior stone. In the process, important features of the building, such as the exterior roof hatch, were revealed. Because of that work, the building will stand for many years to come. Yet there is still much to learn about the site and how it was used. Can we learn the names and stories of the people who used the house for escape? This question motivates continuing research and animates the site with energy whenever people experience it and learn about current research and new findings. An incomplete historical narrative can inspire future historians.

The Johnson House also embodies cultural and symbolic value for the neighborhood. The preservation of an important African American site makes Historic Germantown stand for far more than the colonial period. The story of African Americans taking matters into their own hands and finding their way to freedom before the Civil War is as vital to understanding Germantown's role in American history as the revolutionary-era Battle of Germantown. The Johnson House offers a narrative of uplift that runs counter to the longstanding narrative of neighborhood decline. The neighborhood's traditional history community once mourned its inability to offer more to its neighbors. An officer of the Germantown Historical Society wrote in 1985: "The melancholy condition of much of Germantown is diverse and complex. Unless we work to improve our community, we cannot in the long run even preserve our monuments. They would become like provincial tombs of some long-forgotten local families, and their importance would be lost."[57] The work that identified the Johnson House as a historic site on the Underground Railroad grew out of an energetic approach to history that embraced "diverse and complex" stories.

One of the chief results of this energy and the new narrative of opportunity, hope, and progress was to make more prominent the stories of workers, immigrant groups, and African Americans. The new historic sites, groups, and house museums established from the mid-1960s to the mid-1980s—the Johnson House, Maxwell Mansion, Historic Rittenhouse-Town, Germantown Mennonite Historic Trust—became active in reshaping the Germantown historical narrative to fully integrate the narratives of everyday life and of immigrants and African Americans. But history must have more than symbolic or informational value; it must also play a role in the social and economic life of the neighborhood. It is interesting to look at the impact of the Johnson House in relation to previous attempts to use history to revitalize Germantown, including failed developments on the Colonial Williamsburg model. Clearly, the Johnson House changed the narrative for all of Germantown by highlighting the importance of people outside the elite and demonstrating that a longer chronology is essential to understanding the place. The Johnson House also changed the sense of how history can serve economic goals.

In the 1990s new community development corporations emerged and attempted to challenge Germantown Settlement's control. Settlement had become a powerful group, serving its version of "our people" and favoring projects that benefited its leadership rather than the neighborhood as a whole. Plans involved different neighborhood activists and sought to go beyond the narrow focus of the leadership of the 1960s and 1970s, the era of Colonial Germantown, Inc., and Germantown Settlement under Emanuel Freeman. As these community development organizations produced new plans and recommendations for Germantown Avenue, it became clear that the Johnson House had changed thinking about how history could serve Germantown. The site suggested opportunity rather than decline. Underlying the plans was a new hopefulness: If the Johnson House stood for a story of whites and blacks working together in the cause of freedom and justice, could it galvanize such efforts today? In 2016 the Johnson House rebranded itself as the Johnson House Center for Social Advocacy and works with local businesses to improve the streetscape and offer baskets of coats and books for neighborhood children in the winter.

At the same time the Johnson House was designated a National Historic Landmark in 1997, the National Main Street Center of the National

Trust for Historic Preservation issued recommendations for capitalizing on the broader history of Germantown. The Johnson House was central to this project. "Main Street" became a signature program of the National Trust in 1983. It used neighborhood community revitalization strategies to bring economic investment to older commercial corridors in towns and neighborhoods without destroying historic buildings. The Main Street approach brought volunteers together with preservation and design professionals to develop ways to reuse older buildings, market and promote historic features, and prevent demolition or the kinds of dislocation that have become synonymous with gentrification. Main Street programs train and educate community members to work with public officials and community development corporations to bring in economic benefits without driving longtime residents away. The approach seeks to avoid failures and false starts along the lines of Colonial Germantown, Inc., in the 1950s and 1960s because it stimulates preservation-based economic development strategies involving multiple local partners and regulatory agencies and emphasizes reuse and adaptation of buildings, rather than "condemnation and restoration."

The Main Street Center's recommendations built on many of the plans from the 1950s, 1960s, and 1970s. In 1992 it offered an assessment of economic development planning to that date for the Preservation Coalition of Greater Philadelphia and Historic Germantown Preserved. The assessment extended from Windrim Avenue (near the 1730 Stenton house) north to Sharpnack Street—the entire length of the National Colonial Historic Landmark District. An important challenge for the Main Street approach was that any development in the historic area needed the approval of Germantown Settlement, the community development corporation that controlled public funds and could undermine even the most positive recommendations.[58] The 1992 assessment gathered multiple reports but offered few recommendations.

In 1998, the National Main Street Center commissioned two further reports that built on discussions with business leaders, heads of nonprofit attractions such as house museums, public officials, and staff at community development and housing organizations. The separate reports for Germantown and Mount Airy emphasized the variety of colonial attractions and sites open to the public and offered recommendations about the green squares and parks, Belgian block paving, and the presence of three centuries of historic architecture in an active urban neighborhood. Communities with such features often capitalize on their history, and the 1997 plans urged Germantowners to work together to do so. The plethora of organizations were not serving Germantown Avenue's commercial corridor; it was time to "convene all groups," "network with others," and, in both Mount Airy and Germantown, "continue efforts to coordinate the house museums" and "assist local sites, such as the Johnson House," to build on African American heritage tourism.[59]

The report also looked outside the mansion section: "Lower Germantown has a negative image, that it is dangerous, dirty, and abandoned." To counter that impression, the report recommends building on "Germantown's long proud history stemming from its Quaker and German roots, the Revolutionary War and the Underground Railroad." It continues: "Germantown is truly lucky and unique to have such a long recorded multi-cultural history. History should be more than just plaques and markers. Make history come alive, recreate anti-slavery speeches, show the lives of free blacks in the eighteenth and nineteenth centuries."[60]

According to the report, a staff member of the Central Germantown Housing Development Corporation, a subsidiary of Germantown Settlement, noticed that "traces remain of hidden places used in the Underground Railroad." History, the report says, "should not only be recorded"; it must also "be tangible so it can be experienced." The report continues: "How can existing sites incorporate the history of African Americans in the area? It will provide a wealth of opportunities for events."[61] These reports remain influential in many ways, as various community development corporations pick up the pieces after Germantown Settlement's 2010 bankruptcy and try to restore preservation-based development.

The Main Street reports of the 1990s recognized the component parts of effective public history: research, dialogue, good history, and partnerships—and generating some kind of experience at historic sites that goes beyond curatorial documentation and an urbanist sense of design coherence. Cliveden and the Johnson House offer experiential programming, often making use of dramatic arts, music, and poetry. The Historic Germantown consortium of sites has coordinated the opening of its house museums at the same time for several years; since 2012 a "Second Saturday" promotion has all sixteen sites open to the public at the same time. Coordinated promotion and marketing of neighborhood events involves the historic sites in tandem with neighborhood businesses. The Johnson House has since 2006 sponsored a large Juneteenth festival with the businesses of the 6300 Block Alliance and works with local political leaders to develop the event as an attraction for African American heritage tourists, in partnership with the Concord Schoolhouse, the Mennonite Meeting, and Cliveden.

In September 2017 the National Main Street Center picked the Germantown United Community Development Corporation as a candidate for a "Partners in Preservation" grant, which would assist in the restoration of two buildings associated with twentieth-century African American history: the Trower Building (home to the African American caterer John Trower) and Parker Hall, which offered minority soldiers and sailors social services during World War II. Voting concluded on October 31 and Germantown received the most votes of the contest. Boosted by a savvy social media campaign and aided by coverage from the *Philadelphia Inquirer* and local television and radio stories, and even promoted by the city councilwoman (not a known supporter of that community development corporation), the effort to beat out other Main Street communities transcended Germantown's typical divisions; even Mount Airy and Chestnut Hill community organizations promoted the cause of African American history in Germantown. There is a renewed sense that the community's economic fortunes are connected to all of its history, including the less famous places. In the words of the online promotion for the 2017 contest: "It's time to open doors in Germantown. This project will provide facade and structural improvements to significant twentieth-century African-American historic sites. Replacing these facades will bolster Germantown and increase community pride." This sense of opportunity was nurtured by the same elements that won the Johnson House recognition as an Underground Railroad site: partnerships, uncovering new ways to understand the past, and a desire to bring wholeness to the narrative of Germantown. This 2017 contest, which resulted in $160,000 for Germantown United CDC to manage preservation projects on the Trower Building and Parker Hall, along with the other efforts described here to cooperatively promote historic experiences and highlight the neighborhood's distinctive features, builds on plans and recommendations from the 1990s. Managing change takes time—in this instance, decades.

Germantown, once a place where good plans went to die, has moved steadily ahead, with increase in property values. Public history in Germantown has implemented several recommendations, and the historic sites have devised new models for working together and have enhanced their visibility. It took diligence and effort. The problems are by no means solved, but steady progress has gained traction. In 2008, ten years after the Main Street report came out, we finally had a common map of historic sites. It took fourteen years to get all the historic sites open on a common schedule. Just as it took time to understand that the Johnson House, long slumbering on Germantown Avenue, could tell a different story. It just takes time.

And action.

Fourth of July, 2006

Germantown's Fourth of July program builds on those recommendations of the 1990s: Make a public experience out of a place's history, highlight diversity, and work together to bring the program to the public. In 2006 I moved from directing the Johnson House Historic Site to become the executive director of Cliveden. That year, a month after the first Johnson House Juneteenth festival, we brought Frederick Douglass IV to Germantown for a program called "Ringing Out Freedom and Independence in Germantown." The program connects three sites that were standing on the day the Declaration of Independence was signed and invites visitors to reflect on the meaning of "all men are created equal" in our time. Cliveden, Johnson House, and Concord Schoolhouse are open to the public free of charge, and a first-person interpreter (historical figures have included Harriet Tubman, Richard Allen, and Oney Judge) connected with Germantown's African American heritage delivers an address after the Concord Schoolhouse's bell rings out once for each year since 1776. (The ringing takes about fifteen minutes.) Conventionally the Fourth of July involves fireworks, parades, and concerts, but very little opportunity to reflect on the meaning of independence today. Our 2006 program was notable for two reasons, both of which indicate how far we had come by integrating the historic Johnson House and its neighboring institutions into the life of Germantown.

The celebration became memorable for me when an elderly African American woman climbed up the steps to the Concord Schoolhouse and grabbed my arm. I helped her walk to the burying ground of the schoolhouse, where Israel and Rowland Johnson are buried and where the crowd had gathered for the bell ringing. I asked how she had heard about the event and why she came. She had seen a flier while waiting for a bus across the street and wanted to come because, she said: "I am a Gold Star Mother. And I want to be somewhere that matters on Independence Day." She was standing in a historic cemetery where fifty-eight Revolutionary War soldiers are buried.

After the bell rang 230 times that year, the crowd applauded politely and we walked across the street to hear Douglass read selections from his famous ancestor's 1852 speech, "What to the Slave Is the Fourth of July?" People asked whether the famous Frederick Douglass had ever been at the Johnson House or in Germantown. The answer was: "Maybe. There is some evidence he was in the neighborhood, but we don't really know for sure." A crowd of nearly three hundred filled the yard of the Johnson House, spilling outside the picket fence and onto the sidewalks of Washington Lane and Germantown Avenue—easily the largest crowd we ever had on the Fourth of July in the thirteen years we have done this program. Hundreds peered over the fence—including people I recognized from the bus stop. Some in the crowd even held books written by Frederick Douglass. Amid the sounds of the city, the crowd strained to hear as Douglass brought his ancestor's speech to a close. As he read the words that concluded many of Frederick Douglass's speeches, hundreds of people shouted with him, in unison: "Agitate! Agitate! Agitate!"

The meaning of waiting for the bus at Washington Lane and Germantown Avenue has been forever changed. Activating the Johnson House gave neighborhood history greater integrity by making it more complete. It shows that African American history can deepen and extend Germantown's historic identity not only chronologically but also into a realm of opportunity. The Johnson House represents a story of people taking action—by seeking their freedom, by saving the site, by building a case from many different sources to understand what happened there and why it matters. The Johnson House shows how historical understanding evolves and demonstrates that it need not be defensive or reactive to be useful. Mostly, Johnson House shows the opportunities generated when we seek understanding in history, even if we do not yet know all we want to know about the past.

5

Projections

Empty Buildings of Germantown

P ublic history, as we have seen, drove a wedge between Germantowners in the 1950s and 1960s but also helped to unite and revitalize the
neighborhood. Colonial Germantown, Inc., was rooted in the idea that
Germantown's historical significance rested on its white-dominated colonial and revolutionary period and the buildings that told that story. The
bypass battles of the 1960s grew out of a narrow vision of Germantown's
future as a grand shrine to the eighteenth century—a vision for which
no support could be found among the neighborhood's African American
majority. The significance of the colonial-era Johnson House is based on
many different kinds of evidence, brought forward through a series of
partnerships. Uncovering the house's past enlarged Germantown's system
of public history, opening it up to new history, new perspectives, and narratives of whites and blacks working together in the cause of freedom long
after the colonial period. Germantown's public history in the twenty-first
century has included History Hunters youth programs, discussions among
artists and neighbors about race and class sponsored by the Historic Germantown consortium, and sites, such as Cliveden, that actively seek input
about how to approach and experience difficult topics. All this makes Germantown's public history more accessible and effective—an open system
in which no one pretends to know all the answers. The recent lives of four
empty buildings show something about how Germantown is using this
open system to approach the use of historic spaces.

Several prominent buildings remain vacant in twenty-first-century Germantown. Each in its own way offers an example of how we reckon with the public history practices of the past one hundred years. Empty buildings create their own sort of urgency simply by standing vacant. Empty space raises questions. What will happen to it? What will fill it? Will it be torn down? Who will fix it? What will it take to make it useful? So many unknowns create anxiety in a community. Public history conventionally attempts to deal with such unknowns in ways that create certainty—through designation, documentation, commemoration, and education. When history is used to impose a certainty, however, as it was in Germantown in the 1950s and 1960s, it can contribute a false sense of security or repel people who feel that the history is not about them.

When public history is open to as many questions as answers, the benefits can be great. The four empty buildings profiled in this chapter show what happens when questions about a building's fate are met with misplaced certainty. The process of embracing uncertainty and accepting unknowns has often proved contentious and created a few new battles in Germantown, but it has also given the community new ways to find meaning in those buildings.

There are far too many empty buildings in Germantown to go into detail for all of them. Loudoun, built in 1804, is a former house museum that has been closed since a fire in the 1990s; it is in the process of legally deaccessioning artifacts so the city of Philadelphia can allow a daycare center to use the first floor.[1] The 1914 YWCA building that was central to the planning for Negro Achievement Week in 1928 has been vacant since the 1990s but has attracted a development proposal for a senior housing complex. Germantown High School, closed by the school district in 2013, may be under development too, though its ownership is being challenged in court. The four empty buildings described in this chapter exemplify the ways in which Germantown's public history has evolved beyond treating mere architectural features as the only carriers of historic meaning. The structures take Germantown beyond the tendencies of "building-ism" to trust-building processes that emphasize broader perspectives. When trust is established, the neighborhood has even, at times, moved beyond the idealization of the past that caused the buildings to be preserved but left empty.

The new Town Hall is the most prominent of the four. Its construction was fueled by a strain of Germantown nostalgia that was misplaced and misguided; now it stands dormant, as the most visible symbol of Germantown's sense of itself for most of the past one hundred years. Recent programming suggests progress toward finding a useful meaning for the building, despite its many challenges. Upsala, turned into a house museum that never engaged the community, was sold on the open real estate market in 2017 after a long struggle to find out what the community wanted the 1798 building to be. A high-rise apartment building rose on a potter's field in the 1950s without opposition or community pushback. But when the building was shuttered in 2011 and scheduled to be demolished and replaced, a renewed sense of why the place matters prompted community input that resulted in significant changes to the plans. The story of the 1767 Cliveden kitchen shows how responsible stewardship struggles over forcing a single chronological definition on a work space, as opposed to showing how buildings, especially service spaces, adapt and allow for change. In contrast to prominent buildings such as Town Hall, the potter's field and the kitchen at the back of the house show history from an unseen perspective. Adaptation allowed Cliveden's 1767 kitchen project to move from a planned reconstruction of a colonial hearth to an appreciation of the layers embedded in the space, leading the staff to conclude that if we imposed a single period on it, we would lose the stories of the nineteenth and twentieth centuries. We would obliterate one story to tell another—in a building that might not have survived in the first place had it not been adapted so often.

In these examples lie some lessons for addressing the next public history challenges. Each episode in this chapter shows new ways of thinking rooted in key lessons from this book: about community of memory, experiential learning, engagement with the arts and multiple audiences, and attempts to repair painful chapters of the past. Together they demonstrate that public history must be adaptable in order to be effective. Other business models allow for change, but public history seems to be only just coming to grips with it. Germantown Avenue has many visible, prominent, stark reminders of how important it is for the parts of our shared public history and memory infrastructure to adapt and remain open to change.

Town Hall

A few years ago I had a brief conversation with Chris Matthews, the national political commentator and host of the cable news program *Hardball*. Matthews, a Philadelphia native, was the featured speaker at a gala dinner celebrating the 125th anniversary of the *Philadelphia Tribune*, the

Figure 5.1 "Germantown's Identity, 1967." Town Hall, symbol of Germantown independence, was vacated in 1998 and now stands empty, directly across the street from the vacant Germantown High School. (Special Collections Research Center, Temple University Libraries, Philadelphia, PA; photo by Michael J. Maicher.)

nation's oldest African American newspaper. A formal fundraising affair that was the culmination of a year of special events, the well-attended dinner took place at the Philadelphia Convention Center. At the pre-event mixer, I introduced myself to Matthews, telling him I worked at a historic site in Germantown. He said his mother had come from Germantown, and he was fascinated by the storied history of the neighborhood. "It's always amazed me," he said, "that the Rockefellers wanted to make Germantown into Williamsburg before they settled on Virginia."

The Rockefeller myth is to this day one of Philadelphia's most persistent legends, long after a 1996 scholarly article thoroughly debunked it.[2] Many Philadelphians, and Germantowners especially, cling to the notion that the Rockefeller family, before they went on to found Colonial Williamsburg in Virginia, wanted to invest in Germantown to preserve its colonial history for the nation. The myth simultaneously promotes a claim to historical authenticity and mourns the loss of an opportunity, suggesting that Germantown's leaders somehow fumbled a great opportunity to exploit (especially economically) that connection to America's founding.

What accounts for the myth's staying power?[3] The answer lies in Town Hall, a municipal building that stands as a metaphor for all the dreams of what Germantown might have been.

Germantown's first Town Hall was built in 1854, shortly after Germantown ceased to be a town. Under the Consolidation Act of 1854, Germantown, along with Moyamensing, Kensington, and other districts, was incorporated into the city of Philadelphia. The old Town Hall was used as a Civil War hospital and was the site of the programs celebrating the centennial of the Battle of Germantown in 1877. It had already fallen into disrepair by the time it started offering space for Americanization meetings by various ethnic groups in the 1920s. A new Town Hall was built between 1923 and 1925 amid great fanfare. It was designed to resemble the early nineteenth-century Greek Revival Merchants' Exchange building in Old City Philadelphia. Lacking any of the German or English architectural features of Germantown's own colonial architecture, Town Hall may best be described as "Germantown-y," for it embodied the idealization of classical revival, while its very existence emphasized the neighborhood's independence. The building's disconnectedness from its neighborhood is striking. The question why a building representing Germantown's independent identity needed to resemble a building in Philadelphia's historic district only hints at the multiple inconsistencies wrapped up in Town Hall for nearly a century.

Charles F. Jenkins, president of the Site and Relic Society, used the 1923 cornerstone-laying ceremony to proclaim a lost opportunity. Germantown, he declared, narrowly missed being voted the nation's capital, and this failure doomed it forever. He laid out what might have been: "Here the golden dome of the Capitol would have gleamed across the more beautiful lands below for miles. The Wissahickon would have been the Rock Creek, and the Treasury Building or even the White House might have been placed where we are now standing."[4] This melancholy oration goes beyond the Germantown elite's traditional nostalgia and grieves for a moment that never existed. Even now the building is a prominent symbol of Germantown's struggle to capitalize on its past. Such restorative nostalgia has dangerous implications, compelling leaders to recreate the past in an idealized image that distorts the present. "If only" formulations, in place by the 1920s, have plagued Germantown for generations and are embodied in the empty buildings explored in this chapter.

So disconnected was the new Town Hall that by the 1990s it was no longer used for municipal offices, and the building was left vacant. In 2013 a public art project (part of the Hidden City Festival) stimulated interest in reviving the building, but the projected cost of rehabilitation was estimated at four million dollars by some observers. Town Hall shows Germantown's love/hate relationship with historic buildings and conflicted sense of a shared history.

How did the new Town Hall, which had no direct connection to the colonial past or even the Civil War era, become "historic"? Town Hall became consequential to Germantown history not through a connection to events but because of the way it fed the neighborhood's "if only" worldview, emphasizing what could have almost been over what had actually been. The building never established a sustainable identity of its own or a direct connection to Germantown until it became a ruin.

Recognizing how nostalgia (in all its varieties) forms a "paradoxical dialectic of past, present, and future," goes to the heart of understanding Germantown.[5] Consider that the word "nostalgia" comes from two Greek words that together mean "longing for home." The new Town Hall opened in the 1920s, the decade of Negro Achievement Week. But unlike that progressive and collaborative program, Town Hall remained in public view—keeping alive a narrative of bitter nostalgia about what the neighborhood had become. Germantown leaders tried to bring about a "Colonial Germantown" in wave after wave of futile efforts until the 1970s. The narrative of restoring a past that did not happen, reviving the past to counter the realities of the present, began with Town Hall—a building in a neighborhood that was not a "town" since 1854.

The replacement of Town Hall was marked by the essential contradictions of Germantown's preservation ethic. The 1923 demolition of the 1854 Town Hall presented community leaders with choices. Germantown, with its expanding population, had outgrown the original building, but tearing down one of the neighborhood's landmarks would alter its sense of place. The process of replacing it characterizes how muddled Germantown's approach to preservation had become.

The original Town Hall had its own compelling history. Located prominently at Haines Street and Germantown Avenue, it was Germantown's official center. The wood-framed building was designed by the architect Napoleon LeBrun (1821–1901) and equipped with a large clock tower. The clock came from Independence Hall; the bell had hung in Independence Hall and was cast by John Wiltbank, who had also cast the Liberty Bell. The old Town Hall had been the scene of many important political meetings, and groups as disparate as the Sons of Italy and the Grand Army of the Republic held meetings there.[6] The hall and buildings constructed on its back lawn were used as a hospital during the Civil War; Cuyler Hospital served thousands of the wounded and sick.[7] The scene of 1877 celebrations to commemorate the battle, the old Town Hall was a shared space for the community.

It had also become the object of political tensions between the mayor of Philadelphia and Germantown's progressive Republicans. The community lacked an up-to-date post office; the one it had was "suited to our time as a village" but obsolete now that the combined population of Germantown, Mount Airy and Chestnut Hill numbered eighty thousand. Germantown wanted and needed a new building, even at the expense of historic preservation. Debates about the hall began in 1920—small repairs or massive reconstruction?—and continued for two years.[8] Old though the building was, however, the real issue was that Town Hall was not loved. Some of the building's shortcomings had to do with its functionality, but mostly it was considered inessential because it was not from the right period, the only one that mattered in Germantown: the eighteenth century.

The decision was made to build an entirely new Town Hall, of "pure white marble," with modern amenities, on the spot where the old wooden one stood. Ironically, in a city that often pushed growth and development over heritage, some were arguing to save the old Town Hall. Joseph Wagner, director of the Department of Public Works, argued, "It needs appropriation of $10,000 to put it in 'first class condition.'" But, he went on, sounding almost like a preservationist, "the present Town Hall is a landmark in Germantown. It was built in 1854 and has been an almost historic meeting place during political campaigns in the 22nd ward. It has also been used as a police station and the headquarters and meeting places of the G.A.R. [the Union veterans' fraternity the Grand Army of the Republic] and kindred organizations. The building has fallen into disrepair and it is in an extremely dilapidated condition at the present time."[9]

The old Town Hall arose in the same year in which urban consolidation brought Germantown under the administrative authority of the city of Philadelphia. By the early part of the twentieth century, it was seen as part of an ineffective past, not as the kind of modern municipal building that other sections of the city had. City Hall publicly displayed the architect's model for the new building in the Mayor's Reception Room, as if to proclaim that it was finally meeting the neighborhood's call for infrastructural improvements.[10] The plan conflated so many historical features that it was not clear what it intended to recall or highlight. Designed by the Philadelphia architect John Penn Brock Sinkler, it combined Greek Revival Classicism and the Beaux Arts style, in keeping with the City Beautiful movement of the time, with a Neo-Classical touch in the form of a memorial to the men from the neighborhood who had died in World War I.

According to Edward Hocker, some residents, including a few members of the Site and Relic Society, complained that the design did not reflect the colonial architecture of Germantown's private eighteenth-century houses such as Cliveden and Stenton.[11] The architect could not easily reconcile the tension between the architectural features of a private home and the design of a building intended for public use, as a historical commission would observe decades later: "The form of Town Hall is an adaptation of several Classical models, most notably William Strickland's Greek Revival Merchants Exchange at Walnut and Dock Streets of 1832."[12] Nonetheless, the new design solved the problem of how to place the two hundred-ton tower that was to hold the historic clock and bell from the old Town Hall. It also used a Classical portico of columns with fan-shaped stairs to add dignity and monumentality especially suited to a war memorial.[13] It did not look like any other building in Germantown, yet it was not really modern. It typified the difficulty of preserving historical features in a modern urban neighborhood while still meeting the expressed needs of the citizens.

Germantown did not perceive the demolition of the old Town Hall as a preservation issue, even though the building was almost seventy years old. It was seen as just old, not historic. Yet seventy years was about the gap between John Fanning Watson's antiquarian project and the Revolution. In the early 1830s and 1840s, the buildings Watson sought to preserve were about the same age. And seventy years after the new Town Hall's construction, in 1993, it was nominated for a place on the National Register. How did the Germantown Site and Relic Society consider this issue? The answer shows, in their purest form, all the contradictions inherent in preservation in an urban setting.

In the melancholy address Jenkins gave on the occasion of the laying of the cornerstone, he spoke of Germantown's public history in terms of what could have been. His address is revealing for several reasons. Most significantly, as the neighborhood's chief preservationist, Jenkins had not a word to say about saving the old Town Hall, which was "passing without regret from anybody." Though by this time there was nothing to preserve, the Site and Relic Society had recently pushed to save other structures, sometimes successfully. Passing over the site's connections to the Civil War with but one mention of the nurses and doctors who aided the sick of the "War of Rebellion," Jenkins described the bell and its role in the 1877 commemoration of the Battle of Germantown, when it tolled a hundred times.[14] Town Hall, he was saying, was not historic on its own terms; it was important as a symbol of what could be remembered about the eighteenth century.

Jenkins then turned to Germantown's independence from Philadelphia and reminded everyone that if the Twenty-Second Ward were a city, it would be the "fifth city of Pennsylvania" (meaning the fifth largest in population). But it could have been even greater, if only the founders had not robbed it, if only James Madison, Thomas Jefferson, and Alexander Hamilton had not been able to compromise. "How much different would Germantown have been if it had been the Capital of the United States?" The creation of Germantown's own seat of municipal government in a classical style meant that the new Town Hall represented a restoration of Germantown's perceived importance during the colonial period.

There, in front of a thousand people, Jenkins's conditional language of "would" and "might" and "if only" sealed the interpretation of Town Hall, and with it much of Germantown's outlook for the next hundred years. The speech stamped Town Hall as a monument to Germantown's longing for what might have been. Rather than showing off a grand new building with modern amenities that the community needed and celebrating Germantown's progress and growth over the past few decades, Jenkins idealized "the almost" and signaled bitterness about the past. The preference for glory not gained revealed how sacrosanct the past was for the leaders of the Site and Relic Society.

The construction of the new Town Hall, and the fanfare surrounding it, signified Germantown's belief that it should have its own municipal center—even though it had been reduced to a neighborhood of Philadelphia almost a hundred years before. This sense of identity as separate from the rest of the city would be drawn on again in the 2013 Hidden City art project.

Old Town Hall had functioned as a town square for Germantown, much more than Market Square ever had, and a vital part of the neighborhood's public memory. After its demolition, the true center of Germantown's public sphere was neither the new Town Hall nor Market Square but Vernon Park, the lawn of the Wister Mansion. The history community could not make a place the heart of the neighborhood just by declaring it "historic," in either the 1920s or the 1950s and 1960s. Community use chose Vernon Park as a gathering place rather than either Town Hall or Market Square. The colonial narrative never fit either of these buildings well, despite the projection of them as historically significant. Lasting significance has to be based on a quality or history that many people identify with and connect to, and it has to be based in reality, not fiction or wishful thinking. As of early 2019, the new Town Hall has remained empty, dilapidated, and scarred by vandalism and neglect since the 1990s. Civic leaders of the 1920s were so entranced by the colonial period that they preferred a new building that reminded them of the eighteenth century—and what almost was, what could have been—than an authentically historic building from the nineteenth century.

The Rockefeller Myth

The tale of the Rockefeller family's interest in preserving Germantown has beguiled and deluded the community since the 1920s. The historian David Contosta exposed this legend as unfounded in 1996[15]—and yet the Rockefellers' creation and funding of Colonial Williamsburg, their signature achievement in the area of historic preservation, did have a large impact on Germantown.

The reasons for the myth's persistence are important to consider, for they show Germantown's culture of nostalgia in action on a scale greater than the fate of a single building (Town Hall, for instance). The myth is an important part of Germantown's twentieth-century culture, and it contains kernels of truth. First, one of the Rockefellers' ancestral homesteads was in Germantown, New York, and efforts to preserve an eighteenth-century tavern there in the early 1900s involved them in one of their first acts of preservation.[16] That is, the Rockefellers helped preserve a building in a Germantown. Second, Nelson Rockefeller's first wife, Mary Todhunter Clark, was born in Germantown, Pennsylvania, in 1907 and grew up in the Philadelphia suburb of Bala Cynwyd.[17] They were married in 1930. The Rockefeller name therefore appeared in Philadelphia's society pages during the 1930s, as well as in the news pages that covered their art, real estate, and philanthropic activities.[18] Finally, there was some contact, described by Contosta as "scanty correspondence," between the Germantown Historical Society and curators at Colonial Williamsburg over information in the society's records that might assist Williamsburg's director, the Reverend Dr. W.A.R. Goodwin, in his research.[19] Later the Historical Society asked the Rockefellers for a monetary loan so that it could preserve the Gilbert Stuart studio, two blocks south of Market Square, across from Grumblethorpe; this request went unanswered.[20] These isolated contacts hardly add up to an expression of interest by the Rockefellers in investing in Germantown.

The Rockefeller myth is based in Germantown's culture of nostalgia. Here the distinction between a myth and a legend is significant. A legend is based on stories that cannot be verified; a myth is a group explanation, a popular belief or tradition that has grown up around something (or someone), particularly something that embodies the ideals and institutions of a society or segment of society. The fact that Germantowners have long feared that they have not truly capitalized on its history for the economic well-being of the neighborhood and therefore the supposed failure to attract the Rockefellers confirms and contributes to the community's self-image. The myth's birth and prevalence correspond exactly to the time when Germantowners were coping with economic decline and the neighborhood changed rapidly from a residential suburb to an inner-city ghetto. Its tenacity reflects the inadequacy of resources for public history, a situation that turned desperate as factory jobs and investment moved away—followed by leading institutions such as Germantown Academy. The wishful thinking behind the Rockefeller myth also informed well-meaning volunteers and historical enthusiasts, supplying the bitterness of nostalgia and "if only" formulations. The myth empowered people with a sense of Germantown's authenticity and significance, but it also damned the leadership of the community for having missed its opportunity "to make Germantown Williamsburg before there was Williamsburg."[21] The fact that the Germantown Historical Society aspired to a connection with national saviors like the Rockefellers helps us make sense of the decision for how and why it nearly destroyed the community in the 1950s and 1960s in order to remake Market Square. The resonance of the myth, like the hulk of Town Hall, is as much a part of Germantown's sense of public history as any of its well-preserved buildings are.

"As Goes Town Hall, So Goes the Town"

By the 1980s, the new Town Hall was barely functioning. One or two city offices were left in it, but it lacked modern features such as accessibility for the handicapped. Deferred maintenance had taken a toll, and structural problems were not being addressed. A 1993 a report by the city concluded that the building posed hazards even to passersby; it has been vacant since 1998. Vandals were removing historic features, such as its bronze light standards.[22] A fragile coalition attempted to save Town Hall from the city's plans to close the building entirely.

For better or worse, here was the symbol of Germantown. As one resident noted, "To me, [Town Hall is] a mirror of the community, of things going on in the community."[23] Once it symbolized independence from the city; now it was emblematic of the neighborhood's struggle to make old buildings meaningful to a larger public. The effort to bring this derelict municipal building in line with the larger goals of the neighborhood shows what Germantown is about.

Neighborhood preservationists met with city officials and attempted to bring the building the limited protection of historic designation and greater public attention, with the goal of saving it. Edward Lee, a coordinator of the Friends of Town Hall, remarked, "To have an abandoned, boarded-up building at the center of Germantown would be a huge detriment to the economy. What message does that send to a potential business leader?"[24] Though the building was included in the Historic American Buildings Survey, it was not locally designated. Preservationists hastily and successfully sought designation by the Philadelphia Historical Commission.[25] That designation, rooted in the tenets of building-ism, was based on its decorative features and its architect, John Sinkler. In a final irony, the effort to preserve this symbol of Germantown's independence and strength required begging the city for money.

The strategy to gain funds from the city included a lavish Town Hall Day festival in the spring of 1995. Originally meant to be a simple behind-the-scenes tour by the Friends of Town Hall, the event turned into a characteristically Germantown civic festival, an interesting bookend to other festivals staged on Germantown Avenue, with a parade, speeches, and local experts extolling the building's historical significance. All of this was designed to draw press attention and perhaps put pressure on the city to provide the millions of dollars it would take to restore the building.

The community efforts collided with political realities. Mayor Edward G. Rendell was adamant about the need to trim city expenses during the fiscal emergency of the early 1990s, when the city faced a diminished bond rating and spiraling budget deficits. David L. Cohen, Rendell's chief of staff, said at the time: "It is an important building, important historically and important to Germantown. That combination presents some problems for the government." Nonetheless, he added, "I'm not sure where the money would come from."[26]

Germantown's City Council representative, Al Stewart, brought the project into a wider effort to get more city services for Germantown. He likened the fate of the building to another project that could signal renewal: "If we were serious about trying to restore Germantown Avenue, this would be a good place to start."[27] The council member's interest helped turn the preservation group's original plan—bring a handful of people into Town Hall to show them a faded beauty worth saving—into a sprawling parade with step dancers, African American drummers, and local student groups.

The public festival included songs, speeches, and tours of the building. A member of the Friends of Town Hall even baked a cake in the shape of the building, with a rotunda made of pound cake and frosting.[28] A local storyteller, Ed Stivender, debuted a song called "Once Upon a Town: The Ballad of Olde Town Hall," with the refrain "as the town hall goes, so goes the town." It was composed for Town Hall Day, but it could just as easily serve as a late twentieth-century expression of Germantown's chronic melancholy.

> *Once upon a town there was a town hall*
> *It was beautiful, very historical*
> *A former hospital (during the Civil War)*
> *In '23 they restored it all*
> *And then in '95 they wanted to tear it down*

But as the town hall goes, so goes the town.
Once upon a town there was a trolley line,
And it was very fine,
The old electric kind, they are so hard to find
The number 23, so fine for you and me
And then they came along and shut it down,
As the trolley goes so goes the town.
Once upon a town there was an Avenue
With a very nice view
From the beautiful cupola of old Town Hall.
That hall is a tooth in a smile that stretches for miles
If we knock it out, it will loosen the rest,
So let's do some bonding, but save the best.
So let's repair it, not tear it down.
Cause as the town hall goes, so goes the town.[29]

In 1998, a few years after Town Hall Day, the YWCA closed its doors because of problems of deferred maintenance to its 1914 building, declining membership, and infighting among its leadership.[30] Two of the century's great community institutions now stood empty as symbols of the decline of Germantown's independence and leadership. Town Hall stood for the belief that the neighborhood was large and vital enough to have its own town hall. The YWCA, with professional leaders such as Eva Bowles in the 1920s and Maggie Kuhn in the 1950s and 1960s provided institutional direction and connected neighbors with national initiatives, particularly in civil rights, in a way that other neighborhood associations and community groups could not. The Y had played a major role in Germantown's 1928 Harlem Renaissance event, while the historical community showed no interest in it. Both institutions have been closed now for two decades. Though there is some activity directed at reviving the buildings, replacing the lost leadership may be a greater challenge.

Hidden City's "Germantown City Hall"

I first encountered the inside of Town Hall in 2011 during an arranged tour with city officials, two architects, and representatives from nonprofit organizations that were potential tenants—if a developer could be found to tackle its rehabilitation. The city owns Town Hall under the auspices of the Philadelphia Industrial Development Corporation. In keeping with its complex interpretation and ambiguous place in the larger Germantown historical narrative, rehabilitation will not be straightforward for Germantown Town Hall.

People have to enter the building from the rear, far from Germantown Avenue. The rear entrance is through the basement, and we passed through a narrow back door into a darkened hallway with several rooms and offices beside it. After two decades, the building's floors and walls were caked with dried guano from bats, rats, and birds (among other animals). Puddles of standing water had collected in every corner. Despite boarded windows and doors, vandals had tossed half a dozen car tires on the second floor, which is actually the ground floor in relation to Germantown Avenue. The eeriest feature of the building was a second-floor office, marked by a banner reading, "The Mayor's Action Team," which was, apparently, suddenly abandoned. File cabinets were left open, and desks were covered with papers. A busy office one day—and the next day everyone was gone. No one had even returned to gather items from the office. After we examined the rooms and whatever features we could access safely, I climbed the stairs as far as I could to examine the historic clock mechanism, a replica of the one installed at Independence Hall. Pigeons and bats had nested next to it, and it took considerable imagination to discern its historic features. The architects assured me that the building could be rehabilitated and made functional. Said one, "It's a great building. The problems are nothing that a ton of money couldn't solve." After leaving the building, I threw my shoes into the trash as quickly as possible.

Later that year I got to tour the Town Hall again with a graduate class in conservation science. The graduate students looked at options for the building and conducted surveys, engaging neighbors and stakeholders in a variety of ways to consider what could be done to make Town Hall useful again, and what it would take to accomplish that. They priced out making it part of the high school across the street, establishing a community center, making it once again an office for city services, and even mothballing the entire structure. The students were creative and they wanted to offer the public inventive options, but the building itself got in the way. They could not come up with ways for it to fit the context, serve the neighborhood, or be of use as a building in any way, memorial, educational, or utilitarian—not without significant resources.[31] Its National Register designation gave it curatorial credibility, but it still made no sense in its context. Nor could the public safely experience the building as it has been since the 1990s.

The 1993 National Register listing based its designation on its architectural features: the architect's reputation, the World War I monument, and the mechanics of the clock tower. The larger meaning of the site to the neighborhood did not contribute to the decision. The Town Hall designation fit into the National Park Service's practice of emphasizing building details over significance to the community. Such a designation, however, offers only minimal protection from demolition.

Building-ism reflects the limitations of historic nominations and designations and their inadequacy when it comes to capturing a building's meaning. Town Hall had enough curatorial importance to garner a National Register listing, but it no longer made sense contextually in its urban environment. The experience of the building, boarded up and unused, was one of ruin and neglect, not architectural beauty or historical association. No one could connect with it; it related to Germantown's public history only as a symbol of what might have been. Even the National Register designation was more of an empty honor than a guarantee of protection or path forward. Like the building itself, the designation was considered important, but this was more a perception than reality.

The 2011 graduate preservation studies and community surveys had stimulated an interest in crafting some kind of experience around Town Hall—some link between the building and its contemporary setting, including the people of the neighborhood. In 2013, when Philadelphia's Hidden City Festival included Town Hall in an oddly cerebral art project called "Germantown City Hall," it was time to give artists a chance to imagine the space and its role.

The Hidden City Festival is a public art initiative that brings people into derelict, abandoned, or little-known spaces. Hidden City projects represent the kind of "reflective nostalgia" whereby people consider the past in contemporary language, in settings that allow them to be comfortable with ruins. (Contrast the "restorative nostalgia" of Jenkins's 1923 assertion that Germantown could have been the capital of the United States.) Hidden City's Town Hall project proved slightly contentious, often celebratory, and overall an opportunity to consider the building and what to do with it. In 2013, the building, even empty, was considered an icon, poised to provide the neighborhood with an opportunity to attract attention, and maybe even resources.

That a public art project could even be staged in Town Hall is a testament to Hidden City's dogged work with the city of Philadelphia. The city's Department of Licenses and Inspections approved restricted access to the building, allowed certain activities within it, and helped design entry points and safe passageways around areas with extensive corrosive damage. A temporary entrance allowed access through the Germantown Avenue doors into the rotunda and the World War I memorial. Thus, people could enter from the avenue and immediately be drawn upward by the grandeur of the rotunda. Without the "wow" effect of entering the building through the front door, Hidden City probably would not have gone through with the project.

Hidden City had to secure permits and pay off fines. It makes sense for a city to levy fines and penalties on landlords for buildings left vacant or neglected. In Town Hall's case, the owner is the city of Philadelphia, which was levying fines on itself for not taking adequate care of the structure. Festival organizers had to tackle those fines before a temporary certificate of occupancy could be approved, allowing the project to continue. The city allowed only limited access overall and curtailed operations within the whole structure to a few spaces and rooms. Performance art and drama, important parts of the festival in the past, were not permitted.

The project stimulated a cleanup inside the building and outside. The World War I memorial was scrubbed clean. A friends group was formed, and it cleared debris, washed windows, and provided tables and chairs. People were allowed meeting space in the building during the installation's run of approximately five weeks. Hidden City's plans for the building were exciting at first. Then a very Germantown thing happened: Not many Germantowners were going to be involved.

It turned out that the artist-organizer who had been selected by the Hidden City jurors for the installation, Jacob Wick, was not from Germantown. The festival organizers were taken aback by the public response when it was announced that Wick hailed from Oakland, California. Though he had some support from two local people who were active in the Philadelphia art world, they too were relatively new to Germantown. The diverse neighborhood's working and teaching artists would certainly have welcomed an arts project in Town Hall, had they themselves been welcomed at the planning stage.

By not drawing on the local arts community, Hidden City's Town Hall project alienated many potential supporters and limited its local impact. Like the artists and writers who participated in Negro Achievement Week in 1928, Germantown's artists had, since the mid-twentieth century, pushed its image beyond the quaint and colonial. It was disappointing, then, to local artists—citizens and neighborhood activists, eager to be set loose on making some kind of meaning for the decaying Town Hall—that their talents were overlooked or used only in a limited way. The Hidden City directors met with the local city councilwoman to explain the project and justify the lack of more direct involvement by locals.[32] Next, when Wick called for a meeting of interested neighbors (not in Town Hall but at the Germantown Mennonite Meeting House), most of those who attended thought that the project was going to propose a serious plan for reuse of the building. These contentious meetings at the outset of Hidden City followed the traditional script as Germantown's grassroots groups tried to seize some corner of input and authority over the past. Some neighbors wanted the meetings videotaped so their concerns would be put on the record. That request was voted down on the grounds that these were planning meetings; moreover, the city—the building's owner—would have very little to do with the project. Only to a limited extent would artistic imagination be brought to bear on solving the long-term problems of the neglect and disuse of Town Hall. It was more of a pop-up than a plan.

The project that resulted was what is called "public spatial installation art." Titled "Germantown City Hall," it attempted to create an impression of what the building might be if the neighborhood were truly an independent town. The organizers designed flags for Germantown and posed imaginative ideas about the building's use, but nothing that was intended to be a lasting interpretation. The best parts of the project were the volunteer contributions to the beautification of the site and the community's use of the space for meetings and artists' roundtables. A kind of community of memory arose, with Town Hall taking the role of its shared heritage. In the end, however, the project provided only a short-lived spotlight on Town Hall.

In addition to the "Germantown Artists Roundtable" that took place as part of the festival, several local artists created a separate installation in Vernon Park. The display of T-shirts with the names of Philadelphians murdered in June 2013 drew on news reports of a record-setting homicide rate in Philadelphia that year and presented a sharp contrast with the park's Pastorius Monument, celebrating Germantown's founding. The T-shirt project was a more accurate and honest rendering of the moment than the Town Hall project. And it revealed on a deep level Vernon Park's status in the community: a truer sign of how Germantown goes than Town Hall, or Market Square, ever could be.

During the thirty days of the Hidden City Festival, 1,866 people attended the Town Hall installation, making it the second-best attended of the nine projects that year.[33] The project's true intent, according to Peter Woodall, was realized. The public's acceptance of the building took time, and that proved to be a benefit. People gradually set up their own meetings: a forum to address contemporary housing concerns, a discussion, led by a local businesswoman, about starting retail businesses in the neighborhood. Some came just to see the building, but many others took the project at its word and used it for public and civic activities.

The festival organizers revealed needs on several levels. Germantown has a healthy number of institutional spaces for people to meet, but in Town Hall they could conduct their meetings in a setting that idealized previous eras and conveyed a sense of awe and continuity through its World War I memorial and a kind of Classical architecture associated with the early Republic. For Hidden City, "Germantown City Hall" typified what was "Germantown-y" about the project—it would not have worked in a different neighborhood. The independent-mindedness of Germantown was made evident. The project galvanized interest in the building in ways that the city had not. Germantown High School, just across the street, closed that year, and the already shuttered YWCA was damaged by fire, so even minimal public use of Town Hall counted for something. Hidden City provided its own kind of nostalgia for a municipal building with historic features—an institutional structure that people could now see and enter. It satisfied a need.

I saw the project as having a limited impact, partly because, like Jenkins in his 1923 speech, it seemed to be pushing an alternative history of what might be for the building; partly because the execution of the project reinforced the same kind of disconnect between the community's authentic history and present interests.

As a public history project, Hidden City in Town Hall did not offer factual historical content but treated making history itself as a subject. It brought the "community of memory" into the project, allowing opportunities for debate, criticism, and meaning making by allowing people to discuss possibilities for the site. A friends group formed to try to maintain the energy of the 2013 event, and in 2014 they issued a values statement for the building. In the end, the project solved nothing, but it gave an impetus to different uses of the building as a platform for civic engagement. The artists found it to be a success, while the neighbors still hope that the building can be saved.

As of this writing, the building stands shuttered, with a sign announcing that it is for sale by the city. There are currently no realistic plans for its use.

Historic Upsala: For Sale

In 2016, Upsala, the 1798 Federal-style building that stands prominently on Germantown Avenue at the point where Germantown meets Mount Airy also had a for sale sign. Owned by members of the Johnson family, the house was occupied until the 1920s and then left vacant until a fire destroyed most of the upper floors in 1940. Frances Wister led a neighborhood effort to save the building from being demolished and replaced by a grocery store. The patriotic inclinations derived from the Mount Vernon Ladies Association meant models for using the building were limited; the logical next step was for neighbors to establish a local friends group to restore the building and turn the site into a house museum. The resulting Upsala Foundation managed the site as a nostalgic house museum until its single-digit annual visitation numbers prompted the foundation to seek another way to fulfill its mission to preserve the building. The Upsala Foundation began merger proceedings with Cliveden in 2003.

Cliveden worked for more than a decade to find a way for Upsala to serve Cliveden's mission of making history useful to the neighborhood. In the meantime, it addressed the deferred maintenance, capital projects, and preservation work needed to secure the building from the elements. In 2017 Upsala was sold to a couple who promised to abide by legal protections of the building's features, restore it, and live in it as a private home—its original use. The property has always been zoned residential, even when operated as a house museum. Upsala is a noteworthy example of Federal architecture, but without a compelling history or connection to some larger idea, architectural features alone were not enough to make it sustainable as a historic site open to the public. Not every old building needs to be a house museum. This is the story of how Cliveden and Germantown came to that conclusion.

After the merger in 2005, Upsala was owned by the National Trust for Historic Preservation and managed by Cliveden. In addition to the four buildings on its side of Germantown Avenue, Cliveden now managed Upsala's 2.5 acres directly across the street. Cliveden tried several different approaches to bring life to Upsala. It initially considered turning Upsala into a visitor center for Cliveden. The costs were prohibitive: as much as

Figure 5.2 Historic Upsala for sale, 2016. After a long public process designed to establish preservation protections and find a suitable next use, the National Trust for Historic Preservation placed the former house museum on the market; it eventually sold to a couple who planned to restore it as a private home. (Photo by the author.)

four million dollars for preserving the site and adapting it to full-time use as a welcome area with exhibits and wedding rental space. Weighing this against Cliveden's then-minimal visitation numbers, the board of directors and the National Trust realized that raising four million dollars to serve forty-five hundred visitors was a misguided strategic focus.

Some uses considered for Upsala were preservation-oriented, such as a 2009 attempt to develop it as a center for archaeological work in Germantown. Others would have addressed community needs, such as a meeting space with a community garden. A bookstore's owners considered renting it as a space to hold concerts and run a coffee shop as well as sell books, but they did not have the resources to own and operate it. The project fell through when they retired. A preservation wood contractor looked into using Upsala for offices and a showroom but determined after months of study that the building was too costly to rehabilitate; this firm, too, wanted only to rent the site. Cliveden even offered the space for the headquarters of Germantown Avenue's business improvement district. At over twelve thousand square feet, Upsala was expensive to maintain and secure; a small rental income could never cover the utilities, the needed repairs, and the cost of landscaping its 2.5 acres. All the while, historic woodwork continued to rot, the drainage of the property began to fail, leaving standing water on the grounds, windows were broken, and emergency mold abatement and asbestos removal kept Cliveden's stewardship of the property mired in costly repairs and reactive preservation maintenance. No matter what nonprofit tenant took over and no matter what use they found for the site, it would still cost tens of thousands of dollars each year to run the house and keep it secure. While it worked to repair the wood, windows, roof, and drainage, Cliveden needed better ideas for Upsala's use, and it used its Conversations program to solicit them. The results revealed a good deal about the staying power of the house museum model.

The idea of asking the community what it wanted Upsala to become had not been considered during the merger discussions in 2003; the words "community engagement" were not used in the process at all. Not until an October 2013 Cliveden Conversations meeting that showcased Upsala's historic features were people invited to offer ideas. Most of the suggestions were unworkable or beyond the means of Cliveden's five-hundred-thousand-dollar annual operating budget: another museum for Germantown, such as a banking museum, because the Johnsons had a lot of money; a studio for neighborhood artists; a program for local youths to learn woodworking by restoring the house. Each of the ideas would have kept Cliveden in the role of landlord, when it could no longer afford the tens of thousands of dollars it was spending for ongoing maintenance with little return. Was there another nonprofit organization out there that might be able to use the community's suggestions and give Upsala life?

Working with Cliveden's staff and board of directors, the National Trust for Historic Preservation took steps to find a suitable partner. Besides legally protecting the exterior and setting out public access requirements that the next steward would have to abide by, it issued a Request for Proposals, seeking another entity, perhaps a nonprofit charity, that would be willing to take on the property and preserve it according to the original goals of the Upsala Foundation. That entity would have to be realistic about the capital costs, maintenance, and security measures needed. Not every nonprofit would have the means to manage the site, maintain it to the high standard befitting its status on the National Register, and make it a viably active contributor to life on Germantown Avenue's business corridor. The first public processes drew only two full proposals, neither of which was realistic about the costs of making the site active or abiding by the preservation protections. The third expression of interest came from a local preservation agency, which asked that the site be transferred at no cost, that they be allowed to commit no funds for the adherence to the preservation easement requiring annual inspections, and that all changes made to the site be approved by the National Trust. All three requests proved unworkable.

A second public meeting was held at Cliveden to look at what the managers of historic house museums across the country were considering as alternatives to the use of these houses as nonprofit public museums. Representatives from the National Trust showed examples of shared-use or hybrid models in other communities, where for-profit partnerships kept some public access and historic interpretation even when the site was turned into a restaurant or other commercial venture. Also speaking that night was the preservation consultant Donna Harris, whose 2007 *New Uses for Historic Houses* continued to spark national discussion in what had become a multidecade debate. The audience discussed potential uses and offered suggestions that were impractical, such as a community farm-training center for youths, and would involve prohibitive costs or strain Cliveden's three-person fulltime staff. The last words spoken at the event were Donna Harris's: "Often, the best use is the original use."

Over the next four months, even without a new owner or tenant in view, Cliveden staff and the National Trust's legal department worked on drafting legal protections, including a requirement to host the public on day of the reenactment of the Battle of Germantown. Easements are a creative way to protect preservation features of a building. The National Trust owns 135 easements on private and public properties, including homes and public buildings, and for all sorts of reasons, including viewshed or historic architectural features. An owner must agree to have changes to the property approved by the entity holding the easement, in this case the National Trust, which inspects the property regularly and works with owners on making modern improvements to a house without violating the terms of the preservation protections spelled out in the easement. The easement protects the house in perpetuity.

The Upsala collections were another issue. Few of these colonial-era objects had anything to do directly with the Johnsons or Upsala; they had been acquired around the time of the Bicentennial as part of a project to decorate the property with colonial-era or Colonial Revival artifacts. Cliveden adapted the scope of its collections to include items from Upsala, but the staff also determined that some fell outside that scope because they were unrelated to the Chews, the Johnsons, or the Battle of Germantown. Such objects have to pass through committees at the National Trust and Cliveden; they are then offered to other collecting sites of similar mission, locally, regionally, and nationally. The process of deaccession took thirty months, with many Upsala items going to organizations in Germantown or elsewhere in Philadelphia. The remaining items went to sale, though the value for the entire collection of 135 items amounted to roughly $3,850.[34] Another former house museum on Germantown Avenue, Loudoun, is going through a similar process of deaccession in order to allow adapted use of portions of the building by a nonprofit homeschooling resource center. The center currently rents Loudoun, leaving it under the management of the Fairmount Park Conservancy.

In September 2016 Upsala went on the real estate market. The National Trust had taken pains to avoid this step. Its leadership and Cliveden's held nervous discussions about what public officials would think of the decision and how the community would react. Several people told me bluntly, "It's a disgrace that the National Trust is selling Upsala." Many did not realize that there had been over three years of discussions or that other former house museums had found new owners on the real estate market.[35] Cliveden's board chair joined me to give the news to Germantown's city councilwoman, state representatives, and other public officials. Cliveden's board counsel joined the National Trust attorney to discuss with the Pennsylvania attorney general's office the steps being taken to make sure that the building and its collections were being treated with due diligence and with public transparency. Regular updates to those public officials were part of Cliveden's work with the National Trust to find a suitable steward who could give Upsala its best shot.

The process resulted in nine offers of varying size and with different proposals for end use. Several included elements of the house museum model. The proposed uses included a law office; public galleries devoted to history and art; mixed commercial use with a for-profit school; and residential development combined with gallery space. All the offers were rigorously considered by staff and advisers for Cliveden and the National Trust. The offers were ranked according to the prospective owners' preservation knowledge and experience, their financial resources, and the proposed end use. Because of the easement, no owner can subdivide the land or place siding on the building. The buyer had to be approved—or at least not objected to—by the charitable office of the attorney general.

The real estate process generated far greater interest than the request for proposals had. Unlike the nonprofit proposals, the offers that came forward from the real estate market showed energy and enthusiasm for Germantown. Offers came from as far away Boston and New York as well as from Germantown and Old City. In late March 2017, the attorney general's office announced that it would not object to the sale of Upsala to a preservation-minded couple who planned to readapt the site to its original use as a family home.

Potter's Field

Several blocks off Germantown Avenue, deep in the Pulaskitown section of Germantown, a building much taller and newer than Upsala had stood vacant from 2011 until its implosion in 2014: the housing project tower built in 1955 by the Philadelphia Housing Authority (PHA). The battle over this site shows some of the same tensions we have encountered at other contested sites: Who gets to decide? How is the public to be involved? This time, however, the effort truly showed a community of memory in action.

While public meetings considered the fate of Upsala and Cliveden Conversations sought public input about how to interpret the Chews' slave-owning past, an empty building slated for demolition was also the subject of debate. The PHA had constructed the high-rise housing project on an old public burying ground that had been abused and disrespected for many years: the Pulaskitown potter's field. Purchased by Matthias Zimmerman in 1755, the land was set aside for "all strangers, Negroes, and Mulattoes as die in any part of Germantown forever."[36] In the early twentieth century, neighborhood boys remade the space for playing baseball, using the gravestones for bases. The city health department declared the field a public nuisance in 1916 and closed the grounds to any further burials.

No public objections to disturbing the burial ground were recorded when the PHA began construction on the high rise in the mid-fifties. By 2011, however, the President's House controversy had empowered many to question the use of public funds to commemorate certain histories but not others. For citizen historians passionate about their sense of stewardship, the cultural and symbolic value of the site was very clear. The PHA,

Figure 5.3 Potter's field commemorative marker, installed 2017. The Philadelphia Housing Authority placed this marker on the site of a mid-century high-rise (built in 1955, demolished in 2014) after community members demanded official recognition of the hundreds of unknown people buried there. (Photo by the author.)

despite halting efforts to address their concerns, remained unclear about whether it planned to remove whatever remains might be there without designation or just to build new low-rise housing on top of the site of the old high-rise. It held public meetings packed with people associated with reparations groups, archaeologists, representatives of every neighborhood association in that section of Germantown, ward leaders, and public officials. In the past, whenever the Germantown community challenged the city over history, the effort would typically derail into acrimonious tumult because of diffuse leadership and lack of focus. Plans wound up disintegrating or being shelved.

In 1955, even if the public and the authorities had known about the burials, no grassroots group had the power or connections to make an effective case for the public commemoration, or even the respectful treatment, of this historic site. It did not fit in with the patriotic narrative that Germantown had written for itself. During the 1950s, people overlooked such details to the point of obscuring the past or altering it to avoid anything messy and unpleasant, though at the time, Germantown was formulating plans to remake parts of the neighborhood for a Colonial Germantown, Inc.—construction that would have created more upheaval and likely unearthed other ancestral markings. The potter's field had been established in the mid-eighteenth century, the primary focus of Colonial Germantown, Inc., but it was associated with African Americans and other people considered not significant. Nor did it matter politically in the 1950s that the PHA had trampled over a burying ground. For the twenty-first century, however, the site represented new history: old information made new because ways of understanding had evolved and adapted to consider evidence differently. When the high rise was shuttered in 2011 and plans to remake it were announced, much had changed in Germantown. This time, politics, citizens' ability to marshal the use of historical data, and focused leadership informed by recent public history campaigns could constructively address agreed-on concerns.

Public alarm over the idea that the PHA would further disturb the burying ground, first by imploding the high-rise and then by building over it, produced another neighborhood association. This battle gave birth to the Northwest Neighbors of Germantown, representing the Pulaskitown area. The language of its mission statement directly referred to the earlier fight over the President's House: According to a flyer it shared in the neighborhood, the association was "formed to avenge the Ancestors of the Germantown Potter's Field" and to address local zoning, crime, and quality of life issues. Leaders from the Avenging the Ancestors Coalition (ATAC) and the National Coalition of Blacks for Reparations in America (N'COBRA) were present at the meetings and frequently quoted in the media.

This time the Germantown Historical Society provided crucial assistance and support to neighborhood groups. Newly merged with, and overseen by, the Historic Germantown consortium, the society's archivists helped locate and analyze ownership records and document the historical boundaries of the potter's field site. Making use of this evidence, citizen historians pushed back against the PHA's stated plans. Professional archaeologists and civic leaders, black and white, joined the effort. The group wanted three major steps taken: They wanted ground-penetrating radar used to determine whether any bodies were still buried beneath the parking lot for the high rise, they wanted the PHA to reconsider removing the playground, and they wanted some official commemoration of the potter's field as a site for African American burials. Their argument was

that ancestors had been disrespected in 1955, when construction equipment trampled on and separated human remains, and that such disrespect
called for some sort of official repair.

The politics were different in the aftermath of the President's House
controversy. Though many similar burying grounds exist throughout Philadelphia, filled with the remains of indigents, paupers, and others deemed
unworthy of burial in a churchyard with a headstone, the Pulaskitown
potter's field was framed as an issue involving "our people" because of
the African Americans buried there. When the PHA revealed that it had
decided not to build over the site and would commemorate its use for African American burials, Ari Merretazon, N'COBRA co-chair, called the
agency's shift "a great announcement because it brings forth a lot of possibilities in terms of putting together a burial ground for our ancestors,"
adding, "We would like to engage in that type of discussion."[37] The advocacy groups succeeded also in getting the housing authority's consultants
to work with them on the design of the landscaping. "We want to make
sure we are providing something that is in the community's best interest,"
Brian Schlosnagle, the engineer from the Department of Housing and
Urban Development who was overseeing the consultation, said.[38]

Even if the architects and construction crews of the mid-fifties had
known about the previous use of the site, they and the community would
not have reacted to that knowledge in the same way that advocates did
in the twenty-first century. Cliveden was not directly involved, but I attended some of the public meetings. Historic Germantown's involvement
made a critical difference to the campaign, and its full-time staff allowed
the consortium to weigh in on the historical issues. Archival resources
informed and assisted the process as it moved toward a satisfactory result. Prepared by earlier controversies over the President's House and the
Chew papers and also by Cliveden's use of broad stakeholder engagement
to figure out a solution, the battle over the Pulaskitown potter's field was
resolved somewhat amicably, according to several people involved, notably Lisa Hopkins, leader of the Northwest Germantown Neighbors. The
anger was real. The people buried in the potter's field not so long ago
mattered less than affluent, famous, and pedigreed ancestors. The effort
to address the PHA's decision was framed in terms of social justice and
redress of past wrongs. People were not afraid to fight for the memory of
the anonymous and storyless; as a result, their past was written into the
received narrative of Germantown history.

Public officials saw an advantage to be gained from defending the symbolic value of the site for African Americans. Contacted by active, vocal members of the community, public officials had no problem pushing back against the PHA and adding their names to the effort. Indeed, the state representative and the city councilwoman presided over the dedication of the marker on February 3, 2017. Though it is a local marker (and not a state historical commission sign) installed by the PHA, it represents a substantial addition to the memory infrastructure: a memorial to Germantown's African American history and another landmark in citizen historians' success in extending the narrative, uncovering new layers of history, and making an effort to include all stories.[39] The Germantown potter's field became a worthy counterpart to the Johnson House as a place to remember more of the anonymous people who passed through Germantown. And the process, in which people asserted their own perspectives on previously disrespectful treatment, was as positive as the result.

The potter's field became the antithesis of Rockefeller myth. Germantown has authentic history, and now it has confidence that its history need not be idealized. Even a sad history can be made prominent in everyday spaces such as a housing complex and a playground in a residential neighborhood. Far from being "the historic dregs of the City of Brotherly Love," Germantown is a place that sees history and meaning even when they have been buried for years. Such dregs may contain ways of knowing a more effective history.

Cliveden's 1767 Kitchen

Cliveden has been around for 250 years, and its front façade remains recognizable from famous images such as Howard Pyle's 1898 *Attack upon the Chew House* and Russell Smith's 1843 *Chew House*. As those titles suggest, the site has always been known for its connection with the Chews and its role in the Revolutionary War. At the back of the main house, off to the side, however, is the 1767 Kitchen Dependency, empty now but once the busiest building on the property. That empty kitchen evokes more of the history of the place and all the people involved in it than the memory of one three-hour battle. Yet uncovering the meaning of Cliveden's 1767 kitchen has been a challenge. The building was remodeled (and remuddled) many times to adapt and modernize it, but even in its current spare state, it reveals the complexity of the site in intriguing ways.

The back of the house offers a different way to experience Cliveden's history. Like the potter's field, it is a part of colonial Germantown, even though it was neglected and ignored because it did not fit a glorified narrative. The Kitchen Dependency offers a chance to reexamine the history of Cliveden from the perspective of those who lived and worked in it. The activities that went on in this busy area are essential to the meaning of the site, even though the National Historic Landmark period of significance now goes to only 1825. The 1767 kitchen offers Cliveden the opportunity to tell, in one way or another, more of the site's 250-year history, rather than one specific moment. Though it now stands empty, people find visiting the kitchen exciting because it must be experienced directly.

The 1767 kitchen has been altered so much over the years that revealing its essence has taken the kitchens team into unanticipated areas. The building consists of two stories and a garret, with the kitchen hearth at ground level and a cellar underneath. It was extended during its period of construction (1765–1767), so even the brick cooking hearth is an addition to the original plan. That change to a heavy brick heart forced workers to shore up the floor with separate arches underneath, creating two sections in its small cellar. The Cliveden "Living Kitchens" project team conducted archaeological, archival, and architectural investigations over two years but turned up only limited information. Even the voluminous Chew Family Papers do not explain all the modifications made in the construction of the building. Nor do any records state who worked in the space during the 1700s and 1800s or what duties they had. We know that Benjamin Chew ordered Jacob Knorr to build a coffin for a Negro cook because we have a receipt for Knorr's payment, but we do not know the name or duties of that cook. The enslaved and indentured workers who toiled in the kitchen remain anonymous, at this point known only through hypotheses based on census records, receipts, and scattered correspondence.

We know that modifications to the building began almost as soon as it was built, but the architectural evidence raised as many questions as answers. Did the well pump push water into the kitchen or into an adjacent garden? When the team first visited the kitchen, we thought the iron bars set horizontally next to the cooking hearth formed the basis of a bread oven, but it seems more likely that that held a set kettle. But are we sure? We cannot yet determine when the colonial cooking hearth was filled in with bricks. At the outset of the project, we thought it was filled in when the cooking area was remodeled into a twentieth-century bathroom with a bathtub. Now we understand that the bricks were a backstop for a large Kitchener range installed in the 1860s.[40] The investigations were meant to answer questions posed frequently by visitors after the building was

Figure 5.4 Cliveden mansion, front elevation, 1767 Kitchen Dependency. The Kitchen Dependency preservation project extended the interpretation of the architecture of the original complex and revealed layers of changes that had been made to the site; the Dependency was opened to the public in 2011. (Photo by the author.)

opened to the public in 2011. Instead, the Living Kitchens research has only made it clear that we do not yet know enough to interpret the building fully or with total confidence.

The archival, archaeological, and architectural research, in other words, got us only so far. To supplement the research, Cliveden engaged in multiple listening sessions to gather people's memories of the kitchens in which they grew up. For this project, we changed Cliveden's community forum series to seven Kitchen Conversations, where community stakeholders heard updates about the project, put into context by team members, and then contributed their own input and recommendations in small-group discussions. Each meeting included a meal befitting the topic. For instance, in a program that explored the history of enslaved chefs working for presidents of the United States, people discussed the presentation over pepper pot soup and tavern biscuits. Traditional foods gave strangers a chance to get to know one another by talking over the subject matter and sharing a small meal.

For one of the Kitchen Conversations, Joseph McGill returned to sleep overnight at Cliveden. In 2011, at the beginning of his award-winning Slave Dwelling Project, McGill slept overnight in the Kitchen Dependency and described his experiences to Cliveden Conversations participants. McGill sleeps in extant slave dwellings across the country. Philadelphia was the first northern city he slept in; readers of his project's blog, unaware that slavery existed in northern cities, wondered why he was going there.[41] The Kitchen Dependency was also the first building he slept in as part of the project that was not made of wood and that contained a second story: a purpose-built outbuilding for a mansion, rather than a vernacular structure made of temporary materials. At his presentation he observed that most such buildings, whatever the materials, would not have lasted had they not been altered or remodeled. Kitchens are frequently the first rooms that owners change in a house, so it is not uncommon to see such a building survive by adaptation and change. The slide show McGill presented when he returned to Cliveden in 2015 showcased kitchen buildings he had slept in, providing further comparisons for Cliveden's staff, research team, and stakeholders to consider. At the Kitchen Conversations, people responded to the similarities of those kitchen spaces with the ones they grew up in, noting how many of them connected with work spaces outside and with service quarters where food preparation went on next to laundry work. "Imagine the smell of all those fires boiling all that water," one member said. "My grandmother told me stories of making such fires in her home when the family lived in Carolina before moving to Philly."

Cliveden also solicited information through a community-curated exhibition called "Mixing Memories: Sharing Stories," which collected people's memories of their own kitchens, along with items, images, and recipes, and displayed them in the Cliveden Carriage House, with a timeline of Germantown's food history. The project's oral history component revealed class distinctions and other complexities. For instance, in the 1940s and 1950s, Jell-O became an emblem of social status, signifying that your house had electricity at a time when most people had old-fashioned iceboxes. For many, their childhood kitchen had more in common with the 1767 kitchen than with the 1959 model located inside the mansion. People from around the neighborhood brought their imaginations and connections to the project, and their memories helped fill in gaps in the knowledge we had gained from expensive consultants and professional researchers. For instance, Cliveden staff had never heard of the Kitchener range until a family living near Cliveden on Tulpehocken Street offered to show us theirs because some of our architectural evidence revealed similarities to it. By broadening what we considered sources, we were able to connect some dots.

Originally Cliveden planned to restore the colonial cooking hearth and showcase the history of food preparation at the site. Visits to comparable sites showed that many had restored their kitchens to colonial hearths, often hastily, in the 1970s. Those restorations combined nostalgia and guesswork, so that the kitchens were always much too clean. Information was lost or walled over without proper documentation of the cultural resources that the original cooking spaces contained. Cliveden staff considered kitchens with such infill at Mount Pleasant, Grumblethorpe, Stenton, and other house museums in the area. Why should Cliveden invest considerable resources to reconstruct a colonial cooking space that could be found at other sites—since doing so would impose one period of significance and potentially obliterate others? In the case of the 1767 kitchen, restoring it to its period of construction or period of significance (1767–1825) would obscure the history told in the remains of the Kitchener range and the receipts for it. It would mean losing the story of Abdul Raceed, born in India, who lived in the space and cooked for the Chews in the 1950s, and the story of Elmira and Russell Saunders, who lived there when after it was adapted into an apartment and served as cooks and gardeners during the 1960s and 1970s. We might even miss out on the many connections and memories that are evoked when people see the space.

We went back to stakeholders and the community audience and described the journey of the research and the choices: whether to prioritize one period or several, whether to layer many stories or insist on one. It was clear from the research and the audience feedback that the energy was in the muddle of adaptations and layers. For the audience at the Kitchen Conversations, the stories of caretakers, workers, and the hard work that had gone on in the building were more interesting than replicating a single period. Their recommendations made it clear that the colonial period was not the most important one through which to understand the meaning of the 1767 kitchen. The Cliveden board heard our recommendation and approved it. Then we learned something else.

Work on the kitchen's architecture and interpretation was featured in the food section of the *Philadelphia Inquirer*.[42] Because of the kitchens project, several of the recipes from the Mixing Memories project even made it into the newspaper's article. The response to that news coverage was outstanding. One couple visited Cliveden for the first time with pictures and information about their great-aunt and great-uncle, James Burns and Catherine Crowley Burns, Irish immigrants who worked at Cliveden in the late 1890s as gardener and cook, respectively. We did not know about the Burnses until their descendants saw the article about Cliveden in the newspaper. By telling the story differently and examining the empty buildings in ways that suggest layers of occupation and use, we do not need to have all the answers in order to pose provocative questions. We know that the Kitchen Dependency was the busiest building on the site, and the stories that we have already uncovered show how misguided it would be to ignore them in order to cherry-pick a single, early period in its life. A stereotyped Colonial Revival version of the colonial kitchen does not apply to a grand mansion staffed by enslaved and indentured people and eventually working-class immigrants. People bring their imaginations to the question of what the past was like, and part of the historical experience is to consider many different versions of what the building was. One particular example stood out.

An arts component of the Living Kitchens project brought dancers, musicians, and interpretive artists to Cliveden's grounds one summer weekend to illuminate the 1767 and 1959 kitchens for a neighborhood audience. One of the highlights of the evening program took place in the dark, behind the Cliveden mansion. Projected onto the Kitchen Dependency was a poem, "the ballad of laura nelson," by Yolanda Wisher, a Germantown resident and, at the time, poet laureate of the city of Philadelphia. The poem, about lynching in Pennsylvania, whose words and images were presented silently on the building's exterior to an audience seated on the grounds behind the buildings, revealed that our projections onto these empty buildings gives them meaning.[43] People reading the words experienced the 1767 Kitchen Dependency, at variance with the summer night and the surroundings, prompting a personal, even visceral, understanding of the building's history and ways that it can be changed.

Lessons from Empty Buildings

At Cliveden and elsewhere, the community helped lend meaning to Town Hall, the potter's field, Upsala, and the Kitchen Dependency. They are not so empty now, thanks to arts, advocacy, association, and imagination. An open process that contributes to a shared experience of the spaces takes us beyond building-ism, and because of adaptation we would not have the building. Rigidity made Town Hall and Upsala empty, but flexibility and openness to new approaches keep the potter's field and the Kitchen Dependency empty. The story of how a place or structure came this far and how it got to look as it does is at least as important as whether something historically significant happened in it.

Germantown's empty buildings, perhaps even more than its national historic landmarks filled with fine furnishings, offer lessons that may be transferrable to other communities. Not all neighborhoods have Underground Railroad stations, settings for Revolutionary War battles, or sites of plantation violence. But many communities have a hulking municipal building that reflects values long gone or changed, or the grand home of a wealthy family, beautiful but without a compelling story, or a site where a previously marginalized but newly empowered ethnic group found a way to address past wrongs. Most people have a kitchen, too. All of these places can provide lessons about choices people faced in the past and ways to consider what one would do if confronted with similar circumstances.

One lesson of Germantown's empty buildings is about building trust in a process through which meaning can be found for a site so that, in turn, a use that is helpful to the neighborhood can be devised. By working to establish trust, the advocacy of the Northwest Neighbors group found ways to influence the plans of the PHA. The PHA agreed to several of the advocates' demands, including a landscaping plan that reflects the community's desire for commemorative space and respectful placement of the playground. Compare that outcome with the meaning imposed on the site in 1955. A faulty sense of what the community needed imposed a different meaning on Town Hall in the 1920s. Civic leaders wanted something that would overcome its insecurity at no longer being an independent town. The same stubborn insecurity kept the Rockefeller myth alive way beyond a reasonable lifespan because Germantown's collective identity was bound up in what it thought it could have been. That myth also showed people's distrust in the version of history their leaders had passed down: The myth was never confirmed, but it made sense to people that Germantown's leaders had messed up a great opportunity. The artists and organizers of the Hidden City Festival who brought some life to Town Hall in 2013 had to work to establish trust among community members because of the different ideas about creative uses for the building. This effort, though brief, created momentum and helped promote the work going on in Vernon Park. Using the arts helped make Town Hall a useful place rather than a hulk left to decay because the nostalgia-based way of thinking got in the way of a more community-friendly building.

Even empty buildings and vacant city spaces have been invested with meaning: impressions created, feelings stirred, connections to a place that go far beyond building-ism. There will be many more empty buildings, as there will be many more battles about what do to with them. A public process can help us construct shared answers. It takes hard work to build a trustworthy public process, but the results beat imposing a mythic sense of importance on a site: a decision that doomed the 1925 Town Hall. An open process gives a hearing to multiple perspectives on how to use a space or a structure that stands empty and is in need of adaptation. This openness is essential to evolving our understanding of what to make of buildings, and it is essential to our understanding of history.

Conclusion

I n this book I describe uphill struggles, including my own, to make Germantown history relevant to more kinds of people. These battles have been fought throughout the past one hundred years. Effective public history requires an iterative, ongoing effort that challenges people to extend their personal feelings about the past beyond self-interested promotion in order to connect to something larger: a shared sense of how what happened in the past connects us as human beings. Because people have emotional attachments to history, the battles have been necessary. A book titled *The Battles of Germantown*, however, is difficult to bring to a conclusion. That such battles will surely continue is an essential point of this book, because public history has to be pushed, shared, and explored if it is to remain relevant.

Now, as before, conflicts are played out in board meetings and community forums about historic designation, development plans, and who gets to decide. Examples from 2017 show how the same passions and issues that fueled similar battles in decades past continue to arise. In spring 2017 the Pennsylvania state historical commission considered two historical markers for Germantown. They accepted the one for John Trower (1849–1911), an influential African American caterer and philanthropist whose marker was placed on Germantown Avenue next to Vernon Park. The marker for the famed American tennis player Bill Tilden (1893–1953), the first American to win Wimbledon, was declined. After a storied tennis career in the 1920s, Tilden ran afoul of the law and was convicted of contributing to the delinquency of a minor for soliciting a fourteen-year-old boy; he was later charged with violating his parole when he was found in a car with a teenager. The state historical commission took up the Tilden marker in the wake of the Penn State University pedophilia scandal, when university officials were accused of enabling the football coach Jerry Sandusky's sexual abuse of children. The commission decided that it should consider the entire history of the person being nominated, and therefore bestowing a marker on Tilden "may be perceived to dishonor victims of sexual abuse at a time when Pennsylvanians are especially sensitive to this issue." When the decision was announced, Allen Hornblum, the Tilden biographer who had written the nomination, complained that the state authorities were "acting like politicians afraid of public opinion."[1] It was as if the nominator was asking how public history got so political. As I argue in this book, public history and historic preservation have always been Political, with a capital *P* (as in Criterion P). Recognizing this fact, and being considerate about others' viewpoints, is essential: We have to reckon with all the ways in which the past has been made public in order to expand our knowledge with new discoveries and find different approaches to contemporary problems.

As I write this, another historic Germantown building, the Germantown Boys and Girls Club, is up for designation by the Philadelphia Historical Commission, and the effort has sparked another full-on battle. Advocates for listing the 1886 building want to secure local protection for it because the club has plans for a large, multimillion-dollar ice rink and youth activity center that proposed to demolish the original club building. Some public officials support the ice rink project because it will bring services and construction jobs. Some neighbors do not want it because the building is out of scale with the one-lane neighborhood streets, and the proposed construction will dominate the landscape now occupied by rowhouses and the old boys and girls club. The meeting about designation got political in a very public way. Those who argued against historic designation brought up the fact that the boys and girls clubs had been segregated in Germantown well into the early twentieth century (much as Germantown's YWCA and YMCA had been segregated). The defenders of the development, including public officials, claimed that historic preservation has been racist in Germantown and this incident would be only the latest in a process that has made Germantown what they argued was a segregated Jim Crow neighborhood. When the case originally came before the Philadelphia Historical Commission, the developer had made only one presentation to the neighborhood group. There was no real chance for both sides to be heard—other than on Facebook, through a newly formed Facebook group. When each side gets a hearing and the facts are laid out in terms of agreed-on values, people often find room for give and take. In the case of the boys and girls club, no such opportunity had been organized. As the director of Germantown United community development corporation stated, "We need to have a conversation."[2] Without such conversations, neither side has to face questions based on assumptions and interpretations that might be different from theirs—a feature that is essential to the process of building a community of memory.

In June 2017 leaders of the Johnson House Historic Site complained that the Center City Juneteenth festival was stealing the spotlight from Germantown's festival, which was scheduled for the same weekend. Here was one African American group arguing with another over who controls the history festival.[3] Efforts to control a narrative, impose authority over the commemoration of the past, or present only one version of it are misguided because they close off the chance for partnerships that can bring greater understanding through new perspectives. Public history programs that merely promote the self-interest of a single group are a misuse of kind of energy and result in short-lived projects and partnerships that depend on personalities. If they are to last, programs must be broad-based.

Monument Lab, a major citywide art project run by the Philadelphia Mural Arts Program, produced rancor and criticism in Germantown. From the beginning of September through mid-November 2017, installations in prominent parks and squares, including Philadelphia's City Hall and Rittenhouse Square, played with the form of public statues and monuments. Each was done in a distinctive style by a different artist. For Vernon Park, scene of many public history festivals over the past century, Karyn Olivier, a Germantown resident, blanketed a monument to the 1777 battle with reflective material, inviting people to see themselves in it.[4] Because this was Germantown, the Vernon Park installation generated so much vocal disapproval from colonial-centric tunnel-vision residents that one newspaper called it "the New Battle of Germantown." A neighbor quoted in the article complained: "You covered the monument that is about Germantown! People come from all around the world to see the reenactment. People want to read about Germantown. We are the only park that had its monument covered. Germantown often gets written out, unless it's something bad."[5] Though the first Battle of Germantown lasted

Figure C.1 Karyn Olivier, *The Battle Is Joined*, 2017. Olivier's provocative installation brought Philadelphia's Monument Lab project to Germantown's Vernon Park; the citywide program invited the public to reflect on local historical markers. (Monument Lab 2017. Courtesy of Karyn Olivier.)

only a few hours in the long history of the neighborhood, people are passionate about what they feel belongs to them, including their local history.

This book offers many examples of people wasting passion and energy on an effort to exert control over the past. Releasing control is scary, however, especially when the people involved do not otherwise have much power. Change and difference bring conflict and fear—which can be seen as useful energy if people are willing to stretch themselves to understand. When the passions motivated by the past are applied to experience, dialogue, multiple partnerships, and varied ways of knowing the past, those energies can be better spent on making history useful and making Germantown and places like it better.

The stories in this book show how energies come into conflict when people try to apply the past. Not all of these efforts succeeded—or lasted. But even the attempts that did not work out provide lessons about the limits of public history. Even Germantown's cautionary tales provide hope and information about the potential for effective public history. Let's not hurry bad news, as my ninety-year-old informant advised, but keep in mind that by relinquishing control and allowing more information and perspectives into the conversation about what we think we know about the past, we will find opportunities.

The "battles" of each chapter reflect the neighborhood's sense of urgency about the issues that history is supposed to inform. The architectural historian Jeffrey Cohen said at a meeting about the boys and girls club building: "Perhaps it would be good to know the whole story, even if it reflects badly on the neighborhood."[6] The stories in this book present history in ways that do not always reflect well on the neighborhood, its institutions, or its stewards of historical memory. The efforts of the twenty-first century, however, and our insistence on open discussion and even criticism of what happened in the past, are part of a shared history that can help Germantowners overcome their tendency to be motivated primarily by self-interest. By making the public aware of even the tough stuff of the past, effective public history can turn Germantown's battles—past, present, and future—into constructive experiences.

Negative history is entitled to a seat at the table too. The community of memory is the key, so that people commit to constructing a shared heritage and are willing to celebrate the good and critically examine the bad. The model works if people accept the fact that dialogue and analysis take work, commitment, and follow-through. Only through iterative processes dependent on active listening to points of view other than one's own can public history be a driver of positive results. When the history is applied only in opposition to something—such as change, newcomers, different approaches, new economic pressures—it is harder to push people past their self-interest, but even under these less than ideal conditions, it is possible to craft something different beyond mere opposition.

Emphasizing dialogue, participation, and respect for other points of view should be the work of public history, as much as documentation, conservation, and arresting the decay of the built fabric of a community. The buildings are only as important as the values that their stewards can convey to a visitor, such as whether a place is open, welcoming, and safe, and whether they are willing to consider the possibility that it holds a meaning that is broader than they know. Thus, Cliveden addressed slave owning in very public settings; Historic Germantown worked with churches and students to build a public forum to discuss civil rights in the neighborhood. From November 2015 to May 2017, Historic Germantown brought artists and the public together in historic sites in a program called "Elephants on the Avenue: Race, Class, and Community in Historic Germantown."[7] The name plays on the expression "an elephant in the room." In the last few years we have learned that the neighborhood's challenges resist simple, oppositional descriptions. Respecting the complexity of the past and openly discussing it are what public history needs to be doing. The processes that shaped Cliveden's Conversations have been influential beyond the gates of Cliveden—so much so that both sides of the debate over the boys and girls club even convened at the Cliveden Carriage House late in the summer of 2017 and engaged in a conversation-based approach to mediation.

The arts and artists have greatly enhanced Germantown's history and have been instrumental in making history relevant and accessible. Cliveden's *Liberty to Go to See* and Historic Germantown's "Elephants on the Avenue" continue a tradition that began with Negro Achievement Week, which used collaborative partnerships and a broad community conversation to get people to see African Americans in new ways and address discrimination, segregation, and a rising nativism and racism in Philadelphia. The Germantown artist Benton Spruance led an effort to document discrimination in the mid-1940s and 1950s. Artists provoke dialogue and even heated exchanges whose energy can be used to open up opportunities, as with the 2013 Town Hall project. Even when such programs are temporary—when key institutions do not systematize their cooperation or resources run out—they may be unearthed as history and reexamined in today's light, lending context and informing current battles because Germantown has seen these efforts before.

Mid-century business leaders attempted to craft a colonial experience to address economic decline, using Germantown history as a tool. The project was focused on economic results for a few businesses and was unreceptive to broader viewpoints or creative social partnerships. Thus, the opportunity to address community needs through history-based economic development gained insufficient political support. When the neighborhood timeline was extended beyond the colonial era, new discoveries pushed the Johnson House into the spotlight as a symbol of African American empowerment and a struggle for freedom that whites and blacks engaged in together. J. Gordon Baugh Jr.'s 1913 *Souvenir of Germantown* album had embraced African American history, but the establishment of the Johnson House institutionalized the importance of African American stories, even when they are told in a home that belonged to white people.

Consideration of the broader meaning of events, and recognition that all facts are open to interpretation, brought new partnerships and creative ways to interpret the past—even the same topics that Germantown had always celebrated, such as the colonial era or its architectural beauty. Publicly engaging with history can change what we thought we knew. The process involves bringing meaning and experience, the personal and subjective, into the interpretation. Such uses of effective public history help Germantown's story grow and evolve, even when we do not yet know all the answers, such as the names of the enslaved people at Cliveden or the stories of people who escaped to freedom via the Johnson House. Even without knowing the whole story, it is possible to make connections with people when we become comfortable operating without total understanding, complete information, or a sense of closure. Because not everything has to be a house museum.

A lived-in house is an open system. You can hear conversations in other rooms. Items are not arranged chronologically. People come in and out through different doors, meaning that they have different paths to entry in a room. When we seal off a house by making it a historic house museum, we make it a closed system, with a specific and limited period of significance. Germantown has worked hard to become an open system, to get beyond the building-ism that can close off the public's experience of a place or its story. By pushing open what had been a closed-off, exclusive, and even gated sense of the past, separate from most of the people in the neighborhood, Germantown's public history has generated a sense of hope and opportunity in ways that may help others.

Every place is different, but I believe that many communities are "places like Germantown" and may see parallels and similarities in my neighborhood's numerous battles. Today, when cities such as Charlottesville and Charleston have become sites associated with hate-based violence, local public history is being used as a way to inform people's understanding of the situation. The 2015 shooting at the Emanuel AME Church led historic sites such as Drayton Hall in South Carolina and even the Smithsonian Museum of African American History and Culture to use art, history, and memorial displays and installations to help heal the public. Even as white supremacists in Charlottesville marched to protest the removal of a Confederate monument, Thomas Jefferson's Monticello, James Madison's Montpelier, and other local historic sites were candidly discussing their history of slavery.

Connections are possible, and public history, because it is elementally social, because it is public, must be understood as a point of connection. As individuals, we cannot tickle ourselves or smell our own breath. Only through social interaction can we understand certain things about ourselves, and that includes our understanding of the past. Effective public history actively crafts experiences, such as conversations, in order to overcome the natural tendency to remain in one self-serving narrative and the amnesia that can result; it acknowledges and addresses limits of authority over the past as a way to restore the integrity of the past's ability to lend context to the present; and it makes clear when we project our own needs on to the past in simplistic ways oblivious to the complexity of history which forms the basis of our shared humanity.

———————

In the days after the 2016 presidential election, I received calls from a school, a church, and a college history department asking for suggestions about how to moderate discussions sparked by the election of Donald Trump. The callers wanted to do Cliveden Conversations–style mediated dialogues for people feeling scared, angry, passionate, and desperate to process fear and uncertainty about how the Trump administration's policies (especially on immigration) might affect them. Whom did Cliveden recommend for stimulating dialogue? Which psychologists helped Cliveden bring neighbors into the discussion of slaveholding by the

Chews? What advice could I offer for constructing community discussions or student forums?

Ten years ago, who would have thought of calling a historic site for this kind of advice? The requests show the power of effective public history and what it can do to provide context and inform discussion. The case of the Germantown Boys and Girls Club offers an example. Both sides agreed to participate in conversations based on a common desire to address community needs, allowing each side to see the viewpoint of the other side and perhaps to regard their own side differently once they learned the broader story. With context and open discussion of painful subjects, there is a way forward. In November 2017 a two-day forum explored the 1967 student protest against the lack of African American history in the public school curriculum. The fiftieth anniversary events brought together people who took part in it, public officials and historians of the period, but the program did not commemorate the 1967 event as much as it considered how to change inequities in public funding for Philadelphia schools today—the results of which closed Germantown High School in 2013.[8] The event shows the importance to the public of applying history as context in order to address contemporary challenges. A few weeks after the open process that Cliveden used to bring Upsala under a new form of stewardship by returning it to a private residence, I was contacted by several nonprofit organizations that have too much historic house on their hands and want to understand the "Upsala approach" to adapting the building or finding a new steward for it in a responsible, ethical, sustainable manner.

Germantown remains a parable for and an incubator of public history. In the end, its many battles represent cautionary tales for the field at large but also hopeful, practical examples of people working to overcome the tendencies toward self-interest that are inherent in encounters with the past. Dialogue, partnerships, and openness to new ways of knowing the past make a difference—they have in Germantown. They must become part of regular, iterative routines for stewards of Germantown's public history, or the battles will get harder. If the neighborhood's history, its historic sites and artifacts, are to remain relevant in a place where history matters, the answer lies in our ability to overcome our personal views, consider those of others, and experience new ways of understanding the past. Though difficult, it is important work because effective public history builds a lasting sense of community and a deeper appreciation of the world in which we live.

Acknowledgments

To complete this book was a group effort. I am indebted to many people who supported my writing, listened to my ideas, participated in discussions as my thinking evolved, and even talked me in off the ledge. First and foremost, I thank Aaron Javsicas, along with the Editorial Advisory Board and staff at Temple University Press and Steven Conn, series editor. Their patience and encouragement have been consistent and abiding. I hope this volume serves the series well. Jane Barry worked with me tirelessly to improve the manuscript and offer advice and perspective. I thank Cecelia Cancellaro and the public historians Seth Bruggeman, Ken Finkel, Stephen Hague, Laura Keim, and Michelle McClellan, as well as anonymous reviewers, for reading portions of the manuscript at various stages. Sharon Reid's help in the research and selection of images was invaluable.

At the Germantown Historical Society, Alex Bartlett supported my research and opened doors to further discovery. The staffs and boards at each of the historic sites of Germantown have been a source of constant inspiration. I am grateful, in particular, to Jonathon Burton, Brandi Levine, Dennis Pickeral, John Pollack, Mark Sellers, Stacey Swigart, and Jacqueline Wiggins for their enthusiasm in stewarding all the stories of America's most historic neighborhood. James Duffin answered every one of my calls and queries, usually within minutes; his interest in Germantown's centuries of history is infectious. At the University of Pennsylvania Graduate Program in Historic Preservation, Randall F. Mason and Frank

Matero encouraged my teaching about Germantown. I thank Francesca Ammon, Bill Ewing, Graham Finney, and Mary Ann Tyler for talking me through the intricacies of midcentury urban renewal in Philadelphia.

Cliveden's entire staff and board, past and present, have nourished this project by forging a vision for the site as a life force; I thank, in particular, Jennifer Celata, Mary DeNadai, Erica A. Dunbar, Rick Fink, Darryl Ford, Libbie Hawes, Alan Keiser, Bob MacDonnell, Mimi McKenzie, Randall Miller, Ted Reed, Anne Roller, Carolyn Wallace, and the late Jack Asher and John Chew, as well as the interns and guides who sustained the work that makes Cliveden not just a noun but also a verb in Germantown. The Pew Center for Arts and Heritage generously supported many of the initiatives described in the book; I thank Bill Adair and Laura Koloski for their faith and vision. And I am grateful to every participant in Cliveden Conversations, Germantown Speaks, and other such programs for showing how community involvement can bring forth more effective public history.

At the National Trust for Historic Preservation, David J. Brown, Katherine Malone-France, Tom Mayes, and Stephanie Meeks have nourished this book's journey and many of the projects it describes. The site directors of the National Trust continue to be its greatest national treasure; neither this book nor Cliveden's work would be as effective as they are without the network of directors who bring life to history in the most creative ways possible. Special thanks go to David Janssen, Kevin Kuharic, Erin Carlson Mast, George McDaniel, Therese Pasqual, Greg Sages, and Morris Vogel for the example they have set. I am grateful to the members of the Landmarks Committee of the National Park Service Advisory, especially Cary Carson, Luis Hoyos, Sarah Leavitt, Steven Pitti, and Amber Wiley, for insights and encouragement. This book has benefited from my presentations at the Seminar in Historical Administration (now the History Leadership Institute), run annually by the American Association of State and Local History. I thank Bob Beatty, John Durel, and Max van Balgooy for insisting that I include Germantown projects as live issues for the consideration of emerging leaders.

I thank my family and friends, whose steadfast interest in this book's completion has kept me moving forward. One cannot bring a project like this to fruition without encouragement from one's partners in life. I therefore thank my dogs: Flossie, who showed me the way; Junior, who understood completely; and Grady, who listened to every single word.

Ultimately, though, I owe this book to my wife, Sloan, and my son, Stanton, who both joined me in learning what Germantown really means to all of us.

Notes

INTRODUCTION

1. The continual need to define "public history" has been one of the field's longtime challenges. See, for instance, Robert Weible, "Defining Public History: Is It Possible? Is It Necessary?" *Perspectives: The Newsmagazine of the American Historical Association* 46, no. 3 (March 2008), https://www.historians.org/publications-and-directories/perspectives-on-history/march-2008/defining-public-history-is-it-possible-is-it-necessary; Cathy Stanton, "'What Is Public History?' Redux," *Public History News* 27, no. 4 (September 2007): 1, 14; Ronald J. Grele, "Whose Public? Whose History? What Is the Goal of a Public Historian?" *Public Historian* 3, no. 1 (Winter 1981): 46; Ian Tyrell, "Public at the Creation: Place, Memory, and Historical Practice in the Mississippi Valley Historical Association, 1907–1950," *Journal of American History* 94, no. 1 (June 2007): 19–46.

2. The National Historic Colonial Landmark District also covers Northwest Philadelphia, though the boundaries considered in my book extend farther west into Roxborough and farther east into East Germantown than does the district nomination. See Mark Lloyd and Carl E. Doebley, *National Register for Historic Places Inventory: Nomination Form, Addendum to Colonial Germantown Historic District, Both Sides of Germantown Avenue from Windrim Avenue to Sharpnack Street* (Philadelphia: Clio Group for City of Philadelphia, December 1982).

3. David Contosta, "Philadelphia's 'Miniature Williamsburg': The Colonial Revival and Germantown's Market Square," *Pennsylvania Magazine of History and Biography* 120, no. 4 (October 1996): 286–287.

4. *Wirkungsgeschichte* comes from the work of Hans-Georg Gadamer on philosophy and hermeneutics. Gadamer claims that history or tradition is not simply the past but a process of realization. History conditions our historical understanding. An interpreter is subject to the way in which an object has already been understood in the

tradition to which the interpreter belongs. Any understanding is historically situated and is rooted in prejudice. Thus, understanding is not the act of a subject but an aspect of effective history. See, for instance, Sinead Murphy, *Effective History: On Critical Practice under Historical Conditions* (Evanston, IL: Northwestern University Press, 2010).

5. See, for instance, Melinda J. Milligan, "Buildings as History: The Place of Collective Memory in the Study of Historic Preservation," *Symbolic Interaction* 30, no. 1 (Winter 2007): 105–123; Alon Confino, "Collective Memory and Cultural History: Problems of Method," *American Historical Review* 102, no. 5 (December 1997): 1386–1403; Daniel Levy and Sara Kocher, "Perception of Sacredness at Heritage Religious Sites," *Environment and Behavior* 45, no. 7 (2012): 912–930.

6. See Mat Johnson's fictional depiction of contemporary Germantown, set in a former house museum, *Loving Day: A Novel* (New York: Spiegel and Grau, 2015), 3.

7. My thanks to Dr. Katie Day for this quotation.

8. For a recent initiative see "A Hope for Revival: Apartments Planned for Germantown Landmark," *Philadelphia Inquirer,* February 26, 2017.

9. On Watson, see Deborah D. Waters, "Philadelphia's Boswell: John Fanning Watson," *Philadelphia Magazine of History and Biography* 98, no. 4 (1974): 3–49; Susan Stabile, *Memory's Daughters: The Material Culture of Remembrance in Eighteenth-Century America* (Ithaca, NY: Cornell University Press, 2004), 7.

10. The literature on Germantown history is voluminous. Traditional, antiquarian accounts begin with John Fanning Watson, *Annals of Philadelphia and Pennsylvania in Olden Times,* rev. ed., 2 vols. (Philadelphia: E. Thomas, 1857); Dr. Naaman H. Keyser, C. Henry Kain, John Palmer Garber, and Horace F. McCann, *History of Old Germantown with a Description of Its Settlement and Some Account of Its Important Persons, Buildings, and Places Connected with Its Development,* vol. 1 (Germantown, Philadelphia: H. F. McCann, 1907); papers read before the Site and Relic Society of Germantown, reflecting the attitudes and interests of the upper class, were collected and printed as *Germantown History* (Germantown: Author, 1915); for the history of the township before Mount Airy and Chestnut Hill pursued their separate courses, see Edward W. Hocker, *Germantown, 1683–1933: The Record That a Pennsylvania Community Has Achieved in the Course of 250 Years; Being a History of the People of Germantown, Mount Airy and Chestnut Hill* (Philadelphia, 1933). Stephanie Grauman Wolf's thorough examination of social history in the colonial period, *Urban Village: Population, Community, and Family Structure in Germantown, Pennsylvania, 1683–1800* (Princeton, NJ: Princeton University Press, 1976), has recently been complemented by James M. Duffin's records of the founding of Germantown, *Acta Germanopolis: Records of the Corporation of Germantown, Pennsylvania, 1691–1707* (Philadelphia: Colonial Society of Pennsylvania, 2008). Architectural studies include Harry M. Tinkcom, Margaret B. Tinkcom, and Grant Miles Simon, F.A.I.A., *Historic Germantown from the Founding to the Early Part of the Nineteenth Century: A Survey of the German Township* (Philadelphia: American Philosophical Society, 1955); Joseph Minardi, *Historic Architecture in Northwest Philadelphia 1690 to 1930s* (Atglen, PA: Schiffer Books, 2012).

11. The term "memory infrastructure" was coined by Randall Mason. See "Historic Preservation, Public Memory and the Making of Modern New York City," in *Giving Preservation a History: Histories of Historic Preservation in the United States,* ed. Max Page and Randall Mason (New York: Routledge, 2004), 133–142.

12. Ninety churches and three mosques line an 8.5-mile stretch of Germantown Avenue, averaging more than ten per mile. Katie Day, *Prelude to Struggle: African American Clergy and Community Organizing for Economic Development in the 1990s* (New York: University Press of America, 2002).

13. John Sprinkle, *Crafting Preservation Criteria: The National Register of Historic Places and American Historic Preservation* (New York: Routledge, 2014), 5, 123.

14. Samuel W. Pennypacker, *The Settlement of Germantown, Pennsylvania and the Beginning of Germantown Emigration to North America* (Philadelphia: W. J. Campbell, 1899).

15. The end of the nineteenth century saw many groups proclaim their connections to the early days of Germantown. See, for instance, Julius F. Sache, *The German Pietists of Pennsylvania* (1895); Julius F. Sache, *The German Sectarians of Pennsylvania,* vol. 1 (1889), covering 1708–1742, and vol. 2 (1900); Martin G. Brumbaugh, *A History of the German Baptist Brethren* (Elgin, IL: Brethren Publishing House, 1899); Anne de B. Mears, *The Old York Road and Its Early Associations, 1670–1870* (Philadelphia: Harper and Brother, 1890); A. C. Lambdin, *A Century of Germantown Methodism* (Germantown: Germantown Independent Publishing, 1895); Horace W. Smith, ed., *The History of Germantown Academy* (Philadelphia: Ferguson Brothers, 1882).

16. See Max Page and Marla R. Miller, eds., *Bending the Future: Fifty Ideas for the Next Fifty Years of Historic Preservation in the United States* (Amherst: University of Massachusetts Press, 2016), 11–12.

17. See Franklin D. Vagnone and Deborah E. Ryan, *Anarchist's Guide to Historic House Museums* (Walnut Creek, CA: Left Coast Press, 2016), 38.

18. Ned Kaufman, *Place, Race, and Story: Essays on the Past and Future of Historic Preservation* (New York: Routledge, 2009), 76.

19. For demographic information from the postwar period, see population analysis of the entire German Township in Barbara Ferman, Theresa Singleton, and Don Demarco, "West Mount Airy, Philadelphia," *Cityscape: A Journal of Policy Development and Research* 4, no. 2 (1998): 30.

20. Census figures for Germantown and East Germantown taken from www.city data.com, accessed March 2017.

21. Russell A. Kazal, *Becoming Old Stock: The Paradox of German American Identity* (Princeton, NJ: Princeton University Press, 2004), 6, 58, 64–65.

22. Peter Sager, "Die 'Langen Kerls' in Germantown: Auch sie halten die Tradition noch hoch—vor 300 Jahren kamen die ersten Deutschen nach Amerika," *Zeit Magazin* 18 (1983): 8–22.

23. For readings on the decline of house museums from the past decade, see the essays in *America's Historic Sites at a Crossroads, Forum Journal* 22, no. 3 (Spring 2008). See also Carol B. Stapp and Kenneth C. Turino, "Does America Need Another House Museum?" *History News* 59, no. 3 (Summer 2004): 7–11; Cary Carson, "The End of History Museums: What's Plan B?" *Public Historian* 30, no. 4 (Fall 2008): 9–27.

24. Katharine Gerbner, "'We Are against the Traffik of Men-body': The Germantown Quaker Protest of 1688 and the Origins of America Abolitionism," *Pennsylvania History: A Journal of Mid-Atlantic Studies* 74, no. 2 (Spring 2007): 149–172; "Antislavery in Print: The Germantown Protest, the 'Exhortation,' and the Seventeenth-Century Quaker Debate on Slavery," *Early American Studies: An Interdisciplinary Journal* 9, no. 3 (Fall 2011): 552–575.

25. The contradiction is explored in Donna McDaniel and Vanessa Julye, *Fit for Freedom, Not for Friendship: Quakers, African Americans, and the Myth of Racial Justice* (Springfield, PA: Quaker Press, 2009).

26. David W. Young, "The Battles of Germantown: Preservation and Memory in America's Most Historic Neighborhood" (Ph.D. diss., Ohio State University, 2009), 49–59.

27. Robert Gregg, *Sparks from the Anvil of Oppression: Philadelphia's African Methodists and Southern Migrants, 1890–1940* (Philadelphia: Temple University Press, 1993), 14–25. See also John H. Hepp IV, *The Middle Class City: Transforming Space and Time in Philadelphia: 1876–1926* (Philadelphia: University of Pennsylvania Press, 2003), 34; Kazal, *Becoming Old Stock*, 6, 58–65.

28. Abigail Perkiss, *Making Good Neighbors: Civil Rights, Liberalism, and Integration in Postwar Philadelphia* (Ithaca, NY: Cornell University Press, 2014); Amy E. Hillier, "Spatial Analysis of Historical Redlining: A Methodological Explanation," *Journal of Housing Research* 14, no. 1 (2003): 137–167.

29. See Erika M. Kitzmiller, "The Roots of Educational Inequality: Germantown High School, 1907–2011" (Ph.D. diss., University of Pennsylvania, 2012).

30. Elijah Anderson, *Code of the Street: Decency, Violence, and the Moral Life of the Inner City* (New York: W. W. Norton, 1999); *The Cosmopolitan Canopy: Race and Civility in Everyday Life* (New York: W. W. Norton, 2011).

31. Katie Day, *Faith on the Avenue: Religion on a City Street* (New York: Oxford University Press, 2014), 31–41, 167–168.

32. Richard Handler and Eric Gable, *The New History in an Old Museum: Creating the Past at Colonial Williamsburg* (Durham, NC: Duke University Press, 1997), 222–235.

33. See Max Page, *Why Preservation Matters* (New Haven, CT: Yale University Press, 2016); also, "Beyond Pretty Buildings: How Historic Preservation Can Solve Social Ills," *Chronicle of Higher Education,*" January 13, 2017, where Page argues, "Preservation can have a powerful continuing argument for efforts from the past to achieve a more just society" (1).

34. Consider the essays about community-curated exhibitions in Bill Adair, Benjamin Filene, and Laura Koloski, eds., *Letting Go: Shared Historical Authority in a User-Generated World* (Philadelphia: Pew Center for Arts and Heritage, 2011).

35. Gail Dubrow, "From Minority to Majority: Moving On and Moving Beyond the Politics of Identity in Historic Preservation," in Page and Miller, *Bending the Future,* 72.

36. Ira Berlin, *The Long Emancipation: The Demise of Slavery in the United States* (Cambridge, MA: Harvard University Press, 2015), 1.

37. See Page and Miller, *Bending the Future,* 8, 11–12.

38. Quoted in Richard Rabinowitz, *Curating America: Journeys through Storyscapes of the American Past* (Chapel Hill: University of North Carolina Press, 2016), 8. See also Kaufman, *Place, Race, and Story,* 38–42.

CHAPTER 1

1. See James M. Lindgren, "'A Spirit That Fires the Imagination': Historic Preservation and Cultural Regeneration in Virginia and New England, 1850–1950," in *Giving Preservation a History: Histories of Historic Preservation in the United States,* ed. Max Page and Randall Mason (New York: Routledge, 2004), 108–109.

2. Michael Wallace, "Visiting the Past: History Museums in the United States," in *Presenting the Past: Critical Perspectives on History and the Public,* ed. Susan Porter Benson, Steven Brier, and Roy Rosenzweig (Philadelphia: Temple University Press, 1986), 154–164.

3. See, for instance, J. Freedom du Lac, "Struggling to Attract Visitors, Historic Sites May Have to Face Day of Reckoning," *Washington Post,* December 22, 2012; Ruth Graham, "The Great Historic House Museum Debate," *Boston Globe,* August 10, 2014.

4. The Pew Charitable Trusts' 2005 report estimates the number of organizations in Philadelphia and the four surrounding counties to be between 300 and 400, of which 275 were house museums. See, for instance, Donna A. Harris, *New Solutions for House Museums* (Lanham, MD: Alta Mira Press, 2007), 17n8.

5. The following sites formed the consortium at its founding: Cliveden, Upsala, Concord Schoolhouse, Germantown Mennonite Information Center, Wyck, Ebenezer Maxwell Mansion, Deshler-Morris House, Grumblethorpe, Germantown Historical Society, Loudoun, Stenton, Paley Design Center, and La Salle College Art Museum.

6. See Gerald George, "Historic House Museum Malaise: A Conference Considers What's Wrong," *History News* 57, no. 4 (Fall 2002): 21–25.

7. The omission of any mention of slaves at Cliveden was galling to Gary Nash: see his *First City: Philadelphia and the Forging of Historical Memory* (Philadelphia: University of Pennsylvania Press, 2002), 53. At the time that book was published, only one Chew plantation was well known. Today we know of nine.

8. See Harris, *New Solutions,* 3–78, as well as more recent coverage, such as du Lac, "Struggling to Attract Visitors"; Graham, "Great Historic House Museum Debate."

9. See John Durel and Anita Durel, "A Golden Age for Historic Sites," *America's Historic Sites at a Crossroads, Forum Journal* 22, no. 3 (Spring 2008): 43–51.

10. This account is based on drafts of "History Hunters Youth Report Curriculum" and correspondence between Stenton and Wiggins, History Hunters files, 2001–2002, Johnson House Historic Site, and conversations between members of the History Hunters advisory team and the author, 2004.

11. On the collaboration among the sites of Historic Germantown Preserved, see Stephen G. Hague, "History Revisited," *Context: The Journal of the American Institute for Architects,* Summer 2008, 28–32.

12. As of 2017, the following sites were part of Historic Germantown: Cliveden, Concord Schoolhouse, Johnson House Historic Site, Germantown Mennonite Historic Trust, Wyck, Ebenezer Maxwell Mansion, "Germantown White House" (the Deshler-Morris House), Grumblethorpe, ACES Museum, Germantown Historical Society, Loudoun, Stenton, Hood Cemetery, Historic Fair Hill Cemetery, Historic RittenhouseTown, and La Salle University Art Museum.

13. Molly Lester, "Germantown Speaks: Intergenerational Discussions on the Philadelphia Neighborhood's Past and Present," *Sacred Places: The Magazine of Partners for Sacred Places,* Spring 2010, 15–18.

14. See http://www.freedomsbackyard.com and https://www.youtube.com/user/GermantownSpeaks.

15. Edward Lawler Jr., "The President's House in Philadelphia: The Rediscovery of a Lost Landmark," *Pennsylvania Magazine of History and Biography* 129, no. 4 (October 2002): 371–410.

16. The meeting is summarized in Doris Devine Fanelli, "President's House Civic Engagement Forum," Independence National Historical Park report, October

30, 2004. During the meeting, the National Park Service interpreter Joseph Becton received taunts from activists as he explained the layout of the site's original footprint.

17. Lawler summarizes the research process in "The President's House Revisited," *Pennsylvania Magazine of History and Biography* 129, no. 4 (October 2005): 371–410. See also Roger C. Aden, *Slavery, the President's House at Independence National Historical Park, and Public Memory* (Philadelphia: Temple University Press, 2014).

18. Stephan Salisbury, "Glitches Bedevil President's House," *Philadelphia Inquirer*, September 25, 2011, and "Documents Reveal Longstanding Issues at the President's House," *Philadelphia Inquirer*, August 19, 2012.

19. See Seth C. Bruggeman's review of the exhibition, "The President's House: Freedom and Slavery in the Making of a New Nation," Independence National Historical Park, Philadelphia, Pa., *Journal of American History* 100, no. 1 (June 2013): 158.

20. "Preservation Forward," strategic planning document, National Trust for Historic Preservation and Cliveden, September 22, 1994, Cliveden archives.

21. See Phillip R. Seitz, "Notes and Documents: Tales from the Chew Family Papers: The Charity Castle Story," *Pennsylvania Magazine of History and Biography* 132, no. 1 (January 2008): 66–86.

22. The page remained up for the duration of the processing at the Historical Society of Pennsylvania but was taken down when completed, July 31, 2009.

23. Nash, *First City*, 41, 47.

24. Philip Seitz, "The Slaves of Whitehall Plantation: A True Story of Defiance and Resistance," *Delaware History* 33, no. 3 (Spring–Summer 2011): 123–140.

25. See Gary Nash, "For Whom Will the Liberty Bell Toll? From Controversy to Cooperation," in *Slavery and Public History: The Tough Stuff of American Memory*, ed. James Oliver Horton and Lois E. Horton (Chapel Hill: University of North Carolina Press, 2008), 75–102; Stephan Salisbury, "Remaking History," *Philadelphia Inquirer*, June 30, 2008, and "Beneath Independence Mall: Story of Early Free Black America," *Philadelphia Inquirer*, July 2, 2008; see also Rachel Dukeman, "Unearthing Philly History," *Philadelphia Bulletin*, October 9, 2008.

26. Stephan Salisbury, "An Explosion of Sad History: Ever-growing Chew Archives Tell a Story of the Business of Slavery," *Philadelphia Inquirer*, August 3, 2009.

27. Cliveden Full Board Meeting Minutes, December 2009.

28. For information on ATAC, see http://www.ushistory.org/presidentshouse/links .htm; http://avengingtheancestors.com/info/index.asp.

29. A summary of the project and the list of advisers involved can be found in Philip Seitz and David W. Young, "When Slavery Came to Stay/Transformation at Cliveden," *Museum: A Publication of the American Association of Museums* 90, no. 3 (May–June 2011): 40–47. Seitz's article on his personal journey in relation to the project won an award from the American Alliance of Museums in 2011.

30. Cliveden, All Stakeholders Retreat Minutes, July 14, 2010, Cliveden Interpretive Planning Report.

31. Phillip Seitz, *Slavery in Philadelphia: A History of Resistance, Denial, and Wealth* (CreateSpace, 2014), 123, asserts that the Cliveden project "came to an abrupt end" in 2011. The programs described in this chapter contradict this assessment: ten years of the award-winning Cliveden Conversations, *Liberty to Go to See*, and the recovery of the 1767 Kitchen Dependency, as well as the numerous partnerships that made possible Cliveden's ongoing interpretive expansion.

32. Julia Rose, "Rethinking Representations of Slave Life at Historical Plantation

Museums: Towards a Commemorative Museum Pedagogy" (Ph.D. diss., Louisiana State University, 2006), 230–231.

33. Julia Rose, *Interpreting Difficult Knowledge*, American Association for State and Local History Technical Leaflet 255 (2011).

34. See, for instance, the case studies found in *Interpreting Slavery at Museums and Historic Sites*, ed. Kristin L. Gallas and James DeWolf Perry (New York: Rowman and Littlefield, 2014). Published in conjunction with the Tracing Center on Histories and Legacies of Slavery, the book includes examples from historic sites throughout the country and a guide to the psychological facilitation needed to process the breadth and depth of slavery. For the stress created by such interpretation and organizations' process of deciding whether to interpret such stories, see Amy M. Tyson, *The Wages of History: Emotional Labor on Public History's Front Line* (Amherst: University of Massachusetts Press, 2013), 145–170.

35. Cliveden, All Stakeholder's Retreat Minutes, July 14, 2010.

36. For the reflections of the graduate students who rewrote the Cliveden nomination, see Joseph Cialdella, "A Place of Collaboration: Cliveden and the Merits of Reevaluating a Landmark's Past," *Perspectives on History: The Newsmagazine of the American Historical Association,* December 2013.

37. See also Walter Gallas, "A Second Look at a Landmark's History," *Preservation Leadership Forum* (blog), October 5, 2012, http://blog.preservationleadershipforum. org/2012/10/05/a-second-look/#.VyO4bktsvwJ.

38. Minutes of the National Park System Advisory Board Landmarks Committee Meeting, May 28–29, 2014, Washington, DC: National Park Service, 13–14.

39. Joseph (slave, Whitehall, DE) to Benjamin Chew (Philadelphia), 1804. Chew Family Papers, 2050, box 10, folder 42, Historical Society of Pennsylvania.

CHAPTER 2

1. Caroline W. Shipley to W.E.B. Du Bois, January 22, 1928, Young Women's Christian Association, Germantown, Philadelphia, Pa., Inter-Racial Committee, W.E.B. Du Bois Papers (MS 312), Special Collections and University Archives, University of Massachusetts Amherst Libraries (hereafter cited as Du Bois Papers).

2. W.E.B. Du Bois to Inter-Racial Committee, Germantown Young Women's Christian Association, January 24, 1928, Du Bois Papers.

3. Carole H. Carpenter, "Arthur Huff Fauset, Campaigner for Social Justice: A Symphony of Diversity," in *African-American Pioneers in Anthropology*, ed. Ira E. Harrison and Faye V. Harrison (Urbana: University of Illinois Press, 1998), 213–242; Eric Ledell Smith, "Crystal Bird Fauset Raises Her Voice for Human Rights," *Pennsylvania Heritage* 13, no. 1 (Winter 1997): 34–39.

4. David W. Young, "'You Feel So Out of Place': Germantown's J. Gordon Baugh and the 1913 Commemoration of the Emancipation Proclamation," *Pennsylvania Magazine of History and Biography* 137, no. 1 (January 2013): 79–93.

5. Dr. Naaman H. Keyser, C. Henry Kain, John Palmer Garber, and Horace F. McCann, *History of Old Germantown with a Description of Its Settlement and Some Account of Its Important Persons, Buildings, and Places Connected with Its Development*, vol. 1 (Germantown, Philadelphia: H. F. McCann, 1907).

6. Two major works about German history in Pennsylvania had appeared to mark the anniversaries of the early 1900s. The first was a genealogical study by Samuel

W. Pennypacker, *The Settlement of Germantown, Pennsylvania and the Beginning of Germantown Emigration to North America* (Philadelphia: W. J. Campbell, 1899). A native of Chester County, Pennypacker was a one-term governor of Pennsylvania (1903–1907); his term of office was marred by scandals over the funding of the construction of the Pennsylvania state capitol, led by the Germantown architect Joseph Huston. The second was a book by a professor of German: Marion Dexter Lerned, *The Life of Francis Daniel Pastorius, Founder of Germantown* (Philadelphia: Campbell, 1908), for which Pennypacker wrote the preface.

7. J. Gordon Baugh Jr., *A Souvenir of Germantown Issued during the Fiftieth Anniversary of the Emancipation Proclamation at Philadelphia PA, September 1913* (Philadelphia: author, 1913), 1, African American files, Germantown Historical Society (no pagination in the original). A version annotated by Louise L. Strawbridge, with the assistance of John E. Jones Jr., was reproduced in the *Germantown Crier* 36, no. 1 (Winter 1983–1984) and no. 2 (Spring 1984).

8. Ibid., 21–22. Baugh's list of jobs reads: "Four physicians, 2 trained nurses, 1 dentist, 1 real estate agent, 1 contractor, 3 paperhangers, 3 upholsterers, 1 cabinetmaker, 3 printers, 12 dressmakers, 6 hairdressers, 1 milliner, 1 tailor, 3 laundries, 5 barber shops, 3 restaurants, 12 landscape gardeners, 4 bootblack stands, 1 butter and eggs dealers, 3 caterers, 3 coal and ice companies, 3 grocery stores, 2 garages, 4 expressmen, 18 school teachers, 2 post office employees, 1 custom house employee, 2 policemen, 1 retired policeman, 2 janitors of apt. houses, 3 branch offices of undertakers and embalmers, 1 orchestra, 3 inventors, 3 second hand dealers, 1 dramatic organization."

9. Robert Gregg, *Sparks from the Anvil of Oppression: Philadelphia's African Methodists and Southern Migrants, 1890–1940* (Philadelphia: Temple University Press, 1993), 13–14.

10. Ibid., 14.

11. Estimates come from the entire Twenty-Second Ward (German Township) and are quoted by Gladys Taylor, executive director of the YWCA of Germantown, in "Experiences in Neighborhood Building through the YWCA," May 16, 1949, "Integration, 1928–1950," YWCA Germantown records, box 24, folder 27, Urban Archives, Temple University Libraries, Philadelphia.

12. *The Beehive* 17, no. 3 (July 1930): 1–3.

13. For an excellent summary of the ethnic composition of Germantown during this period, see Russell A. Kazal, *Becoming Old Stock: The Paradox of German American Identity* (Princeton, NJ: Princeton University Press, 2004), 226–230.

14. J. Thomas Scharf and Thompson Westcott, *History of Philadelphia 1609–1884* (Philadelphia: L. H. Everts, 1884), 663. See also Samuel Rezneck, "The Social History of an American Depression, 1837–1843," *American Historical Review* 40, no. 4 (1935): 667.

15. Cornelius Weygandt Jr., "Thank God for Germantown," Weygandt Papers: Writings, Essays, Incomplete Sets 11, box 4, folder 27, University of Pennsylvania Archives and Records Center, UPT 50 W547.5, Philadelphia. The speech was given in 1940 and used as a basis for a chapter in a book two years later. See Cornelius Weygandt, *The Plenty of Pennsylvania: Samples of Seven Cultures Persisting from Colonial Days* (New York: H. C. Kinsey, 1942), 58–82.

16. Weygandt, "Thank God for Germantown."

17. Kazal, *Becoming Old Stock*, 230–231; Philip Jenkins, *Hoods and Shirts: The Extreme Right in Pennsylvania, 1925–1950* (Chapel Hill: University of North Carolina

Press, 1997), 72, 76. James Wolfinger, in *Philadelphia Divided: Race and Politics in the City of Brotherly Love* (Chapel Hill: University of North Carolina Press, 2007), 187, states, "The Klan had several hundred members during WWII and was growing under the direction of Samuel Stouch, the personnel director for the community's police department."

18. Kazal, *Becoming Old Stock,* 231. See also Jenkins, *Hoods and Shirts,* 72, 76.

19. The Germantown Historical Society's Subject file contains articles clipped from unnamed newspapers: "Ku Klux Klan Starts Organization Here: Largely Attended Meetings Held in Old Odd Fellows' Hall on Wister Street: No Hooded Parade Yet," 1926; "Another Klan Meeting," describing a 1924 picnic at a Mount Airy farm with an estimated three hundred attendees.

20. See Louetta Ray Hadley, "My Family and Community," *Germantown Crier* 52, no. 1 (2002): 33, also included in *Remembering Germantown: Sixty Years of the* Germantown Crier, ed. Irvin Miller and Judith Callard (Charleston, SC: History Press, 2008), 124–126.

21. Baugh, *Souvenir of Germantown;* see also Strawbridge's collections of African American responses to her research, Pamphlet box: African American, Germantown Historical Society.

22. David Contosta, "Philadelphia's 'Miniature Williamsburg': The Colonial Revival and Germantown's Market Square," *Pennsylvania Magazine of History and Biography* 120, no. 4 (October 1996): 285–290.

23. Wolfinger, *Philadelphia Divided,* 16–20.

24. *The Beehive* 17, no. 2 (March 1930): 19.

25. Ibid., 1–2.

26. See Wolfinger, *Philadelphia Divided,* 2, 14–80. On cooperation in Philadelphia, see Jonathan Farnham, "A Bridge Game: Constructing a Co-operative Commonwealth in Philadelphia, 1900–1926" (Ph.D. diss., Princeton University, 2000).

27. "Mayor Would Stop Exodus to Suburbs; United Support of Transit Plans Will Do It, He Tells Germantown Businessmen, a Plea for the Avoidance of Sectionalism," *Philadelphia Bulletin,* April 17, 1928, 22.

28. Contosta, "Philadelphia's 'Miniature Williamsburg,'" 290.

29. David Glassberg, *American Historical Pageantry: The Uses of Tradition in the Early Twentieth Century* (Chapel Hill: University of North Carolina Press, 1990), 110–150.

30. On the Colonial Revival and the Sesquicentennial, see Morris J. Vogel, *Cultural Connections: Museums and Libraries of the Delaware Valley* (Philadelphia: Temple University Press, 1991), 131–157; Steven Conn, *Museums in American Intellectual Life,* 1876–1926 (Chicago: University of Chicago Press, 1998), 238–244.

31. Vogel discusses the movement of Sulgrave Manor, a 1926 replica of Washington's ancestral home in Oxfordshire, England, to a residential street in Chestnut Hill, in *Cultural Connections,* 149–157.

32. John Bodnar, *Remaking America: Public Memory, Commemoration, and Patriotism in the Twentieth Century* (Princeton, NJ: Princeton University Press, 1992), 14.

33. "Germantown Women Organize to Study Political Situation; Celebrate Achievement Week," *Philadelphia Tribune,* April 19, 1928, 12. See also "Achievements of Negro Feature Program," *Philadelphia Tribune,* April 19, 1928, 3; "Record Breaking Audiences Greet Achievement Week Orators," *Philadelphia Tribune,* April 26, 1928, 12.

34. "Integration, 1928–1950."

35. "Colored Artists Show Their Work: Paintings, Manuscripts, and Rare Documents in Negro Achievement Work Exhibition, Ogden Chorus Heard," *Philadelphia Bulletin*, April 17, 1928. The article describes the work of Tanner and Waring and refers to "art and historical documents pertaining to the colored race . . . on exhibition this week in the auditorium of the free library, Vernon Park, Germantown."

36. "Democracy in America," April 1928, Du Bois Papers (MS 312).

37. Shipley quoted in Beulah McNeill, "Negro Achievement Week Report," in "Integration, 1928–1950."

38. "Record Breaking Audiences Greet Achievement Week Orators; Germantown News," *Philadelphia Tribune*, April 26, 1928, 12.

39. Clarence Cameron White (1880–1960) was born in Tennessee and trained as a violinist and composer at Oberlin College. See Cary D. Wintz and Paul Finkelman, *The Encyclopedia of the Harlem Renaissance* (New York: Routledge, 2004), 1248.

40. McNeill, "Negro Achievement Week Report."

41. Ibid.

42. For the development of Woodson's reasoning, see C. G. Woodson, "The Celebration of Negro History Week, 1927," *Journal of Negro History* 12, no. 2 (April 1927): 103–109; "Negro History Week—the Fourth Year," *Journal of Negro History* 14, no. 2 (April 1929): 109–115.

43. See Lisa Meyerowitz, "The 'Negro in Art Week': Defining the 'New Negro' through Art Exhibition," *African American Review* 31 (Spring 1997): 7–90.

44. Quoted in James Weldon Johnson, "Race Prejudice and the Negro Artist," *Harper's* 157 (1928): 669–676.

45. From Charles P. T. Banner-Haley's study of Philadelphia, *To Do Good and to Do Well: Middle-Class Blacks and the Depression, Philadelphia 1929–1941* (New York: Garland, 1993), 5–6. On this period, see also H. Viscount Nelson, *Black Leadership's Response to the Great Depression in Philadelphia* (Lewiston, NY: Mellen, 2006), 25–28.

46. On Alain Locke, see Leonard Harris and Charles Molesworth, *Alain L. Locke: The Biography of a Philosopher* (Chicago: University of Chicago Press, 2009). For perspective on Du Bois's Philadelphia study, see Elijah Anderson's introduction to W.E.B. Du Bois, *The Philadelphia Negro: A Social Study,* first published 1899 (Philadelphia: University of Pennsylvania Press, 1996).

47. On Ishmael Locke, see David W. Young, "The South Jersey Influences on a Great African American," *Salem Sunbeam*, February 24, 2003, 7.

48. Mary Ann Calo, *Race, Nation, and the Critical Construction of the African American Artist, 1920–1940* (Ann Arbor: University of Michigan Press, 2007), 74–75.

49. Ibid., 72–74; Meyerowitz, "'Negro in Art Week.'"

50. Program flyer for Negro Achievement Week, in "Integration, 1928–1950."

51. Betty Livingston Adams ties Negro Arts Week events to combating the rise of the Ku Klux Klan in post–World War I cities in *Black Women's Christian Activism: Seeking Social Justice in a Northern Suburb* (New York: New York University Press, 2016), chap. 4, "'Unholy and Unchristian Attitude': Interracial Dialogue in Segregated Spaces, 1920–1937," in which she cites "Church Women in Interracial Cooperation, Prepared by the Continuation Committee of the Interracial Conference of Church Women Held at Eagles Mere Pa, 21–22, 1926," pamphlet no. 7, December 1926. See also Bettye Collier-Thomas, *Jesus, Jobs, and Justice: African American Women and Religion* (New York: Knopf, 2010), 312–325.

52. McNeill, "Negro Achievement Week Report."

53. Eva Bowles (1875–1943) was born in Ohio and attended Ohio State University and Columbia University. In 1917 she was appointed national director of the YWCA's Colored Work Committee. She saw the YWCA as a "pioneer in interracial experimentation." Stephanie Yvette Felix, "Committed to Their Own: African American Women Leaders in the YWCA; The YWCA of Germantown, Philadelphia, Pennsylvania, 1870–1970" (Ph.D. diss., Temple University, 1999), 78–80. On the level of professional leadership in the Germantown YWCA, see ibid.

54. From the program flyer for Negro Achievement Week.

55. See Felix, "Committed to Their Own," 127–129.

56. *Philadelphia Tribune*, March 1, 1928, 12.

57. On the rifts between African Americans during the Great Migration in Philadelphia, see Banner-Haley, *To Do Good*, 6, 48–50; the subject is also covered in Gregg, *Sparks from the Anvil of Oppression*, 50–64.

58. "Negro Achievement Week in Germantown," *The Beehive* 13, no. 1 (April 1928).

59. Felix, "Committed to Their Own," 99–100.

60. "Negro Achievement Week in Germantown," 1–2.

61. Ibid., 17. See also Shirley Turpin-Parham, "A History of Black Public Education in Philadelphia, Pennsylvania 1864–1914" (Ph.D. diss., Temple University, 1986), 240–247.

62. Quoted in McNeill, "Negro Achievement Week Report."

63. Ibid.

64. Ibid.

65. The only references to Negro Achievement Week appear in the local press of the time and, briefly (with the incorrect date of March 1928), in a booklet by Lucy P. Carner, *YWCA: The First 100 Years in Germantown 1870–1970* (Philadelphia: Press of International Print Co., 1970), 57; Felix, "Committed to Their Own," 128–129.

66. "Observe Negro History Week," *Philadelphia Tribune*, February 14, 1929.

67. Sarah Campbell, "Germantown," *Philadelphia Tribune*, February 20, 1941.

68. W.E.B. Du Bois to George A. Updegraff, August 22, 1930, Du Bois Papers.

69. Calo, *Race, Nation*, 75.

70. Ibid.

71. Caroline W. Shipley to Du Bois, April 19, 1928.

CHAPTER 3

1. For the impact of separating the township's neighborhoods on issues such as education and housing, see Erika M. Kitzmiller, "The Roots of Educational Inequality: Germantown High School, 1907–2011" (Ph.D. diss., University of Pennsylvania, 2012), 350–364; Abigail Perkiss, *Making Good Neighbors: Civil Rights, Liberalism, and Integration in Postwar Philadelphia* (Ithaca, NY: Cornell University Press, 2014), 10–89.

2. Jane Jacobs, *The Death and Life of Great American Cities* (New York: Random House, 1961).

3. After visiting one of the Philadelphia city planner Edmund Bacon's more successful projects, Jacobs asked, "Where are the people?" Bacon was involved in plans for Germantown in the 1950s and 1960s, part of the Model Cities projects that built on attempts to create a "miniature Williamsburg" on Germantown Avenue. Jacobs's view

of the Society Hill urban renewal process is recounted in Alice Sparberg Alexiou, *Jane Jacobs: Urban Visionary* (New Brunswick, NJ: Rutgers University Press, 2006), 39–40.

4. Jacobs, *Death and Life of Great American Cities*, iv.

5. Perkiss, *Making Good Neighbors*, 22–23.

6. Matthew J. Countryman, *Up South: Civil Rights and Black Power in Philadelphia* (Philadelphia: University of Pennsylvania Press, 2005), 73.

7. The number of organizations grew to thirty. The Germantown Historical Society did not take part. See "Outside Agencies Germantown Community Audit," YWCA Germantown, box 30, folder 11, Urban Archives, Temple University Libraries, Philadelphia; "Human Relations Audit Planned in Germantown Area: Twenty-Five Major Agencies to Seek Facts on Social Adjustments, Relationships," *Germantown Courier*, June 16, 1949.

8. Other communities used similar audits to assess religious, ethnic, and racial discrimination in the housing market. Montclair, New Jersey, started one in December 1947; Baltimore conducted one in 1950 through the Baltimore Urban League. Rose Helper, *Racial Policies and Practices of Real Estate Brokers* (Minneapolis: University of Minnesota Press, 1969), 349–350.

9. "Community Audit."

10. The 1940 U.S. census tallied 108,083 people in the Twenty-Second Ward, 10,044 of them black (500 more than in 1930). The 1950 census showed that, collectively, the German Township (Germantown, Mount Airy, and Chestnut Hill) contained 105,334 people, of whom approximately 10 percent were black. In 1950 the wards of Germantown proper (i.e., not the entire Twenty-Second Ward) numbered 69,615 (61,448 white, 8,167 nonwhite). This number represented a decrease of more than 13,000 white residents. The increase in the black population was in part explained by the fact that Germantown had "become a destination for 'moneyed blacks.'" Stephanie Yvette Felix, "Committed to Their Own: African American Women Leaders in the YWCA; The YWCA of Germantown, Philadelphia, Pennsylvania, 1870–1970" (Ph.D. diss., Temple University, 1999), 155, 245; Francis X. Delany, "Germantown and Its Civic Organizations 1946–1981: A Community in Search of Effective Form," *Germantown Crier* 52, no. 1 (Spring 2002): 4–22. For a population analysis of the entire township, see Barbara Ferman, Theresa Singleton, and Don Demarco, "West Mount Airy, Philadelphia," *Cityscape: A Journal of Policy Development and Research* 4, no. 2 (1998): 30.

11. See Lloyd M. Abernethy, *Benton Spruance: The Artist and the Man* (Cranbury, NJ: Associated University Presses, 1988), 116.

12. Ibid., 43.

13. See Ruth E. Fine and Robert F. Looney, *The Prints of Benton Murdoch Spruance* (Philadelphia: University of Pennsylvania Press, 1986), 114.

14. Quoted in Abernethy, *Benton Spruance*, 79.

15. See Elizabeth Robins Pennell and Joseph Pennell, *Our Philadelphia* (Philadelphia, 1914). On Spruance's influence on Germantown, see David Contosta, "Philadelphia's 'Miniature Williamsburg': The Colonial Revival and Germantown's Market Square," *Pennsylvania Magazine of History and Biography* 120, no. 4 (October 1996): 302.

16. Marguerite de Angeli, *Bright April* (New York: Doubleday, 1946).

17. *Bright April* was praised as one of the few books of the 1940s to "look head-on at racial discrimination and injustice." Quoted in Elizabeth Goodenough, Mark A. Heberle, and Naomi B. Sokoloff, *Infant Tongues: The Voice of the Child in Literature* (Detroit, MI: Wayne State University Press, 1994), 241–242.

18. William W. Adam, board member of the Germantown Historical Society, to Otis W. Balis, treasurer of the Germantown Community Council, August 19, 1948, Stradley Papers, Germantown Historical Society (hereafter Stradley Papers).

19. *Germantown Crier* 1–5 (1949–1953).

20. Stradley was an expert on corporate taxes. His economic history of Pennsylvania, *Early Financial and Economic History of Pennsylvania* (New York: Commerce Clearing House, 1942), covers colonization to 1873.

21. Leighton Stradley to Rev. Ellsworth Jackson, August 10, 1948, Stradley Papers. Stradley made repeated references to Williamsburg in correspondence about the project. See also Leighton Stradley to Carl W. Fenninger, August 3, 1948, ibid.

22. Contosta, "Philadelphia's 'Miniature Williamsburg,'" 302.

23. "We have assurances from all of the adjoining owners on the square except the church and the properties on the south side of the square that they will cooperate in conforming their properties to architects' plans for the restoration, which will largely be on the Williamsburg model. This gives us some justification in assuming that Market Square will be nationally known and will be on the itinerary of many visitors to this section of the country following historical interests. Accordingly it will not only benefit Germantown but Philadelphia as well." Stradley to the Civil War Ellis Legion Post, 1805 Pine St., Philadelphia, October 21, 1948, Stradley Papers.

24. *Germantown Crier* 1 (January 1949): 2.

25. Contosta, "Philadelphia's 'Miniature Williamsburg,'" 304–305.

26. Edward Hocker to Leighton Stradley, December 1948, Stradley Papers.

27. William Emhardt to Leighton Stradley, November 14, 1949, ibid.

28. Stradley to editors of local papers, December 1949, ibid.

29. Contosta, "Philadelphia's 'Miniature Williamsburg,'" 310n67.

30. "East Mount Airy Opposes Bypass," *Germantown Courier*, August 31, 1967.

31. Contosta, "Philadelphia's 'Miniature Williamsburg,'" 310.

32. Ibid., 310–312.

33. For instance, see Arnold R. Hirsch, *Making the Second Ghetto: Race and Housing in Chicago, 1940–1960* (New York: Cambridge University Press, 1983).

34. Thomas J. Sugrue, *The Origins of the Urban Crisis: Race and Inequality in Postwar Detroit* (Princeton, NJ: Princeton University Press, 1998), 262–265.

35. Arnold R. Hirsch, "Urban Renewal," in *The Encyclopedia of Chicago*, ed. James R. Grossman, Ann Durkin Keating, and Janice L. Reiff (Chicago: Newberry Library and Chicago Historical Society, 2004), 1295.

36. Clarence N. Stone, *Regime Politics: Governing Atlanta, 1946–1988* (Lawrence: University of Kansas Press, 1989), 190–195.

37. New Haven received more federal funds under Model City and other urban renewal programs than other city during the 1950s and 1960s. See Mandi Isaacs Jackson, *Model City Blues: Urban Space and Organized Resistance in New Haven* (Philadelphia: Temple University Press, 2008), 28–35.

38. James Robert Saunders and Renae Nadine Shackelford, *Urban Renewal and the End of Black Culture in Charlottesville, Virginia: An Oral History of Vinegar Hill* (Jefferson, NC: McFarland, 1998), 87–110.

39. Michael Wallace, "Reflections on the History of Historic Preservation," in *Presenting the Past: Critical Perspectives on History and the Public*, ed. Susan Porter Benson, Steven Brier, and Roy Rosenzweig (Philadelphia: Temple University Press, 1986), 183–184.

40. See Gregory T. Heller, *Ed Bacon: Planning, Politics, and the Building of Modern Philadelphia* (Philadelphia: University of Pennsylvania Press, 2013); Scott Gabriel Knowles, ed., *Imagining Philadelphia: Edmund Bacon and the Future of the City* (Philadelphia: University of Pennsylvania Press, 2009).

41. On funding for urban renewal in Philadelphia, see Countryman, *Up South*, 300–307.

42. For an oral history of the displaced residents, see August Tarrier, Susan B. Hyatt, and Neighborhood Action Research Group, *The Forgotten Bottom Remembered: Stories from a Philadelphia Neighborhood* (Philadelphia: New City Press, 2002).

43. On Society Hill's urban renewal process, see Alexiou, *Jane Jacobs*, 39–40.

44. See Joseph S. Clark Jr. and Dennis J. Clark, "Rally and Relapse 1946–1968," in *Philadelphia: A 300 Year History* (Philadelphia: Barra Foundation, 1982), 678. On urban renewal, see 662–665.

45. Countryman, *Up South*, 223–255.

46. Quoted in ibid., 307.

47. City of Philadelphia Planning Commission, G. Holmes Perkins, Chair, "Morton Area Redevelopment Plan," January 1958. The Morton Redevelopment Project was rooted ideas from the late 1940s with planners working closely with the Morton neighbors and using Germantown Settlement as its community corporation to distribute federal funds. Highlighted for years after as a successful example of urban renewal, it was profiled at the 1964 New York World's Fair. "Germantown Renewal Project on Display at World's Fair," *Philadelphia Evening Bulletin*, October 8, 1964.

48. Clark and Clark, "Rally and Relapse," 662.

49. Jane Wilson McWilliams, *Annapolis, City on the Severn: A History* (Baltimore, MD: Johns Hopkins University Press, 2011), 291–360.

50. Quoted in Delany, "Germantown and Its Civic Organizations," 13.

51. The 1960 study, by Henry S. Churchill, Jack M. Kendree, and Ty Learn, "A Preliminary Study of Germantown," prepared for Concern for Germantown and described as "an extension and up-dating of a study of part of Germantown made in 1956 for the Planning Commission of Philadelphia," lists its working committee: Earle N. Barber Jr., realtor with an office on Germantown Avenue, who was involved with Germantown Historical Society and Concord Schoolhouse; John W. Bodine, lawyer and reform advocate during the Joseph S. Clark–Richardson Dilworth era of the late 1940s; Robert M. Browning, lawyer who served on the board of Germantown Hospital and Germantown Friends meeting; Clarence L. Cave, pastor of Faith Presbyterian Church, the lone African American in the group; Elias Charry, rabbi who served the Germantown Jewish Center from 1942 to 1983; Donald E. Hamilton, executive director of the Germantown Community Council, 1957–1960; Dwight S. Large, who directed the American Friends Service Committee's relief operations in Palestine in 1949, held several administrative posts with Amnesty International, and was a United Methodist pastor in Germantown; Marguerite L. Riegel, executive director of the Germantown Community Council, 1948–1955, and founder of Center in the Park; Harold D. Saylor, judge and president of the Germantown Historical Society; Allen M. Woodruff, lawyer. The same report listed Concern for Germantown's sixteen sponsoring organizations in June 1959: First Methodist Church, Unitarian Church of Germantown, Germantown Historical Society, Colonial Market Square, Inc. (as Colonial Germantown, Inc., was sometimes called), Lankenau Public School, William Penn Charter School, Germantown Friends School, Wissahickon Boys Club, Coulter Street Friends Meeting, Friends Free Library,

Faith Presbyterian Church, Second Presbyterian Church, Germantown Jewish Center, YWCA, Greene Street Friends School, School House Lane Friends Meeting.

52. The plans include Henry J. Magaziner, "Germantown Avenue in Germantown," May 1952, a report written for the community group Concern for Germantown; Henry Churchill and Jack M. Kendree, Philadelphia City Planning Commission, "Germantown: A Planning Study," 1956; Churchill, Kendree, and Learn, "Preliminary Study"; Henry J. Magaziner, AIA, and Wright, Andrade, and Amenta, AIA, architects, "A Proposal for the Revitalization of the Heart of Germantown," prepared for Philadelphia Planning Commission on behalf of the voluntary civic group "Concern for Germantown," May 1960; Henry Magaziner, "Study of Central Germantown for the Philadelphia City Planning Commission," May 1963 (hereafter cited as "Study of Central Germantown," pt. 1); Henry Magaziner, "Areas of Opportunity for Renewal of Germantown: Part 2 of the Study of Central Germantown for the Philadelphia City Planning Commission," March 1964 (hereafter cited as "Study of Central Germantown," pt. 2). All in Germantown Community Groups, box 30, folder 13, Urban Archives.

53. Churchill, Kendree, and Learn, "Preliminary Study for Germantown," map 12.

54. Magaziner, "Study of Central Germantown," pt. 1, 35.

55. The seven buildings remained unidentified in Magaziner's plans, an indication only that they would come from the southern part of Germantown Avenue. That likely meant Mehl House, the Christopher Sower building, and perhaps even Grumblethorpe, which was undergoing a restoration during the 1950s.

56. Magaziner, "Study of Central Germantown," pt. 1, 11, 30–35.

57. Magaziner, "Germantown Avenue in Germantown," 3.

58. Ibid.

59. Magaziner et al., "Proposal," 45.

60. Wallace, "Reflections," 153–154.

61. Alison Isenberg describes efforts to restore a historic appearance to downtown commercial buildings as a practice that started in the 1970s; the trend in the 1950s was to modernize older buildings. Isenberg, *Downtown America: A History of the Place and the People Who Made It* (Chicago: University of Chicago Press, 2004), 164–165.

62. Contosta, "Philadelphia's 'Miniature Williamsburg,'" 313.

63. "City Commission Is 'Cautious' on Germantown's Planning," *Philadelphia Inquirer*, March 5, 1964.

64. Ibid.

65. Dexter C. Hutchins, "Passage of Renewal Bill Fund Bolsters Germantown Hopes; Fast Action Is Expected on Project," *Philadelphia Inquirer*, September 6, 1964.

66. Churchill, Kendree, and Learn, "Preliminary Study," 9.

67. Magaziner, "Study of Central Germantown," pt. 2, 35.

68. Ibid., 36.

69. Ibid.

70. Delany, "Germantown and Its Civic Organizations," 14.

71. Magaziner, "Study of Central Germantown," pt. 1, 1.

72. Magaziner et al., "Proposal," 38–39.

73. Magaziner, "Study of Central Germantown," pt. 1, 5.

74. Churchill, Kendree, and Learn, "Preliminary Study," 12.

75. Magaziner et al., "Proposal," 39–40.

76. Quoted in Nancy Love, "The Second Battle of Germantown," *Philadelphia Magazine*, September 1967, 46.

77. Ibid., 43–45.

78. Churchill, Kendree, and Learn, "Preliminary Study," 11–12.

79. Ibid.," 12.

80. William Will, "The Germantown Renewal Program of 1958–1968: A First-Hand Account," *Germantown Crier* 52, no. 1 (Spring 2002): 25.

81. Hornung was educated at Harvard and worked in urban planning in Philadelphia in the 1960s and 1970s before settling in the Pacific Northwest. He co-wrote *The Citizen's Guide to Urban Renewal* with Alfred P. Van Huyck (West Trenton, NJ: Chandler-Davis, 1962). See also Jake Ellison, "Jack Hornung: Urban Planner Helped Set Up Greenway Corridor," *Seattle Post-Intelligencer*, July 4, 2005.

82. Delany, "Germantown and Its Civic Organizations," 15.

83. Quoted in Nancy Love, "Second Battle," 107.

84. Delany, "Germantown and Its Civic Organizations," 12. For the rest of the old German Township, the change was equally rapid. East Mount Airy was 33 percent black in 1960, 56 percent black in 1970, and 75 percent black in 1990. West Mount Airy was 19 percent black in 1959, 38 percent black in 1970, and 46 percent black in 1980. See Juliet Saltman, *A Fragile Movement: The Struggle for Neighborhood Stabilization*, Contributions in Sociology 86 (New York: Greenwood Press, 1990), 295–300.

85. Delany, "Germantown and Its Civic Organizations," 15.

86. Ibid., 16.

87. Wallace, "Reflections," 184.

88. Margaret B. Tinkcom, "Germantown's Market Square," report for Colonial Germantown, Inc., December, 23, 1966; see also Contosta, "Philadelphia's 'Miniature Williamsburg," 314–315.

89. Love, "Second Battle," 112, speculates that the reason the *Germantown Courier* did not run any letters or articles opposing the plan is that Colonial Germantown, Inc., had threatened to withdraw precious advertising funds.

90. Salvatore Mastriano, letter to the editor, *Germantown Courier*, August 17, 1967, was the first letter critical of the plan published by the *Courier*.

91. Wallace, "Reflections," 183.

92. "Germantown Bypass Faces Court Battle," *Philadelphia Inquirer*, June 12, 1969.

93. Michael deHaven Newsom, "Blacks in Preservation," *Law and Contemporary Problems* 36 (Summer 1971): 428–429.

94. Delany, "Germantown and Its Civic Organizations," 14.

95. John A. Bower Jr. and Frederick M. Fradley, *Central Germantown Urban Renewal Area Technical Report* (Philadelphia: Redevelopment Authority of the City of Philadelphia, 1966), 46–47.

96. Love, "Second Battle," 110.

97. Quoted in "Community Council Will Fight for Renewal," *Germantown Courier*, July 6, 1967. Another report warned: "Traffic flow is estimated to increase by 22% by 1985." Quoted in "Philadelphia Redevelopment Authority Approves Central Germantown Renewal," *Germantown Courier*, July 27, 1967; "East Mount Airy Opposes the Bypass," *Germantown Courier*, August 31, 1967.

98. Quoted in Delany, "Germantown and Its Civic Organizations," 17.

99. David J. Umansky, "Battle of Germantown to Reach City Council Urban Renewal Hearing," *Philadelphia Inquirer*, September 3, 1967.

100. Ronald DeGraw, "Germantown Bypass Rapped as 150 Ask for Recreation, Aged," *Philadelphia Inquirer*, September 9, 1967.

101. They were right about being deliberately shut out, since the newspapers in Germantown reported only one side of the dispute over planning. The *Germantown Courier* had for years "clamped a lid on unfavorable coverage of urban renewal" in response to a request from Jack Hornung and Colonial Germantown for fairer treatment. Love, "Second Battle," 112. The money the group spent on advertising in the paper bought the favorable coverage Hornung wanted. Delany, "Germantown and Its Civic Organizations," 17.

102. The traffic study, "Analysis of Proposed Traffic Circulation Plans—Central Germantown Urban Renewal Area, April 1966," by Simpson and Curtin, an engineering firm, was part of the Planning Commission's study and was included in the December Redevelopment Authority plan. See Love, "Second Battle," 107.

103. "Germantown Bypass Accord Balked as Civic Groups Split over Route," *Philadelphia Inquirer,* August 6, 1967.

104. Love, "Second Battle," 108.

105. When the City Hall hearings began in the first week of September 1967, the tally of groups for and against Colonial Germantown, Inc., and the Redevelopment Authority was as follows: in favor were Germantown Business Men's Association, Germantown Dispensary and Hospital, Institute for Urban Studies of La Salle College, YMCA and YWCA, Germantown Friends School, Germantown Lutheran Academy, Germantown Historical Society, Germantown Religious Council, St. Luke's Episcopal Church, First United Methodist Church of Germantown, First Presbyterian, Unitarian Church, Germantown Citizens for Renewal Now, Germantown Lions Club, and Covenant House. Civic groups endorsing the plan were West Central Germantown Neighbors and West Price Street Neighbors (both members of the Germantown Community Council) as well as the Lions Club and Covenant House. Opposing the plan were the Germantown Community Council board of directors, West Side Neighborhood Council, Wayne-Harvey Neighbors, Price-Knox Civic Association, and Neighbors of Germantown Heights, formerly Penn Area Neighbors, Morton Neighborhood Council, East Mount Airy Neighbors, Wayne-Harvey Area Civic Association, Southwest Germantown Civic Association, Germantown and Chelten Retail Businessmen's Association, the Urban League, and the Northwest NAACP chapter. Umansky, "Battle of Germantown to Reach City Council Urban Renewal Hearing."

106. "City Council Holds Two Day Hearing On Central Gtn. Renewal," *Germantown Courier,* September 14, 1967, 1–12.

107. Quoted in "City Council Passes Amended Renewal Bill," *Germantown Courier,* October 12, 1967. See also Contosta, "Philadelphia's 'Miniature Williamsburg,'" 317.

108. "Council Officials Clash over Belfield Bypass," *Philadelphia Inquirer*, April 11, 1968.

109. Delany, "Germantown and Its Civic Organizations," 19–20.

110. Cohen's remarks were part of a rules committee meeting in City Council. "Council Officials Clash."

111. James Eady, "Community Coalition Formed to Strengthen Role in Urban Renewal," *Philadelphia Inquirer,* September 14, 1969.

112. Alan L. Phillips, "Citizens Planning Office Is Proposed to Tackle Germantown Problems," *Philadelphia Inquirer,* January 29, 1970.

113. James Eady, "District Court Halts Acquisition of Lands for Belfield Bypass," *Philadelphia Inquirer,* December 3, 1969, 9.

114. The court's ruling on *Germantown Community Council, Inc., et al. v. The Department of Housing and Urban Development et al.,* U.S. District Court, East-

ern District Pennsylvania, was made on April 7, 1971, https://www.leagle.com/deci
sion/19711054324fsupp7301916.

115. Margaret Halsey, "Rittenhouse Bypass Could Be Killed by City," *Philadelphia Bulletin*, 14 May 1972; Delany, "Germantown and Its Civic Organizations," 19–20; see also "Neighborhood Development Program 1970," records of the Wister Area Committee, Accession 343, Series II, boxes 1–2, Urban Archives.

116. See William W. Cutler III, "The Persistent Dualism: Centralization and Decentralization in Philadelphia, 1854–1975," in *The Divided Metropolis: Social and Spatial Dimensions of Philadelphia, 1800–1975*, ed. William W. Cutler and Howard Gillette (Westport, CT: Greenwood Press, 1980), 249–277.

117. Ibid., 274.

118. See Ferman, Singleton, and Demarco, "West Mount Airy Philadelphia," 29–59; Saltman, *Fragile Movement*, 295–300; Leonard Franklin Heumann, "The Definition and Analysis of Stable Racial Integration: The Case of West Mount Airy, Philadelphia" (Ph.D. diss., University of Pennsylvania, 1973).

119. Heumann, "Stable Racial Integration," chap. 2; Saltman, *Fragile Movement*, 295–297.

120. The KKK held rallies in Germantown in 1927. See James Wolfinger, *Philadelphia Divided: Race and Politics in the City of Brotherly Love* (Chapel Hill: University of North Carolina Press, 2007), 22–23, 187; Philip Jenkins, *Hoods and Shirts: The Extreme Right in Pennsylvania, 1925–1950* (Chapel Hill: University of North Carolina Press, 1997), 72, 76, 128.

121. See Countryman, *Up South*, 223–255.

122. Ibid., 242–243; Delany, "Germantown and Its Civic Organizations," 15, 20. Countryman's study relies on oral histories of African American community organizers conducted in 1977.

123. Countryman, *Up South*, 242–243, 317–318.

124. Minutes of the board of directors of the Germantown Community Council, May 22, 1969.

125. Germantown Community Council to Shelton Granger, executive director of the Health and Welfare Council, April 17, 1972, cited in Delany, "Germantown and Its Civic Organizations," 22.

126. Contosta, "Philadelphia's 'Miniature Williamsburg,'" 318.

127. Countryman, *Up South*, 305–308.

128. Ibid., 306–307.

129. From "Germantown Settlement: History and Structure," contained in the consultant report *Creating Resident-Led Governance Structures: Peer Technical Assistance Match between Boston and Philadelphia* (Baltimore, MD: Annie E. Casey Foundation and the Center for the Study of Social Policy, 2003), 8. The report does not mention Settlement's financial status; rather, it paints a positive picture of specific youth education programs supported as part of a multiyear project funded by the Annie E. Casey Foundation. Germantown Settlement gained support for programs stressing the needs of the neighborhood.

130. The programs run by Germantown Settlement are described in articles that chronicle investigations into the organization. See "Cash-strapped Germantown Charter Lent Money," *Philadelphia Inquirer*, August 1, 2008; "Germantown Charter School's Use of Taxpayer Funds Being Investigated," *Philadelphia Inquirer*, October 12, 2008; Jason Fagone, "Emannuel Freeman: The Man Who Duped City Hall," *Phil-*

adelphia Magazine, September 24, 2010, http://www.phillymag.com/ articles/emanuel-freeman-the-man-who-duped-city-hall/?all=1.

131. According to IRS Form 990 for Germantown Settlement, Freeman made $158,814 in 2008 and paid his wife $94,818. Cited in Kristen Mosbrucker, "Germantown: Settlement Begins to Crumble," *Philadelphia Neighborhoods* (blog), November 10, 2010, philadelphianeighborhoods.com.

132. On the lack of accountability after the liquidation, see Brian Hickey's October 22, 2012, report for Newsworks.org: "When bankruptcy Judge Stephen Raslavich ordered Germantown Settlement, the disgraced 125-year-old social service and housing agency, to liquidate in 2010, he said leaving executive director Emanuel Freeman in charge was the equivalent of 'leaving a fox in a henhouse.' The politically connected Freeman helmed Germantown Settlement as it received massive levels of public and private funding in the 1990s" (https://whyy.org/articles/foster-inquires-about-germantown-settlement-probe-at-corruption-hotline-launch-event/).

CHAPTER 4

1. Upper Burying Ground of Germantown Burial Records book, located at Concord Schoolhouse and Upper Burying Ground Association of Germantown.

2. Svetlana Boym studied the fate of public monuments in the Soviet Union and draws a distinction between restoring a story and reflecting on a story without destroying it. See Svetlana Boym, *The Future of Nostalgia* (New York: Basic Books, 2001), 33.

3. For Boym's definitions of restorative nostalgia, see ibid., 41–44; for reflective nostalgia, see 47–51.

4. Important studies of African American and abolition history in Philadelphia from the period include Emma Jones Lapsansky, "'Since They Got Those Separate Churches': Afro-Americans and Racism in Jacksonian Philadelphia," *American Quarterly* 32, no. 1 (Spring 1980): 54–78; Harry Silcox, "Philadelphia Negro Educator: Jacob C. White, Jr.," *Pennsylvania Magazine of History and Biography* 97 (January 1973): 75–98; Jean Soderlund, *Quakers and Slavery: A Divided Spirit* (Princeton, NJ: Princeton University Press, 1985); Vincent P. Franklin, *The Education of Black Philadelphia: The Social and Educational History of a Minority Community, 1900–1950* (Philadelphia: University of Pennsylvania Press, 1979).

5. Ellen Fitzpatrick reminds us that the 1960s and 1970s did not invent social history and historians wrote from a wider perspective in the nineteenth and early twentieth centuries, too. See Fitzpatrick, *History's Memory: Writing America's Past, 1880–1980* (Cambridge, MA: Harvard University Press, 2004), 12.

6. Even a partial list of works by Gary Nash suggests this broader approach to Philadelphia's urban history. See "Slaves and Slaveowners in Colonial Philadelphia," *William and Mary Quarterly,* 3rd ser., 30, no. 2 (April 1973): 223–256; *The Urban Crucible: Social Change, Political Consciousness, and the Origins of the American Revolution* (Cambridge, MA: Harvard University Press, 1979); *Forging Freedom: The Formation of Philadelphia's Black Community, 1720–1840* (Cambridge, MA: Harvard University Press, 1988).

7. See, for instance, Billy G. Smith, *The "Lower Sort": Philadelphia's Laboring People, 1750–1800* (Ithaca, NY: Cornell University Press, 1990).

8. See, for instance, Dennis Clark, *The Irish in Philadelphia: Ten Generations of Urban Experience* (Philadelphia: Temple University Press, 1982); Richard N. Juliani,

The Social Organization of Immigration: The Italians in Philadelphia (New York: Arno, 1980); Allan F. Davis and Mark H. Haller, eds., *The Peoples of Philadelphia: A History of Ethnic Groups and Lower Class Life, 1790–1940* (Philadelphia: Temple University Press, 1973).

9. See, for instance, Theodore Hershberg, "Free Blacks in Antebellum Philadelphia: A Study of Ex-Slaves, Freeborn, and Socioeconomic Decline," *Journal of Social History* 5, no. 2 (Winter 1971–1972): 183–209; Theodore Hershberg et al., "A Tale of Three Cities: Blacks and Immigrants in Philadelphia, 1850–1880, 1930, and 1970," in *Philadelphia: Work, Space, Family, and Group Experience in the Nineteenth Century*, ed. Theodore Hershberg (New York: Oxford University Press, 1981), 461–491.

10. See the profile of Hershberg, "Perspective: After 30 Years, Where Does Penn Stand?" *Daily Pennsylvanian*, September 17, 2002.

11. On criticism of the project, see William G. Thomas III, "Computing and the Historical Imagination," in *A Companion to Digital Humanities*, ed. Susan Schreibman, Ray Siemens, and John Unsworth (New York: Blackwell, 2004), 61–62.

12. See, for instance, the example of this trend in Philadelphia: Gary Nash, "Behind the Velvet Curtain: Academic History, Historical Societies, and the Presentation of the Past," *Pennsylvania Magazine of History and Biography* 114 (1990): 3–26; Barbara Clark Smith, "The Authority of History: The Changing Public Face of the Historical Society of Pennsylvania," *Pennsylvania Magazine of History and Biography* 114 (1990): 37–66.

13. Dolores Hayden, *The Power of Place: Urban Landscapes as Public History* (Cambridge, MA: MIT Press, 1995), 14–15.

14. Robert F. Ulle, "A History of St. Thomas' African Episcopal Church, 1794–1865" (Ph.D. diss., University of Pennsylvania, 1986). See also Richard K. MacMaster with Samuel L. Horst and Robert F. Ulle, *Conscience in Crisis: Mennonites and Other Peace Churches in America, 1739–1789* (Harrisonburg, VA: Herald Press, 1979); John L. Ruth, *Maintaining the Right Fellowship: A Narrative Account of Life in the Oldest Mennonite Community in North America* (Harrisonburg, VA: Herald Press, 1984).

15. Stephanie Grauman Wolf, *Urban Village: Population, Community, and Family Structure in Germantown, Pennsylvania, 1683–1800* (Princeton, NJ: Princeton University Press, 1976).

16. Ibid., 3.

17. See Benjamin Filene, "Passionate Histories: 'Outsider' History-Makers and What They Teach Us," *Public Historian* 34, no. 1 (Winter 2012): 11–33.

18. Edward Lawler Jr., "The President's House in Philadelphia: The Rediscovery of a Lost Landmark," *Pennsylvania Magazine of History and Biography* 129, no. 4 (October 2002): 371–410.

19. John Sprinkle, *Crafting Preservation Criteria: The National Register of Historic Places and American Historic Preservation* (New York: Routledge, 2014), 5, 123.

20. See Edward Robinson's popular guides: *The World of Africans and Afro-Americans* and *Journey of the Songhai People* (Philadelphia: Pan African Federation Organization, 1970). Shortly before his death, a collection of his essays was published: Edward Robinson with Frederick L. Bonaparte, *No Man Can a-Hinder Me: A Message of Defiance from My Plantation Mothers and Fathers* (Philadelphia: CreateSpace, 2011).

21. Louise Strawbridge, "I Have Had a Great Privilege," manuscript, n.d., "Afro-Americans," box 1, Germantown Historical Society.

22. Ibid., 1.

23. See Ron Avery, "Taking the Mystery Out of History: Old-Timers Clue in Germantown Buff," *Philadelphia Daily News*, March 22, 1990.

24. *Philadelphia Courthouse Mural* is a ninety-six-foot-long panoramic view of Philadelphia, installed in 1995 in the lobby hallway of the Philadelphia Justice Center. Douglass Cooper, the artist, created similar works in other cities. See Melissa Dribben, "Oral Histories Paint a Picture," *Philadelphia Inquirer*, August 21, 1995.

25. 1977 National Historic Landmark nomination, Germantown Avenue National Historic Landmark District, Section 7.

26. The Underground Railroad had a far lower profile in Germantown's public memory than the 1688 Germantown Protest and other antislavery activity. Other than the Johnson House, only the Rock House has been regularly associated with the Underground Railroad in Germantown sources. It and the house next it to are mentioned in stories related to Moses Lewis, whose wife escaped from slavery and was arrested in 1837. That incident was covered in 1837 by the *Germantown Telegraph* and is recounted in Charles J. Wister's memoir, *The Labour of Long Life* (Germantown, Philadelphia), vol. 1 (1862) and vol. 2 (1886), and reprinted as "Slave Catcher Thwarted," *Germantown Crier* 43, no. 2 (1991): 45. The house is mentioned in some news clippings, which describe it as an ancient house with some association with escaping slaves that was about to be torn down in 1927. See "The Rock House: Additional Facts Concerning the Ancient Structure," and "The Passing of the Rock House," African American file, Germantown Historical Society. See also Gloria Davis Goode, *African American Heritage Guide to Philadelphia's Historic Northwest* (Philadelphia: Germantown Historical Society, 2007), 5–6.

27. For instance, among the histories of Germantown houses, even recent ones, the Johnson House is mentioned as an Underground Railroad station only in Harry M. Tinkcom, Margaret B. Tinkcom, and Grant Miles Simon, F.A.I.A., *Historic Germantown from the Founding to the Early Part of the Nineteenth Century: A Survey of the German Township* (Philadelphia: American Philosophical Society, 1955), 95. It is listed solely as a Revolutionary War site—with no mention of the Underground Railroad—in every festival week or walking tour brochure until the 1972 flyer for the annual spring walking tour sponsored by the Germantown Historical Society. References to the Johnson House in the following works, similarly, fail to note the connection to abolitionism or the Underground Railroad: S. F. Hotchkin, *Ancient and Modern Germantown* (Philadelphia: Ziegler, 1889), 323–325; Harold D. Eberlein and Cortlandt Van Dyke Hubbard, *Portrait of a Colonial City* (Philadelphia: Lippincott, 1939), 380–382; the WPA guide to Philadelphia, *Philadelphia: A Guide to the Nation's Birthplace* (first published 1937; rev. ed., Philadelphia: University of Pennsylvania Press, 1988), 485–486; Roger Moss, *Historic Houses of Philadelphia* (Philadelphia: University of Pennsylvania Press, 1998), 126–127.

28. See Russell Weigley, "The Border City in the Civil War," in Weigley et al., *Philadelphia: A Three-Hundred-Year History* (New York: Norton, 1982), 387.

29. S. J. Bumstead, *The Riversons: A Tale of the Wissahickon* (New York: Welch, Fracker, 1890).

30. Samuel Josiah Bumstead studied in Philadelphia and later moved to Macon County, Illinois. See Leigh Page, "A Biographical Memoir of Henry Andrews Bumstead (1870–1920)," in *National Academy of Sciences of the United States of America Biographical Memoirs,* vol. 13, part 2, which mentions his father, Samuel Josiah Bumstead. On Bumstead's connection to Hiram Corson, see Papers of John Bingham Roberts (1852–1924), MSS 2/0024, College of Physicians, Philadelphia.

31. See "Lost Cave in the Wissahickon," *The Beehive* 10, no. 4 (July 1926): 5: "These fugitives were taken to Flat Rock Dam, on the Schuylkill; thence over Domino Lane, Ridge Road, Crease's Lane, Livezey's Lane, and Township Line to the Blue Bell, then secreted in the cavern and there cared for by Mennonites and Friends."

32. Blockson's reference credits Robert Ulle's accounts. Blockson's books reproduce the errors of the *Beehive* report, despite its obvious errors, such as its identifying the author as "Umstead" (a familiar name in Germantown, and a Rittenhouse descendant), not "Bumstead," and its having been written in 1890, twenty-five years after the Civil War had ended. These issues do not seem to have been factored into Blockson's account, which became the standard for Philadelphia's Underground Railroad history. Many sources have relied on his books, *The Hippocrene Guide to the Underground Railroad* (New York: Hippocrene Books, 1994), and *The Underground Railroad in Pennsylvania* (Jacksonville, NC: Flame International, 1981), 14. See, for instance, William J. Switala, *Underground Railroad in Pennsylvania* (Mechanicsburg, PA: Stackpole, 2001), 150, 168–170, which treats as an actual map the route described in *The Beehive*.

33. The list of organizations to which Johnsons and their immediate relatives belonged is very long. Besides the Longwood Progressive Yearly meeting, immediate Johnson family members participated in important antislavery organizations, including the American Anti-Slavery Society, the Pennsylvania Abolition Society, the Philadelphia Free Produce Society, and the Vigilance Committee of Philadelphia. Adding cousins of theirs who lived in Germantown and belonged to antislavery organizations would make an even longer list. See William M. Dorsey, "Appendix B: Johnson Family Organizational Associations," in *Johnson House Agenda for Action: A Plan for the Institutional Development of the Johnson House Historic Site,* prepared by Avi Decter, director of History Now, Interpretive Planning and Consulting firm, January 1997, 49–55.

34. Israel Johnson to Ellwood Johnson, May 22, 1838, in Johnson Family Papers: Correspondence, Germantown Mennonite Historic Trust. The letter mentions that the light of the fire could be seen in Germanton, eight miles away. After the Civil War, Israel Johnson served with Still on the board of the Home for Aged and Infirm Colored Persons in Philadelphia.

35. W. Edmund Claussen*, Wyck: The Story of an Historic House: 1690–1970* (Philadelphia: M. T. Haines, 1970), 21–22. Wyck, located near the Johnson House, was built in 1690 by the daughter of Dirk Johnson. It has been owned and operated since the seventeenth century by Johnson family descendants associated with the Wistar and Haines families.

36. For the role of Johnsons as wagon-drivers: "The two buildings above the Kirk and Nice were Underground Railroad stations. The next stop was Dreshertown. They would be driven up the drive which ran along the North side of the Knorr House and hidden in the back buildings to await a chance to be carried onward. Usually at night by some interested neighbor usually one of the Johnsons." "Washington Lane Courier," *Germantown Journal*, May 1927.

37. Blockson, *Hippocrene Guide* 85–86; Switala, *Underground Railroad in Pennsylvania*, 168.

38. J. Thomas Scharf and Thompson Westcott, *History of Philadelphia 1609–1884* (Philadelphia: L. H. Everts, 1884), 663. See also Samuel Rezneck, "The Social History of an American Depression, 1837–1843," *American Historical Review* 40, no. 4 (1935): 667.

39. An article in the *Germantown Telegraph,* December 20, 1837, noted the capture of Margaret Brooke, later known as Margaret Brooke Lemon; the memoirs of Charles J. Wister Jr. provide an eyewitness account: see Wister, *The Labour of a Long Life,* 2:12–13, and "Slave Catcher Thwarted," 45.

40. See William E. Cadbury, "A History of Negro Membership in the Society of Friends," *Journal of Negro History* 21 (1936): 151–213. Israel Johnson in 1840 was a clerk of the Willings Alley School for Association of Friends for Free Instruction of Adult Colored Persons.

41. "There was a direct connection between Norristown and the anti-slavery office in Philadelphia, via night-trains on the Norristown Railroad." Theodore W. Bean, ed., *History of Montgomery County Pennsylvania* (Philadelphia: Everts and Peck, 1884), 306. The railroad's Germantown office stood at the corner of Price Street and Germantown Avenue.

42. Edward T. Johnson, "Washington Lane formerly Abington Lane," manuscript, 1909, Germantown Historical Society. The detailed description of the use of the house as a station (63–67) links Underground Railroad activity to neighboring houses and families, such as William Dorsey's family (63–65) and the Knorrs and the Keysers, and includes references to leading abolitionists such as the Motts, the Whartons, and Miller McKim (60–63).

43. William Still, *The Underground Railroad* (Philadelphia, 1872; repr. ed., Medford, NJ: Plexus, 2005), 421. Charles Kirk was also a member of the Abington Meeting during the 1830s and 1840s and was known to receive runaways from Germantown. See *Recollections of Charles Kirk* (Philadelphia: Friends Book Association, 1892), 27–28.

44. Thomas Shoemaker's scrapbook, n.d. (likely 1884–1885), contains articles clipped from the *Germantown Telegraph* and other local newspapers and collected by a late nineteenth-century antiquarian. The unknown author is referred to as "An old gentleman." Shoemaker Scrapbook, vol. 1, document 2, Historical Society of Pennsylvania.

45. For the trapdoor in the back garret, see Martin Jay Rosenblum, R.A., and Associates, *John Johnson, Jr., House Historic Structure Report,* prepared for the Germantown Mennonite Historic Trust, April 1995, 51. Family lore comes from Gay Johnson and Elizabeth Johnson Hood in personal communication with the author.

46. "Recalls Incidents of Slavery Days: B. F. Kirk Tells of the Underground Railway's Operation in the Eastern Pennsylvania Abolition Talks Here," newspaper article, newspaper unknown, Johnson House files, Germantown Historical Society.

47. Blockson, *Hippocrene Guide,* 86. Both newspaper sources put the meetings at Pomona Grove, across the street from Johnson House, with speakers such as Tubman and Frederick Douglass.

48. See Kate C. Larson, *Bound for the Promised Land: Harriet Tubman, Portrait of an American Hero* (New York: Random House, 2004), 127–129.

49. Johnson Family Papers: Correspondence.

50. Shoemaker Scrapbook, vol. 1, document 2; "Recalls Incidents."

51. Robert Ulle, manuscript and 1850 U.S. Census, Germantown Mennonite Historic Trust. Out of 118 or 119 African American residents of Germantown, 50 (42 percent) were born in the slave states of Maryland, Delaware, Virginia, North Carolina, or Mississippi. The 1860 U.S. Census gives the proportion as 38 out of 143 (26 percent).

52. See, for instance, *The Present State and Condition of the Free People of Color of the City of Philadelphia and Adjoining Districts, As Exhibited by the Report of A*

Committee of the Pennsylvania Society for Promoting the Abolition of Slavery (Philadelphia: Merrihew and Gunn, 1838); also "1847 Census: A Statistical Inquiry into the Condition of the People of Colour in the City and Districts of Philadelphia" (Philadelphia: Kite and Walton, 1849).

53. On Susan Lewis, see Charles Kirk, "A slave girl received into his home," in *Recollections of Charles Kirk*, 27–28.

54. Concord School and Upper Burying Ground, Treasury Records, 1775–1945, MS 2001, Historical Society of Pennsylvania.

55. The evolution of the source material and the ability of local historians and scholars to make sense of it would have been impossible without funding. The Mennonite Historic Trust approached the William Penn Foundation, a prominent local foundation, about helping with the Johnson House. Cliveden–William Penn Foundation correspondence, April 22, 1997–June 2, 1999, Cliveden archives.

56. Johnson House Advisory Committee meeting minutes, January–March 1997, in ibid. Members included the museum professionals Sandy Lloyd, Romona Riscoe (later the director of the African American Museum in Philadelphia), and Kate Stover; Mennonite Trust director Galen Horst-Martz; Cliveden board members Carol Giles, Ann Green, and Richard Snowden; Cliveden director Jennifer Esler; and community members Gladys Hall and Arthur Johnson.

57. Michael B. Mann, "Society News," *Germantown Crier* 37, no. 4 (Fall 1985): 91.

58. Jennifer B. Goodman, preservation planner, and Deborah Marquis Kelly, assistant director of the National Trust for Historic Preservation Mid-Atlantic Regional Office, *The Germantown Avenue Study: 4500–6533 Germantown Avenue*, vols. 1–2 (Philadelphia: Preservation Coalition of Greater Philadelphia and Historic Germantown Preserved, 1992). One goal was to create a detailed inventory of resources in the study area that would provide thorough documentary evidence and serve as a preservation planning tool. The work would involve analyzing planning data, such as ownership, zoning, land use, and preservation regulatory techniques to assess preservation needs.

59. Quotations are from recommendations in Manuel Ochoa and R. MacDuffie Nichols, *Mount Airy Assessment Report* (Philadelphia: National Trust for Historic Preservation National Main Street Center, 1998). The Mount Airy report lists numerous advisers: staff of historic sites including Cliveden, and public officials, such as the local councilwoman, business owners, and employees of the Mount Airy USA Community Development Corporation.

60. Recommendations from Manuel Ochoa and R. MacDuffie Nichols, National Trust for Historic Preservation, National Main Street Center to Stephen Kazanjian, executive director of Greater Germantown Housing Development Corporation (GGHDC), memorandum, "Assessment for Lower Germantown Neighborhood," March 15, 1998. GGHDC was a subsidiary of Germantown Settlement until 2010.

61. Ibid.

CHAPTER 5

1. City of Philadelphia's petition requesting Orphans' Court approval to modify the city's use of Loudoun Mansion and to deaccession various objects from the Loudoun Collection, filed December 7, 2015. Loudoun Mansion had been accepted into the city's ownership by the Fairmount Park Commission. It was a bequest of Maria Dickenson Logan, along with $150,000, "as long as the real estate shall maintain its present

condition as a museum and headquarters for such historical and patriotic enterprises as the Commission shall deem appropriate" and the museum and grounds "were maintained for the use and enjoyment of the citizens of the community."

2. See David Contosta, "Philadelphia's 'Miniature Williamsburg': The Colonial Revival and Germantown's Market Square," *Pennsylvania Magazine of History and Biography* 120, no. 4 (1996): 296–299, on the persistence of, and lack of foundation for, the myth.

3. A 2014 comment by "Madeline of Germantown" on one of many Germantown-related Facebook pages typifies the lingering power of the Rockefeller myth: "One aside, Germantown was considered for development, but Williamsburg was chosen. Sigh."

4. Charles F. Jenkins, "Address Delivered at the Laying of the Corner Stone of the New Town Hall in Germantown, December 18, 1923," *The Beehive* 4 (January 1924): 1, 17–20.

5. Svetlana Boym, *The Future of Nostalgia* (New York: Basic Books, 2001), 33.

6. "Italians Celebrate, Meet in Germantown to Observe Anniversary of Italy's Unity," *Philadelphia Inquirer,* September 19, 1921.

7. On the Cuyler Hospital, see Eugene G. Stackhouse (with the help of the Germantown Historical Society), *Germantown in the Civil War* (Charleston, SC: History Press, 2010), 96–98, 101–106, 141.

8. "Germantown Asks Town Hall Repairs; Famous Building Will Be Used for City Offices in Twenty-Second Ward," *Philadelphia Inquirer,* June 9, 1920; "Germantown Asks New Post Office Site in Front of Town Hall Plaza to Be Urged on City Council," *Philadelphia Inquirer,* July 3, 1920; "Germantown Town Hall Backers Win Ordinance Reported to Council after Heated Argument on Reprisal," *Philadelphia Inquirer,* March 22, 1921.

9. "Germantown Town Hall Backers Win Ordinance."

10. "Model Is Displayed; Visitors at Mayor's Office Note Plan of Proposed Germantown City Hall," *Philadelphia Inquirer,* October 10, 1922.

11. For this discussion see Edward W. Hocker, *Germantown, 1683–1933: The Record That a Pennsylvania Community Has Achieved in the Course of 250 Years; Being a History of Germantown, Mount Airy and Chestnut Hill* (Philadelphia, 1933), 218–221.

12. Nomination for Germantown Town Hall, 5928 Germantown Avenue, Philadelphia Register of Historic Places, prepared by Ira Kauderer, executive secretary, Philadelphia Historical Commission, February 17, 1993.

13. Paul M. Hesser Jr., "The Municipal Building of Germantown, Mount Airy and Chestnut Hill: An Appropriate Setting for World War Memorials," in *The Beehive* 7, no. 2 (February 1925): 3.

14. Jenkins, "Address," 20.

15. See Contosta, "Philadelphia's 'Miniature Williamsburg,'" 296–299.

16. On the Rockefeller family's roots there, dating to 1733, see Ron Chernow, *Titan: The Life of John D. Rockefeller, Sr.* (New York: Vintage Books, 1998), 3–4; Joseph Giovanni, "Rockefeller Tavern: The Toast of a Town," *New York Times,* July 28, 1988.

17. Eric Pace, "Mary C. Rockefeller, Governor's Former Wife, Dead at 91," *New York Times,* April 22, 1999.

18. The *Philadelphia Inquirer* announced the Bala Cynwyd wedding of Rockefeller and Clark on the day it took place and ran a front-page photo of the couple above

the fold on the day after. "Scion of Rockefeller Will Wed Here Today; Mary Todhunter Clark to Be Bride of Second Son of John D., Jr.," *Philadelphia Inquirer,* June 23, 1930, 2; "Rockefeller Scion and Bride," *Philadelphia Inquirer,* June 24, 1930.

19. Contosta, "Philadelphia's 'Miniature Williamsburg,'" 296.

20. Ibid., 295–297.

21. Ibid.

22. Daniel Rubin, "Historic Building's Light Standards Stolen: The Bronze Fixtures Stood outside Germantown Town Hall for 70 Years: Two City Workers Are Suspected," *Philadelphia Inquirer,* March 21, 1995.

23. Quoted in Suzanne Sataline, "In the Heart of Germantown, an Effort to Rescue History," *Philadelphia Inquirer,* May 8, 1995. See also "Community Mobilizes to Save Germantown's Historic Town Hall," *Chestnut Hill Local,* January 29, 1995.

24. Quoted in Sataline, "In the Heart of Germantown."

25. Application for designation, City of Philadelphia Historical Commission, August 11, 1993.

26. Quoted in Daniel Rubin, "Making Preservation of an Old Building More Palatable," *Philadelphia Inquirer,* February 2, 1995.

27. Quoted in ibid.

28. Ibid.

29. Ed Stivender, "Once Upon a Town: The Ballad of Town Hall," 1995, Pamphlet file, "Town Hall," Germantown Historical Society. Lyrics reprinted courtesy of Ed Stivender.

30. "A New Board Ousts the Old in an Attempt to Save YWCA," *Germantown Courier,* May 29, 1999. See also "Doubts? Debts? The Beat Is Up at Germantown Y," *Philadelphia Inquirer,* August 18, 1999.

31. Latishia Allen, Molly Lester, Kalen McNabb, Monica Rhodes, Michael Shoriak, Matthew Wicklund, and Courtney Williams, "Germantown Town Hall Preservation Plan," Preservation Studio, Susanna Barucco and Randall Mason faculty advisers, Fall 2011.

32. Based on discussions with Hidden City project director Peter Woodall.

33. Interviews with Peter Woodall. The Natatorium project had the highest number of visitors, at 1,964.

34. Catalogue of sale, Stephenson's Auction New Year's Antiques and Decorative Arts Auction. Southampton, PA, January 1 and 2, 2018.

35. Examples include Casa Amesti Foundation, which went from stewardship as a house museum owned by the National Trust for Historic Preservation to management by another nonprofit, the Old Capitol Club, as a private club; the Nantucket Historical Association, which reprogrammed some of its buildings; and the Robert E. Lee Boyhood Home, sold to private owners with preservation protections. See Donna A. Harris, *New Solutions for House Museums* (Lanham, MD: Alta Mira Press, 2007), 81–102, 107–117, 196–197, 212–215.

36. The original Matthias Zimmerman deed and map, quoted here, are reprinted in Eugene G. Stackhouse, "Potter's Field," in *Remembering Germantown: Sixty Years of the* Germantown Crier, ed. Irvin Miller and Judith Callard (Charleston, SC: History Press, 2008), 6–8.

37. Vernon Clark, "PHA Scraps Plans to Build on Burial Ground," *Philadelphia Inquirer,* January 7, 2012.

38. Quoted in "Commemorating a Colonial-Era Burial Ground for Blacks in Germantown," *Germantown Beat*, March 10, 2016 (La Salle University journalism school website), http://wp.lasalle.edu/gb/2016/03/10/commemorating-a-colonial-era-burial-ground-for-blacks/.

39. "Historical Marker Designates Potter's Field in Germantown," *Mt. Airy Times-Express*, February 11, 2017.

40. In 1868, Anne Sophia Penn Chew had cast-iron range, the "American Kitchener," installed in the old cooking hearth. She purchased it from a dealer named James Wood. "Sept. 6 pd Alberger & wood for copper boiler & plumbing." Chew Family Papers, 2050, vol. 28, box 697, folder 21, Historical Society of Pennsylvania.

41. On Joseph McGill's stay at Cliveden, see "They Lived Where They Worked," November 16, 2015, http://slavedwellingproject.org. On the Slave Dwelling Project, see Tony Horwitz, "One Man's Epic Quest to Visit Every Former Slave Dwelling in the United States, *Smithsonian Magazine*, October 2013; and Jennifer Schuessler, "Confronting Slavery at Long Island's Oldest Estates," *New York Times*, August 12, 2015.

42. Rick Nichols, "Historic Cliveden Expands Its Story Beyond Its Famous Battle to . . . Kitchens," *Philadelphia Inquirer*, May 12, 2016.

43. See Lisa Kraus's review, "Cliveden, Animated," August 10, 2016, http://thinkingdance.net/articles/2016/08/10/3/Cliveden-Animated/.

CONCLUSION

1. Quoted in William Bender, "Tennis Star 'Big Bill' Tilden Denied His Plaque Again," *Philadelphia Daily News,* March 28, 2017.

2. Quoted in Inga Saffron, "Century-Old Club Building Shouldn't Be Razed, Replaced," *Philadelphia Inquirer*, May 5, 2017.

3. Mensah M. Dean, "Juneteenth Is Growing, with Friction," *Philadelphia Inquirer*, June 12, 2017.

4. On Olivier's project, see http://monumentlab.muralarts.org/karyn-olivier.

5. "The New Battle of Germantown: Art Project Cloaks Germantown Monument on Anniversary of Historic Battle," *Metro Philadelphia*, October 6, 2017.

6. Quoted in Saffron, "Century-Old Club Building."

7. For "Elephants on the Avenue," see Natalie Pompilio, "Traveling on Germantown's Historic Path," *Philadelphia Inquirer*, January 17, 2016.

8. Kristen A. Graham, "These Philly Schoolkids Marched against Injustice 50 Years Ago, and Police Responded with Nightsticks; Today, They Inspire a New Generation," *Philadelphia Inquirer*, November 18, 1967. See also Dale Mezzacappa, "A History Lesson on Historic Day for School Reform Commission," *The Notebook*, November 16, 2017, http://thenotebook.org/articles/2017/11/16/a-history-lesson-on-historic-day-for-school-reform-commission.

Selected Bibliography

These works were selected because of their significant conceptual or historical influence on the thinking in this text.

Adair, Bill, Benjamin Filene, and Laura Koloski, eds. *Letting Go: Shared Historical Authority in a User-Generated World.* Philadelphia: Pew Center for Arts and Heritage, 2011.

Anderson, Elijah. *Code of the Street: Decency, Violence, and the Moral Life of the Inner City.* New York: W. W. Norton, 1999.

———. *The Cosmopolitan Canopy: Race and Civility in Everyday Life.* New York: W. W. Norton, 2011.

Banner-Haley, Charles P. T. *To Do Good and to Do Well: Middle-Class Blacks and the Depression, Philadelphia 1929–1941.* New York: Garland, 1993.

Benson, Susan Porter, Steven Brier, and Roy Rosenzweig, eds. *Presenting the Past: Critical Perspectives on History and the Public.* Philadelphia: Temple University Press, 1986.

Berlin, Ira. *The Long Emancipation: The Demise of Slavery in the United States.* Cambridge, MA: Harvard University Press, 2015.

Blockson, Charles L. *The Underground Railroad in Pennsylvania.* Jacksonville, NC: Flame International, 1981.

Bodnar, John. *Remaking America: Public Memory, Commemoration, and Patriotism in the Twentieth Century.* Princeton, NJ: Princeton University Press, 1992.

Boym, Svetlana. *The Future of Nostalgia.* New York: Basic Books, 2001.

Clemens, Thomas. *East Germantown: A New Name for Ancient Villages.* Philadelphia, 1936.

Collier-Thomas, Bettye. *Jesus, Jobs, and Justice: African American Women and Religion.* New York: Knopf, 2010.

Conn, Steven. *Museums and American Intellectual Life, 1876–1926.* Chicago: University of Chicago Press, 1998.

Contosta, David. "Philadelphia's 'Miniature Williamsburg': The Colonial Revival and Germantown's Market Square." *Pennsylvania Magazine of History and Biography* 120, no. 4 (October 1996): 264–320.

————. *Suburb in the City: Chestnut Hill Philadelphia 1850–1990.* Columbus: Ohio State University Press, 1992.

Countryman, Matthew J. *Up South: Civil Rights and Black Power in Philadelphia.* Philadelphia: University of Pennsylvania Press, 2005.

Davis, Susan G. *Parades and Power: Street Theatre in Nineteenth-Century Philadelphia.* Philadelphia: Temple University Press, 1986.

Day, Katie. *Faith on the Avenue: Religion on a City Street.* New York: Oxford University Press, 2014.

Du Bois, W.E.B. *The Philadelphia Negro: A Social Study.* First published 1899. Philadelphia: University of Pennsylvania Press, 1996.

Farnham, Jonathan E. "A Bridge Game: Constructing a Co-operative Commonwealth in Philadelphia, 1900–1926." Ph.D. diss., Princeton University, 2000.

Felix, Stephanie Yvette. "Committed to Their Own: African American Women Leaders in the YWCA; The YWCA of Germantown, Philadelphia, Pennsylvania, 1870–1970." Ph.D. diss., Temple University, 1999.

Ferman, Barbara, Theresa Singleton, and Don Demarco. "West Mount Airy, Philadelphia." *Cityscape: A Journal of Policy Development and Research* 4, no. 2 (1998): 29–59.

Fitzpatrick, Ellen. *History's Memory: Writing America's Past, 1880–1980.* Cambridge, MA: Harvard University Press, 2004.

Franklin, Vincent P. *The Education of Black Philadelphia: The Social and Educational History of a Minority Community, 1900–1950.* Philadelphia: University of Pennsylvania Press, 1979.

Gallas, Kristin L., and James DeWolf Perry, eds. *Interpreting Slavery at Museums and Historic Sites.* New York: Rowman and Littlefield, 2014.

Glassberg, David. *American Historical Pageantry: The Uses of Tradition in the Early Twentieth Century.* Chapel Hill: University of North Carolina Press, 1990.

Gregg, Robert. *Sparks from the Anvil of Oppression: Philadelphia's African Methodists and Southern Migrants, 1890–1940.* Philadelphia: Temple University Press, 1993.

Handler, Richard, and Eric Gable. *The New History in an Old Museum: Creating the Past at Colonial Williamsburg.* Durham, NC: Duke University Press, 1997.

Harris, Donna A. *New Solutions for House Museums: Ensuring the Long-Term Preservation of America's Historic Houses.* Lanham, MD: AltaMira Press, 2007.

Hayden, Dolores. *The Power of Place: Urban Landscapes as Public History.* Cambridge, MA: MIT Press, 1995.

Hepp, John H., IV *The Middle Class City: Transforming Space and Time in Philadelphia: 1876–1926.* Philadelphia: University of Pennsylvania Press, 2003.

Hocker, Edward W. *Germantown, 1683–1933: The Record That a Pennsylvania Community Has Achieved in the Course of 250 Years; Being a History of the People of Germantown, Mount Airy and Chestnut Hill.* Philadelphia, 1933.

Hosmer, Charles B., Jr. *Preservation Comes of Age: From Williamsburg to the National Trust, 1926–1949.* Charlottesville: University Press of Virginia, 1981.

Isenberg, Alison. *Downtown America: A History of the Place and the People Who Made It.* Chicago: University of Chicago Press, 2004.

Jackson, Mandi Isaacs. *Model City Blues: Urban Space and Organized Resistance in New Haven.* Philadelphia: Temple University Press, 2008.

Jacobs, Jane. *The Death and Life of Great American Cities.* First published 1961. New York: Random House, 1993.

Jenkins, Charles F. *Germantown History: Consisting of Papers Read before the Site and Relic Society of Germantown.* Germantown: Author, 1915.

Jenkins, Philip. *Hoods and Shirts: The Extreme Right in Pennsylvania, 1925–1950.* Chapel Hill: University of North Carolina Press, 1997.

Johnson, Mat. *Loving Day: A Novel.* New York: Spiegel and Grau, 2015.

Kammen, Michael. *The Mystic Chords of Memory: The Transformation of Tradition in America.* New York: Vintage, 1991.

Kaufman, Ned. *Place, Race, and Story: Essays on the Past and Future of Historic Preservation.* New York: Routledge, 2009.

Kazal, Russell A. *Becoming Old Stock: The Paradox of German American Identity.* Princeton, NJ: Princeton University Press, 2004.

Keyser, Dr. Naaman H., C. Henry Kain, John Palmer Garber, and Horace F. McCann. *History of Old Germantown with a Description of Its Settlement and Some Account of Its Important Persons, Buildings, and Places Connected with Its Development.* Vol. 1. Germantown, Philadelphia: H. F. McCann, 1907.

Kitzmiller, Erika M. "The Roots of Educational Inequality: Germantown High School, 1907–2011." Ph.D. diss., University of Pennsylvania, 2012.

Lapsansky, Emma J. "Patriotism, Values and Continuity: Museum Collecting and Connectedness." *Pennsylvania Magazine of History and Biography* 114 (1990): 61–82.

Larson, Kate C. *Bound for the Promised Land: Harriet Tubman, Portrait of an American Hero.* New York: Random House, 2004.

Lawler, Edward, Jr. "The President's House in Philadelphia: The Rediscovery of a Lost Landmark." *Pennsylvania Magazine of History and Biography* 129, no. 4 (October 2002): 371–410.

Lerned, Marion Dexter. *The Life of Francis Daniel Pastorius, Founder of Germantown.* Philadelphia: Campbell, 1908.

Levin, Amy K, ed. *Defining Memory: Local Museums and the Construction of History in America's Changing Communities.* Lanham, MD: Alta Mira Press, 2007.

Lloyd, Mark Frazier. "Historic Germantown." *Antiques,* August 1983, 253–300.

McDaniel, Donna, and Vanessa Julye. *Fit for Freedom, Not for Friendship: Quakers, African Americans, and the Myth of Racial Justice.* Springfield, PA: Quaker Press, 2009.

McWilliams, Jane Wilson. *Annapolis, City on the Severn: A History.* Baltimore, MD: Johns Hopkins University Press, 2011.

Meyerowitz, Lisa. "The 'Negro in Art Week': Defining the 'New Negro' through Art Exhibition." *African American Review* 31 (Spring 1997): 7–90.

Minardi, Joseph. *Historic Architecture in Northwest Philadelphia 1690 to 1930s.* Atglen, PA: Schiffer Books, 2012.

Mires, Charlene. *Independence Hall in American Memory.* Philadelphia: University of Pennsylvania Press, 2002.

Moss, Roger. *Historic Houses of Philadelphia.* Philadelphia: University of Pennsylvania Press, 1998.

Murphy, Sinead. *Effective History: On Critical Practice under Historical Conditions.* Evanston, IL: Northwestern University Press, 2010.

Nash, Gary. "Behind the Velvet Curtain: Academic History, Historical Societies, and the Presentation of the Past." *Pennsylvania Magazine of History and Biography* 114 (1990): 3–26.

———. *First City: Philadelphia and the Forging of Historical Memory.* Philadelphia: University of Pennsylvania Press, 2002.

Nelson, H. Viscount. *Black Leadership's Response to the Great Depression in Philadelphia.* Lewiston NY: Mellen, 2006.

Newsom, Michael deHaven. "Blacks in Preservation." *Law and Contemporary Problems* 36 (Summer 1971): 423–431.

Page, Max. *Why Preservation Matters.* New Haven, CT: Yale University Press, 2016.

Page, Max, and Randall Mason, eds. *Giving Preservation a History: Histories of Historic Preservation in the United States.* New York: Routledge, 2004.

Page, Max, and Marla R. Miller, eds. *Bending the Future: Fifty Ideas for the Next Fifty Years of Historic Preservation in the United States.* Amherst: University of Massachusetts Press, 2016.

Pennypacker, Samuel W. *The Settlement of Germantown, Pennsylvania and the Beginning of Germantown Emigration to North America.* Philadelphia: W. J. Campbell, 1899.

Perkiss, Abigail. *Making Good Neighbors: Civil Rights, Liberalism, and Integration in Postwar Philadelphia.* Ithaca, NY: Cornell University Press, 2014.

Philadelphia: A Guide to the Nation's Birth Place. Works Progress Administration, Federal Writers' Project. Philadelphia: William Penn Association of Philadelphia, 1937.

Rabinowitz, Richard. *Curating America: Journeys through Storyscapes of the American Past* (Chapel Hill: University of North Carolina Press, 2016).

Saunders, James Robert, and Renae Nadine Shackelford. *Urban Renewal and the End of Black Culture in Charlottesville, Virginia: An Oral History of Vinegar Hill.* Jefferson, NC: McFarland, 1998.

Scharf, J. Thomas, and Thompson Westcott. *History of Philadelphia 1609–1884.* Philadelphia: L. H. Everts, 1884.

Shelton, Cynthia. *The Mills of Manayunk: Industrialization and Social Conflict in the Philadelphia Region 1787–1837.* Johns Hopkins University Press, 1986.

Smith, Barbara Clark. "The Authority of History: The Changing Public Face of the Historical Society of Pennsylvania." *Pennsylvania Magazine of History and Biography* 114 (1990): 37–66.

Soderlund, Jean. *Quakers and Slavery: A Divided Spirit.* Princeton, NJ: Princeton University Press, 1985).

Sprinkle, John. *Crafting Preservation Criteria: The National Register of Historic Places and American Historic Preservation.* New York: Routledge, 2014.

Stabile, Susan. *Memory's Daughters: The Material Culture of Remembrance in Eighteenth-Century America.* Ithaca, NY: Cornell University Press, 2004.

Sugrue, Thomas J. *The Origins of the Urban Crisis: Race and Inequality in Postwar Detroit.* Princeton, NJ: Princeton University Press, 1998.

———. *Sweet Land of Liberty: The Forgotten Struggle for Civil Rights in the North.* New York: Random House, 2008.

Switala, William J. *The Underground Railroad in Pennsylvania,* Mechanicsburg, PA: Stackpole Books, 2001.

Tinkcom, Harry M., Margaret B. Tinkcom, and Grant Miles Simon, F.A.I.A. *Historic Germantown from the Founding to the Early Part of the Nineteenth Century: A Survey of the German Township.* Philadelphia: American Philosophical Society, 1955.

Tyson, Amy M. *The Wages of History: Emotional Labor on Public History's Front Line.* Amherst: University of Massachusetts Press, 2013.

Vagnone, Franklin D., and Deborah E. Ryan. *Anarchist's Guide to Historic House Museums.* Walnut Creek, CA: Left Coast Press, 2016.

Vogel, Morris J. *Cultural Connections: Museums and Libraries of the Delaware Valley.* Philadelphia: Temple University Press, 1991.

Wallace, Michael. *Mickey Mouse History, and Other Essays on American Memory.* Philadelphia: Temple University Press, 1996.

Webster, Richard. *Philadelphia Preserved: Catalog of the Historic American Buildings Survey.* Philadelphia: Temple University Press, 1981.

West, Patricia. *Domesticating History: The Political Origins of America's House Museums.* Washington, DC: Smithsonian Institution Press, 1999.

Weygandt, Cornelius, Jr. *The Plenty of Pennsylvania: Samples of Seven Cultures Persisting from Colonial Days.* New York: H. C. Kinsey, 1942.

Wolf, Stephanie Grauman *Urban Village: Population, Community, and Family Structure in Germantown, Pennsylvania, 1683–1800.* Princeton, NJ: Princeton University Press, 1976.

Wolfinger, James. *Philadelphia Divided: Race and Politics in the City of Brotherly Love.* Chapel Hill: University of North Carolina Press, 2007.

Young, David W. "The Battles of Germantown: Preservation and Memory in America's Most Historic Neighborhood." Ph.D. diss., Ohio State University, 2009.

———. "'You Feel So Out of Place': Germantown's J. Gordon Baugh and the 1913 Commemoration of the Emancipation Proclamation." *Pennsylvania Magazine of History and Biography* 137, no. 1 (January 2013): 79–93.

Index

Page numbers followed by the letter *f* indicate figures.

DAVID W. YOUNG is the Executive Director of the Delaware Historical Society. He previously served as Executive Director of Cliveden, a historic site of the National Trust for Historic Preservation, and the Johnson House Historic Site, both located in the Germantown section of Philadelphia. He received his Ph.D. in history from Ohio State University.